MODERN ENGLISH STRUCTURES

SECOND EDITION

MODERN ENGLISH STRUCTURES

FORM, FUNCTION, AND POSITION

SECOND EDITION

BERNARD T. O'DWYER

broadview press

BROADVIEW PRESS
is an independent, international publishing house, incorporated in 1985.

NORTH AMERICA

PO Box 1243
Peterborough, Ontario
Canada K9J 7H5

PO Box 1015
3576 California Road
Orchard Park, New York
USA 14127

tel (705) 743-8990
fax (705) 743-8353
customerservice
  @broadviewpress.com

UK, IRELAND AND CONTINENTAL EUROPE
NBN International
Estover Road, Plymouth
PL6 7PY, UK
tel 44 (0) 1752 202300
fax order line:
44 (0) 1752 202330
orders:
enquiries@nbninternational.com

AUSTRALIA
UNIREPS University of
New South Wales
Sydney, NSW 2052 Australia
tel: 61 2 96640999
fax: 61 2 96645420
infopress@unsw.edu.au

www.broadviewpress.com

Copyright © 2006 Bernard T. O'Dwyer

CANADIAN CATALOGUING IN PUBLICATION DATA
O'Dwyer, Bernard
    Modern English structures: form, function and position/Bernard T. O'Dwyer.—2nd ed.

Includes bibliographical references and index.
ISBN 1-55111-763-0

1. English language—Grammar. I. Title.

PE1112.O38 2006   425   C2006-902547-9

Broadview Press gratefully acknowledges the financial support of the Ministry of Canadian Heritage through the Book Publishing Industry Development Program.

Original design by Zack Taylor, Black Eye Design, Inc. Second Edition by Liz Broes, Black Eye Design, Inc. Typeset in Bembo, Agenda, and Filosofia. Cover Design by: Lisa Brawn

10 9 8 7 6 5 4 3 2 1

Printed in Canada

TABLE OF CONTENTS

PREFACE

Modern English Structures began as a compilation of notes, supplementing a number of grammar texts that I used in an introductory grammar course at the university level. As these texts went out of print, I began using my own manuscript as the basis for my course. Encouraged by good results and constructive comments from my students, the manuscript underwent several revisions to improve its clarity for presentation and discussion. From the revisions evolved a book of exercises, parallelling each of the text chapters, to put theory into practice. Ultimately, the grammar text went into its first publication.

Current grammar books illustrate that there are varied approaches for analyzing modern English grammar. Some grammarians follow a holistic approach, breaking down larger structures, paragraphs into sentences, sentences into clauses, clauses into phrases, and phrases into words. Others follow a serialist approach, starting with words, moving up to phrases, then to clauses, finally building sentence structures. Both approaches are accepted as valid; *Modern English Structures*, however, follows the latter one.

Structurally, this grammar book is divided into three parts: what a sentence constituent **IS**, what a sentence constituent **DOES**, and where a sentence constituent **GOES**—Form, Function, and Position. Form structures are affixes, words, phrases, and clauses that generally express lexical meaning; they are the first and simplest modes of classification. Functions are the grammatical relationships that sentence constituents have with one another as they express grammatical meaning. Position marks constituents within sentences based on their form and function. All constituents make up sentences—our largest syntactic structure.

My objective is to bring students to a better understanding of sentence constituents and sentence structures, providing them with appropriate terminology to discuss these forms and relationships. I realize that there is a great deal of structural analysis to be learned beyond the grammatical structures presented here, but this is a basic course in English grammar. It differs from other grammars currently on the market in the ways that the analyses are structured by moving beyond form and function to position.

Now that I have stated what *Modern English Structures* is, let me say what it is not. This is not a linguistics text, and therefore I do not attempt to analyze modern English grammar from a linguistic perspective of phonology, morphosyntax, and semantics. Yes, there are times when I overlap with linguistic terminology (especially in the first chapter on morphemes), but I operate from the premise that students using this book have no training in linguistics.

To illustrate the use of grammar, I have selected examples from nineteenth, twentieth, and twenty-first century authors. These vary in style from literary writers, academic authors, and newspaper journalists. My reason for selecting examples in this way is to introduce students to the multiple styles of written English. *Structure plus style is really the basis of understanding language in use.*

Wherever possible I have taken complete sentences from these authors; at times, however, because of grammatical focus and the sentence length, I have taken only independent clausal structures for illustrative purposes. Where such examples could not be found, contrived examples are used. All examples have been documented and precise references are available upon request.

There is never a more humbling experience than authoring a text for your students, especially when you asked for their comments, and comments they gave. All the more humble for the experience and thankful for the corrections and improvements, I acknowledge my students for their suggestions, which brought about many improvements to this second edition.

I also acknowledge my colleagues, Dr. William Kirwin (Professor Emeritus), Professor Robert Hollett, and Dr. George Casey for their many suggestions in this second edition. Thank you.

Bernard T. O'Dwyer
Memorial University
St. John's, NL

ABBREVIATIONS
AND SYMBOLS

aj	=	adjective
app	=	apposition
av	=	adverb
c	=	complement
cj	=	conjunction
cl	=	clause
cn	=	connector
cp	=	comparative
Do	=	direct object
ex	=	example
Gk	=	Greek
gr	=	gerund
HAdj	=	head adjective
HAv	=	head adverb
HG	=	head gerund
HI	=	head infinitive
HN	=	head noun
HP	=	head participle
HPP	=	head present participle
HPRP	=	head preposition
HPTP	=	head past participle
HV	=	head verb
HW	=	head word
Ido	=	indirect object
I	=	infinitive
I-ph	=	infinitive phrase
ITV	=	intransitive verb
L	=	Latin
LV	=	linking verb
M	=	modifier
NP	=	noun phrase
NP^2	=	second noun phrase
NP^3	=	third noun phrase
OC	=	objective complement

OP	=	object of preposition
P	=	predicate
3 p sg	=	third person singular
p-aj	=	predicate adjective
ph	=	phrase
pl	=	plural
p-n	=	predicate noun
pp	=	present participle
pr	=	pronoun
prp-ph	=	prepositional phrase
ps	=	possessive
pt	=	past tense
ptp	=	past participle
S	=	independent sentence
sg	=	singular
Sj	=	subject
sp	=	superlative
TV	=	transitive verb
V	=	verb
VP	=	verb phrase
VP^2	=	verb phrase two
▌	=	point in time
→	=	produces
→→→	=	progression
★	=	ungrammatical
ø	=	zero ending
/	=	primary stress
\	=	mid stress
^	=	secondary

[Note: Upper and lower keys are not distinctive.]

INTRODUCTION
ENGLISH GRAMMAR

To perceive how language works ... is to comprehend a crucial aspect of the complicated business of living the life of a human being.[1]

Why do we study grammar? This is a question often debated today in our secondary and post-secondary educational institutions. It is a very valid question and one that should receive some consideration here if we are going to propose a course of grammar, *Modern English Structures*.

Among those who challenge the benefits of studying grammar, George Hillocks and Michael Smith conclude that research over a period of nearly 90 years has consistently shown that the teaching of school grammar has "little or no effect" on students.[2] This is not a single observation nor a new one; in recent years we have seen such similar statements, as follows:

The impressive fact is ... that in all these studies ... the results have been consistently negative so far as the value of grammar in the improvement of language expression is concerned. Surely there is no justification in the available evidence for the great expenditure of time and effort still being devoted to formal grammar in American schools.[3]

Diagramming sentences ... teaches nothing beyond the ability to diagram.[4]

The teaching of formal grammar has a negligible or, because it usually displaces some instruction and practice in actual composition, even a harmful effect on the improvement of writing.[5]

For most students, the systematic study of grammar is not even particularly helpful in avoiding or correcting errors.[6]

Systematic practice in combining and expanding sentences can increase students' repertoire of syntactic structures and can also

1 S.I. Hayakawa and A.R. Hayakawa, *Language in Thought and Action*, 5th ed. (Orlando, FL: Harcourt Brace Jovanovich, 1990), p. viii.

2 G. Hillocks, Jr., and M.W. Smith, "Grammar and Usage," in J. Flood, J.M. Jensen, D. Lapp, and J.R. Squires (eds.), *Handbook of Research on Teaching the English Language Arts* (New York: Macmillan, 1991).

3 J.J. DeBoer, "Grammar in Language Teaching," *Elementary English* 36 (1959): 413–421.

4 *Encyclopedia of Educational Research*, 4th ed. (New York: Macmillan, 1960).

5 R. Braddock, R. Lloyd-Jones, and L. Schoer. *Research in Written Composition* (Urbana, IL: NCTE, 1963).

6 W.B. Elly, I.H. Barham, H. Lamb, and M. Wyllie. "The role of grammar in a secondary English curriculum," *Research in the Teaching of English* 10 (1976): 5–21; F. McQuade, "Examining a grammar course: the rationale and the result," *English Journal* 69 (1980): 26–30; G. Hillocks, Jr., *Research on Written Composition: New directions for teaching* (Urbana, IL: NCTE, 1986).

improve the quality of their sentences, when stylistic effects are discussed as well.[7]

Although there is some disagreement between *Encyclopedia of Educational Research* and Hillocks and Smith regarding sentence analysis, all comments focus on the theme that we study grammar for the sole purpose of writing better sentences. This is a rather narrow view of a great discipline. Before challenging this argument, let us first briefly review why grammar has been studied.

Greek philosophers, the first to systematically study grammar, focussed on sounds, words, and their meanings. It was not until the 5th century BC that language was classified into parts of speech, inflections, and moods. Soon afterwards, these classifications gave way to the development of the first written systematic grammars as we have come to understand them. The basis for these grammars, however, arose initially not out of language/linguistic questions, but out of philosophical discussions. The question centred on whether language was *natural* (instinctive, that is, natural or an inborn tendency to speak) or *conventional* (acquired or learned).

Grammarians, during *Pax Romana* 31 BC to 180 AD, focussed more on language rules by writing simple and practical descriptions of their languages. These were the first steps in developing grammar into the discipline as we know it. Furthermore, rhetoricians (those who studied the art of prose composition) and grammarians began to use grammar to teach ideas of correctness, style, and effectiveness in language use. Indeed, for many, grammar became the key to all learning.

During the Scholastic Period, the 13th to 14th centuries, grammarians probed further into whether the knowledge of grammar could illuminate our minds, especially the parts of speech. This source of enquiry eventually gave way to the idea of a universal grammar—the view that all languages have linguistic structures in common. Many grammarians at that time thought all languages reflected certain enduring categories in our minds and in the world around us. They promoted the idea that languages were essentially the same and differed only accidentally. Rhetoric (the art of using words effectively) and pedagogy (the art or science of teaching), following the traditions of the Greeks and Romans, began to recede, especially during the 18th century. Internal rules of thought as expressed in language became a major grammatical focal point and the idea of a universal grammar continued.

During the 18th and 19th centuries other approaches for analysing language became popular. Most important among these was *comparative philology*, which studied the historical relationships of words. This process began as early as the 16th century, but it was not until the 18th century that philologists were able to show relationships among Germanic[8] and other Indo-European[9] languages. Soon after that, they were able to trace relationships among Greek, Latin, and Sanskrit languages as well.

The most important discovery leading to this hypothesis was the recognition that Sanskrit, a language of ancient India, was one of this

7 Hillocks, Jr., and Smith, pp. 591–603.

8 Germanic means languages of the Germanic family: Norwegian, Icelandic, Faeroese, Swedish, Danish, German, Yiddish, Dutch, Flemish, and English, for example.

9 Other Indo-European languages are those spoken throughout western and eastern Europe and beyond, from Ireland to India.

group [Indo-European languages]. This was first suggested in the latter part of the eighteenth century and fully established by the beginning of the nineteenth century.[10]

Through this comparative process, philologists refocused their view of language. They now saw the study of language as more than a rationalistic science; it became a historical science.

Throughout the history of grammar, many models for language use arose. Most popular among the traditional grammars was the *prescriptive* approach.

In its most general sense, prescriptivism is the view that one variety of language has an inherently higher value than others, and that this ought to be imposed on the whole of the speech community. The view is propounded especially in relation to grammar and vocabulary, and frequently with reference to pronunciation. The variety which is favoured, in this account, is usually a version of the "standard" written language, especially as encountered in literature, or in the formal spoken language which most closely reflects this style. Adherents to this variety are said to speak or write "correctly"; deviations from it are said to be "incorrect."[11]

Other traditional models followed only some of the prescriptive rules, but cut corners. A second model for analysis, which gained prominence in the early part of the 20th century, is called the *descriptive* model.

Descriptive Linguistics is concerned with the documentation of all aspects of individual languages, including their sound structure (phonetics and phonology), word structure (morphology), phrase and sentence structure (syntax), semantics, discourse patterns, and pragmatics of use.[12]

Today most language scholars agree that the study of grammar should follow the descriptive model.

We now return to our opening question—*why do we study grammar?*—and to the suggestion that studying grammar does not result in writing better sentences. We saw from the Greeks that an interest in grammar grew out of an interest in language itself, rather than out of an interest for writing. During the past century, however, the focus has shifted and, generally, we now study grammar for the wrong reasons.

Grammar might be studied for many reasons, and least among them should be simply to improve sentence structures. First, we have two modes of expression: speech is the older and more frequently used one; and writing is the more recent and static one. Grammar is first found in speech, in how we use and classify words, and in how we group them to express our thoughts. We study grammar to understand how we structure and use language. Grammar flows from language, not language from grammar. Grammar existed long before we began

10 Baugh, Albert C. & Cable, Thomas. *A History of the English Language.* 3rd ed. (Prentice-Hall, Inc: New Jersey, 1978), p. 18.

11 Crystal, David. *The Prescriptive Tradition.* www.sebsteph.com/ Professional/ Bart's%20class/Readings /crystal.htm – 19k

12 Department of Linguistics, University of Oregon. logos.uoregon.edu/ research/descriptive_ linquistics.html – 47k

to write our speech down in graphic form. So why restrict the study of grammar to "writing down sentences"?

Studying the grammatical structure of one's language can be very helpful in using that language and learning the origin and the power of words for all modes of communication, not just for writing. It is most helpful in learning other languages using a similar structure. Understanding the structure of one's own language opens up the whole discipline of linguistics and the investigation of other languages. Most important, studying grammar goes beyond just teaching a skill; it teaches us to think more analytically.

LANGUAGE STRUCTURE

Native speakers of English learn the structures and relationships of language constituents subconsciously as young children. We listen to and speak with other native speakers, and in this way we learn what is communicative in our language and what is not. Too frequently, however, we do not learn enough about these structures and relationships at a more conscious level. We know only *when* an expression is articulated correctly and meaningfully; we do not *why* this is so. *Modern English Structures* focuses on the *whys* of our language structure and offers a basic descriptive analysis of Modern English.

When analysing a language like Modern English, we see an infrastructure of relationships called grammar. To understand these relationships we subdivide language into three focal areas for analysis. The first of these is the spoken language or speech sounds (phonology/phonetics), which are used to form larger meaningful units. These units are morphemes (morphology/morphemes), from which we construct words (lexicon/vocabulary). Words are then combined to produce phrases and clauses (syntax). The latter three (words, phrases, and clauses) are constituents from which we form our largest syntactic unit— the sentence. The focus of sentence structures is to convey completed meaning (semantics). Figure 0.1 illustrates these areas for language analysis.

Spoken language (phonology/phonetics) is the process of producing sounds in an organized and meaningful way for the purpose of communication; it involves a speaker and a hearer/audience. This *speech event* or *act* is quite a complicated process, which has several levels of analysis. Written language (orthography), however, refers to the process of recording language using a (standard) system of written symbols; it is the visual representation of the sounds for that language. Some languages are *phonemic* in that they use one orthographic symbol per sound (phoneme); both Finnish and Turkish come very close to this

FIGURE 0.1 ✿ LANGUAGE STRUCTURE

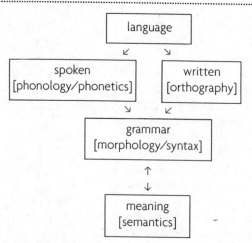

process. English and most languages show great inconsistencies in the graphic to sound representations of their speech; however, English is standardized and from that perspective it is useful for most regional standards.

Grammar (morphology/syntax) is that component of language categorized under *form*; it is distinct from sound (phonology/phonetics) and meaning (semantics). Although combined under grammar, morphology (the study of words) and syntax (the study of phrases, clauses, and sentences) will be studied separately here. In English the terms *grammar* and *syntax* are often used interchangeably, although syntax is the more significant feature of *grammatical structure*.

Semantics (from Gk. semantikos, or *significant meaning*; derived from sema, *sign*) is the study of *lexical* meaning as it occurs in morphemes, words, phrases, and sentences. It is often contrasted with syntax, which studies the formal structure or patterns in which something is expressed, spoken, or written. This is called *grammatical* meaning.

SPOKEN VS. WRITTEN GRAMMAR

Spoken and *written* forms of language differ more than just *sound* versus *symbol*. Spoken language is constantly in a *state of flux* (changing in both sounds and structure). Written language or spelling is more *fixed* or archaic, generally dating back to earlier stages of the language. This raises the question of two possible grammars—spoken and written. Grammarians have long been aware of these differences. "Unfortunately, awareness of this dichotomy has often resulted in spoken forms being looked upon as poor cousins of the written, aberrations from canonical 'correct' forms as it were."[13] In this text we restrict our analyses to traditionally written English; spoken grammar deals with a varied set of structures often different from that of its written grammar. The examples used to illustrate grammatical rules and structures here will be taken from traditional and contemporary texts. *Contrived* examples have their place, but they do not generally reflect actual language use and are definitely static in style. For that reason, contrived examples have been avoided (with a very few necessary exceptions).

GRAMMATICAL TERMINOLOGY

Terminology can be very confusing when analysing grammar, because it is not consistent. One grammarian may use the term *noun* to identify a phrase with a head noun, and another grammarian may refer to it as a *nominal* phrase. Do they mean the same thing? One dictionary shows that nominal applies to, "4. *ling* noun or word or phrase used as a noun"; adjectival applies to "1. adjective; 2. *sing* many adjectives."[14] *Modern English Structures* is very precise about its use of grammatical terminology. By form, for example, a word may be a *verb*, by function it is a *predicate*, and by position it is *verbal*; similarly, a word may be an *adjective* by form, a modifier by *function*, and an *adjectival* by position. Emphasis is given to categorizing the terminology according to this structure.

13 Guest, M. (1996). *Spoken Grammar as a Bridge between Languages*. Unpublished Master's Degree Dissertation, Aston University, Birmingham, UK.

14 *The Scribner-Bantam English Dictionary*. Bantam Books: New York, 1991.

SENTENCE CONSTITUENTS

CONSTITUENTS
are language elements
forming part of a larger
syntactic unit.

Form is the first of the three fundamental areas of this text; *grammatical function* and *grammatical position* follow from this to give us a full syntax of Modern English grammar.

FORM

FORM
is the shape of a
sentence constituent,
or what it is.

Form structures identify what a sentence constituent **IS**. They can be meaningful parts of words (as *morphemes*) or words, phrases, and clauses that combine to express grammatical meaning.

They are the simplest mode of classification for identification purposes. As we identify each of the above groups, we learn the characteristics of that group, and this, in turn, enables us to identify other members that belong to that group. Form often reveals the grammatical relationship of constituents to one another within sentences.

Morphemes

Morphemes are minimal distinctive units and generally have little or no apparent meaning by themselves. They are generally recognized in association with other morphemes (free or bound) at the word level. If free, a morpheme is identical to a word and stands alone with meaning (ex. dog); if bound, it relies on other free or bound morphemes to express meaning (ex. dog + *s*). Morphemes are also derivational, in that they can create new words or change word categories (ex. happy [adjective] + *-ness* = happiness [noun]). They can also be inflectional (ex. talk + *-ed*), that is, they can limit the grammatical significance of other morphemes. In this last example the grammatical meaning of the word is restricted by the *-ed*, meaning past tense. Morphemes form the infrastructure of words, build vocabulary, and extend grammatical meaning.

Words

As a working definition (that is, one sufficient to give meaning to our discussion), words are free forms and stand alone with meaning. We categorize them into form class and structure class words. Form words are *nouns, verbs, adjectives,* and *adverbs*; they are called *open class* because they readily accept new members. Structure words are *pronouns, determiners, auxiliaries,* and *conjunctions*; they are called *closed class* because they rarely admit new members. *Parts of speech* is the traditional name for such classifications.

Phrases

Phrases are word groups having internal cohesion and forming syntactic units with a head word (HW). A head word is the single word around which other words group for meaning. For example, a noun phrase has a head noun (HN), a verb phrase has a lexical head verb (HV), and a participle phrase has a head present or past participle (Hpp or Hptp). Identifying the head word is helpful when classifying a phrasal structure.

We identify nine types of phrases: *noun, verb, adjective, adverb, participle, gerund, infinitive, prepositional,* and *absolute*. Noun and verb phrases occur most frequently because they are essential to the structure of every sentence and clause. Other phrases vary in their occurrences depending upon the structure of the sentence.

Clauses

Clauses are more complex in structure than phrases. They are similar to sentences in that they must contain a noun phrase (subject) and a verb phrase (predicate/finite verb). Independent (main) clauses stand alone with completed meaning as syntactic structures, while dependent (subordinate) clauses need other independent or dependent clauses to complete their meanings.

Independent clauses should not be equated with sentences. All independent clauses are sentences, but not all sentences are of themselves independent clauses. Most sentences comprise of more than one clause; usually they have one or more dependent and one or more independent clauses. Dependent clauses are identified as *noun,*[15] *relative adjective, relative adverb,* and *adverb clauses.*

15 The noun clause is a very simple description here. There are other classifications, e.g., temporal, final, causal, hypothetical clauses, but these distinctions are reserved for a more in-depth study of English syntax.

FUNCTIONS

Grammatical function identifies what a sentence constituent **DOES.** Specifically, this means the role that a word or word group (phrase or clause) has within the larger syntactic unit—the sentence. This special role signals the grammatical meaning for that sentence constituent.

Grammatical functions will be divided into major and minor functions. Major functions are *subjects, predicates, direct,* and *indirect objects;* minor functions are *adjective* and *adverb modifiers, appositives, complements, connectors,* and *objects of prepositions.* Each of these functions will be discussed in detail, showing how various categories of words, phrases, or clauses can carry out their respective roles.

GRAMMATICAL FUNCTION
is the role a constituent has within a sentence, along with its relationship to other constituents within that sentence.

POSITIONS

GRAMMATICAL POSITION

marks constituents within sentences based on their form and function.

Grammatical position identifies where a sentence constituent **GOES**. Sentence constituents occupy four grammatical positions: *nominal, verbal, adjectival,* and *adverbial.* Depending on the sentence structure, however, one or more words, phrases, or clauses can occupy these positions. Within a sentence, grammatical positions are generally not difficult to identify, and knowing them is particularly helpful when narrowing down grammatical function. Position is useful in treating problematic forms like infinitives, gerunds, and participles, where the form and function information can "conflict."

SENTENCES

SENTENCE

is the largest syntactic structure made up of constituents, but it is not a constituent of a larger syntactic structure.

A sentence is the largest syntactic structure, consisting of constituents structured as a noun phrase and a verb phrase; it is not a constituent of a larger syntactic structure. Traditionally they have been identified as *simple, compound, complex,* and *compound-complex.* A simple sentence consists of only one independent clause; this clause contains only one finite verb. A compound sentence has two or more main clauses linked by a coordinating conjunction. A complex sentence contains one main clause and at least one subordinate clause. A compound-complex sentence consists of two or more main clauses and at least one subordinate clause. Today, however, grammarians identify sentences according to their constituent patterns.

A sentence, like the clause, has two essential components, a noun phrase (subject) and a verb phrase (predicate). Depending on the verb type, a third component may occur, a second noun phrase or complement (objects, subjective or adverbial complements). Noun phrases and complements can be made up from a word, a phrase, or a clause; the verb phrase can be either a word or a phrase, but it cannot be a clause. We express this structure as:

Sentence = Noun Phrase + Verb Phrase ± Noun Phrase^2 or Complement.

As a guide for sentence patterns, we can formulate this structure as follows:

$$S \rightarrow NP + VP \pm NP^2 / C$$

The focus of *Modern English Structures* is to identify all sentence constituents, noting their grammatical relationships. To do this, each constituent is labelled according to its grammatical form, grammatical function, and grammatical position.

The following sentence is simple in structure and therefore its constituents are easily identified. Most sentences are more complex and will be more difficult to analyze, because they have larger phrase and clause structures. Figure 0.2 illustrates a typical analysis.

FIGURE 0.2 ✿ SENTENCE ANALYSIS

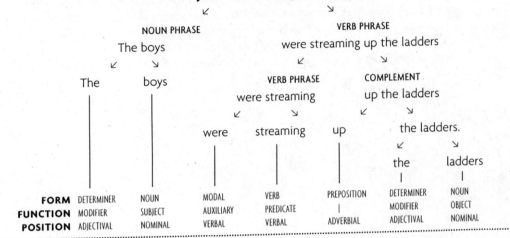

FORM	DETERMINER	NOUN	MODAL	VERB	PREPOSITION	DETERMINER	NOUN
FUNCTION	MODIFIER	SUBJECT	AUXILIARY	PREDICATE		MODIFIER	OBJECT
POSITION	ADJECTIVAL	NOMINAL	VERBAL	VERBAL	ADVERBIAL	ADJECTIVAL	NOMINAL

This introduction has focused on presenting an overview of the organization of *Modern English Structures,* giving special emphasis to its underlying structures—grammatical form, function, and position.

STYLE

Structure plus style is really the basis of understanding language in use. To ignore the latter would be like *flying on one wing.* Yet if we have to follow an order for analysis, structure precedes style because it leads into style.

Traditional literary scholars say that style is the *deliberate use of written or spoken language for a particular effect.* Style, however, is not restricted to poetry, drama, and novels for example; rather it is the personal use that individuals make of language in their speech and writing. It is how words, phrases, and clauses are brought together to express meaning. Just as there are many types of individuals, there are many types of styles. We may contrast a *formal* with an *informal* style; we may speak of an *ornate* or a *comic* style. In literature we may identify a period by its writers' style: an example of this would be the style of Augustan poetry.

To focus in depth on style would add considerable complexity to the aim of this book, so I will leave that area of analysis for further study. Indirectly, I

FIGURE 0.3 ✿ SUMMARY OF GRAMMATICAL STRUCTURES

structures
↓

morphemes
words
phrases
clauses
↓
grammatical
↓

forms	→	what a constituent **IS**
functions	→	what a constituent **DOES**
positions	→	where a constituent **GOES**

introduce you to style by offering you a wide variety of sentence structures taken from current national and international newspapers, popular cultural magazines, and contemporary and traditional literature. Just seeing and reading these sentences will make you aware of the simplicity and complexity of sentence structures, and therefore styles. In itself, it is an excellent context in which to analyse grammar, because this is *real* language in recent and current use. With the exception of a very small number, the examples here have not been written for the purposes of providing grammatical examples; rather, they have been selected from "real life."

form

1   MORPHEMES

MORPHEMES

Morphemes are basic meaningful units in our grammatical system. Understanding morphemes is important: not only do they carry meaning, but they help create new words, move words from one grammatical category to another, and even extend grammatical meaning of words. Figure 1.1 illustrates the variation of morphemes.

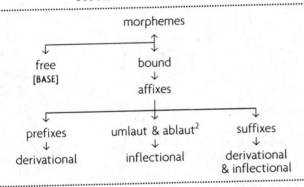

FIGURE 1.1 ✿ MORPHEMES

To analyze morphemes, however, we usually do so at the lexical or word level, that is, units carrying the denotative (dictionary) meaning of words. We look words up in dictionaries to find their meanings, and frequently to learn their composition from other meaningful units (morphemes). Therefore, through our lexicon (words) we learn to understand morphemes.

At this point we can then look up morphemes themselves as parts of words (affixes: prefixes, and/or suffixes) in many dictionaries, to learn their various meanings. In essence these individual segments are themselves morphemes—not words—but they combine to create words.

To illustrate a single morpheme that is not a word, let us examine the word *happiness*—Figure 1.2.

Happiness has two morphemes: the first, *happy*, is easily identified as a word; the second, *-ness*, may cause some difficulty because it is not a word. The morpheme, *-ness*, however, does occur in other words, for example: *foulness, fullness, laziness, strangeness*; it has the meaning "*the quality of*" what it accompanies. By adding *-ness* to

FIGURE 1.2 ✿ MORPHEME BREAKDOWN

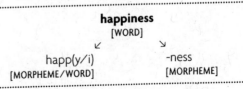

the word *happy* (*an adjective*), we have also created a new word—*happiness* (*a noun*)—meaning "*the quality of being happy.*" The meaning of *happy* does not change by adding the morpheme *–ness*.

Happy can take other morphemes to create more new words, by attaching them either at the beginning or at the end of the base morpheme. In this way we can expand our vocabulary and even change word categories. Consider the variations on the base *happy* in the following paradigm, and note where the morpheme changes a word from one category to another.

Listing variations of morphemes around a single base, as shown in Figure 1.3 creates a *paradigm* (from Greek *para-*, "beside" plus *deigma*, "example"), that is, a model of variations.

FIGURE 1.3 ✿ MORPHEME PARADIGM

	WORDS	BASE	PREFIX	SUFFIX	CATEGORY
			MORPHEME		
1.	happy	happy	—	—	adjective
2.	happiness	happy(y/i)	—	+ ness	noun
3.	happier	happy(y/i)	—	+ er	adjective
4.	happiest	happy(y/i)	—	+ est	adjective
5.	happily	happy(y/i)	—	+ ly	adverb
6.	unhappy	happy	un +	—	adjective
7.	unhappiness	happy(y/i)	un +	+ ness	noun
8.	unhappier	happy(y/i)	un +	+ er	adjective
9.	unhappiest	happy(y/i)	un +	+ est	adjective
10.	unhappily	happy(y/i)	un +	+ ly	adverb

Morphemes changing spelling

A spelling adjustment sometimes occurs to a word when a new morpheme is added at the end of it. *Happy*, for example, changes its final letter *–y* to an *–i–* to accommodate *–ness*: *happ + y* becomes *happ + i + -ness*. To note this variation we show both spellings, *happ + (y ~ i).*[1] Spelling changes can become more complicated with other morphemes. Consider the following examples in Figure 1.4.

1 The symbol "~" means in variation with.

FIGURE 1.4 ✿ SPELLING CHANGES

BASE	MORPHEME	BASE + MORPHEME	CHANGES
abate	+ **-ing**	abat**ing**	loss of final -e
abdomen	+ **-inal**	abdom**inal**	-en becomes -in
brilliant	+ **-cy**	brillian**cy**	-t is replaced by -c
constitute	+ **-ent**	constitu**ent**	loss of final -te
prognosis	+ **-icate**	prognos**ticate**	-t- is added and -is becomes -ic

Such changes are sometimes difficult to explain, probably because they are rooted in historical spelling practices.

Morphemes and words

Most morphemes are *free* and so they are *words*; others are *bound* and require another free or bound morpheme for it to exist at the word level. To understand this difference, we need to distinguish between two levels of analysis, the *morphological* level and the *word* level. The former identifies the internal patterning of words, the base/stem, and affixes (prefixes and suffixes), generally noting only the partial meaning of a word. The latter focuses on the word as a vocabulary item that appears in a dictionary; these units carry the complete denotative (dictionary) meanings. It is through our lexicon that we understand the composition of morphemes. When a morpheme and a word are identical in form, the level of analysis needs to be identified, because a *word* can also refer to structures made up of two or more morphemes. For example, the free form *dog* is a single morpheme at the morphological level, and simultaneously it is a word at the lexical level. It is a morpheme because it cannot be broken down further without losing its word meaning, and it is a word because it is a free form and can stand alone. Note the following example in Figure 1.5.

If we break down the morpheme *dog*, we quickly lose its meaning as a unit. In the first example, the result is a *d* and an *og*, and neither has meaning on its own. In the second example, we end up with a *do* and a *g*. Now the first part *do* has meaning on its own, for it can be a verb; however, the *g* part does not have meaning on its own. Furthermore, to accept *do* as a meaningful unit changes the original meaning of the morpheme/word. The meanings of *dog* and *do* are not in any way similar. The morpheme *dog*, therefore, cannot be further broken down without destroying the original meaning of that morpheme/word.

FIGURE 1.5 ✿ FREE MORPHEME/WORD BREAK DOWN

	dog		dog	[FREE MORPHEME / WORD]
1.	↙ ↘	2.	↙ ↘	
	d og		do g	

The simplicity of the one syllable English word is not a contributing factor here; many polysyllabic words are indivisible along the same lines as *dog*. Consider the following words in Figure 1.6 as representative examples:

FIGURE 1.6 ✿ ONE-MORPHEME WORDS

belligerent	follicle	crescendo	immerse	diamond
mahogany	extreme	mushroom	fluctuate	pioneer

To break any of these words down further would result in losing the lexical meaning of the free morpheme.

Base and stem

BASE
is a lexical morpheme
minus all affixes.

STEM
is a lexical
morpheme with or
without an affix.

Two other terms that require clarification are *base* and *stem*. Base is a morpheme without an affix (prefix and/or suffix); stem is one or more morphemes with or without an affix. These terms are sometimes confused because they overlap at the stage of *without an affix*. A base is identical to a stem without an affix; once the base takes on an affix it can only be called a stem.

A base is a free or bound morpheme carrying the lexical meaning for that unit. It is a word or that part of a word that we look up in a dictionary to find its meaning. The following example illustrates a base/stem and then a stem with affixes.

1. [base/stem]
   consider

To begin with, **consider** is a base/stem, that is, a single morpheme. It belongs to the verb category and lexically has the meaning (to think about). Any further division of this unit and the lexical meaning will be lost. At this point base and stem are identical in form, that is, they are one and the same.

2. [base/stem]   +   [morpheme]   [stem/singular noun]
   consider   +   *(at)ion*   =   consideration

With the addition of the morpheme -*(at)ion*, we now have a stem because an affix has been attached—**consideration**. The unit has lost its base status because we have more than one morpheme; the stem is a singular noun meaning (careful thought). The added suffix also changes the word category from a verb to a noun.

3. [base/stem]   +   [morpheme] + [morpheme]   [stem/plural noun]
   consider   +   *(at)ion*   +   **s**   = considerations

The addition of a second suffix (three morphemes altogether counting the base) creates a new stem, **considerations**, a plural noun meaning (careful thoughts). The grammatical meaning of the word is extended from *singular* to *plural*.

4. [morpheme] + [base/stem] + [morpheme] + [morpheme]   [stem/plural noun]
   re   + **consider**   + *(at)ion*   +   **s**   = reconsiderations

Again, we have a new stem, **reconsiderations**, a noun (to think about again) with a slight variation of the previous lexical meaning. We have created three new words from the single base/stem **consider**, and we have changed the word category. That is probably as far as one would go with this word base; however, you could be very imaginative and ask is *non-reconsiderations* a word? This would be adding yet another prefix.

Knowing the number and order of affixes added to a base/stem, either prefixes or suffixes, is very helpful in understanding the composition of words.

Here is a rare example of a base/stem with a derivational prefix and four derivational suffixes: *deinstitutionalization*.[2]

```
 1              2     3     4     5
de + institut + ion + al + iz + ation
```

Free morphemes

Free morphemes are exactly that—"free"—because they do not require a second free or bound morpheme to express full meaning at the word level. When we first see them, we think of them as words because that is our general level for grammatical analysis. Only when we consider them as morphemes do we recognize the difference. This is illustrated in the following Figure 1.7.

First we see *black* and *bird* as two free morphemes/words; yet when combined they create only one word. In combination they are still two free morphemes. In the second example, *black* is a free /word; combined with *-ness*, a bound morpheme, it is still only one word.

Next we see *up*, *and*, *about* as three separate free morphemes/words; yet when combined they create a single compound word. Combined they are still free morphemes.

FIGURE 1.7 ✿ FREE MORPHEMES

EXAMPLES	MORPHEME TYPE	WORD
black	free morpheme	one word
bird	free morpheme	one word
blackbird	two free morphemes	one word
up	free morpheme	one word
and	free morpheme	one word
about	free morpheme	one word
up-and-about	three free morphemes	one compound word

Bound morphemes

Bound morphemes, in contrast to free morphemes, cannot stand alone at the word level, and for this reason it may appear that they do not have meaning. This, however, is not the case, for bound morphemes, as we have seen, do have meaning. It may be at the word level that this meaning is not apparent. If we look up the whole word in a dictionary, we can seen if it consists of more than one morpheme to note its breakdown. Many bound morphemes can also be looked up individually as affixes (prefixes or suffixes) in many dictionaries. For examples, *com-* or *col-* or *con-* as prefixes mean: 1. *Together, with; joint; jointly*[3]; *-ation, -tion* or *-ion* as suffixes mean: 1. *Action* or *process*: *strangulation*.[4] It is important to note the position of the dash: (-) after the morpheme notes a prefix, and the dash before the morpheme notes a suffix. Without the acknowledged dash (-) what may appear to be a morpheme affix may be, indeed, a free morpheme in its own right; for example, from the above *con* without the dash can be a free morpheme meaning: 1. As a verb "to con a person"; or, 2. as a noun it is the slang word for "convict."

FREE MORPHEMES can stand alone with meaning.

BOUND MORPHEMES do not stand alone with meaning; they join other free or bound orphemes to create a word.

2 Hope, Majorie and James Young, "The Homeless: On the Street, on the Road." *Christian Century*, January 18, 1984, p. 48.

3 *The American Heritage College Dictionary*, 3rd edn. Houghton Mifflin: New York, 1993, p. 277.

4 Ibid, p. 86.

FIGURE 1.8 ✿ BOUND MORPHEMES

WORDS	BOUND PREFIX MORPHEMES		BOUND BASE MORPHEME
abject	ab-	= *from, away, of*	-ject
deject	de-	= *down, away from*	-ject
eject	e(x)-	= *out of*	-ject
inject	in-	= *in, into*	-ject
object	ob-	= *to, toward, before*	-ject
project	pro-	= *in front of*	-ject
reject	re-	= *again, back*	-ject
subject	sub-	= *lower in position*	-ject

Comparing similar words in a paradigm is most helpful to fully understand the concept of bound morphemes. Consider examples in Figure 1.8.

The highlighted bound morphemes are formed on the base/stem *–ject* meaning, *to throw or cast*, to create new words. Each of the prefixes has a distinctive meaning, while the base morpheme remains constant. If we look up *eject* we will find its meaning is *to drive or force out*, and we can compare this with *reject* and its meaning *to throw back*. The meaning of the bound base is evident in both words. Taking this further we can create a paradigm: *abject, deject, inject, object, project*, and *subject*. For the most part we can work out the meaning of each of these words because of the base; only the prefixes need to be given meaning.

A problem with many bound morphemes is that their meanings are not readily apparent, and therefore we have to consider the etymology (the origin and development) of the morpheme(s)/word. Often this means the unpacking of a dead or dying metaphor coined in another language, or simply looking up the root (the base/stem within a word which carries the main lexical meaning) in a foreign language. The following Figure 1.9 illustrates bound morphemes.

In the first example, *ten-* and *-ant* (from Latin *tenere*, "to hold" and *-ant* "one that"), we have two bound morphemes; the base is *ten-* and the suffix morpheme is *-ant*. Neither can stand alone as a complete word with meaning; yet, combined they form a single word *tenant*. Here is where the dash is most important; without it we have two free morphemes/words. *Ten* is a number; *ant* is an insect. Neither, however, reflects the original meaning "to hold."

For the second example, *cosm-* and *-ic* (from Greek *Kosmos*, "the universe" and *-ikos*, "like to") the same applies. To understand the meaning of either of these bound morphemes, we really need to study the etymology of the word and to find its meaning in its originating language.

The single bound morpheme, *ten-*, can occur in a derivational paradigm, which makes its meaning easier to understand. Consider the paradigm in Figure 1.10.

FIGURE 1.9 ✿ BOUND BASE MORPHEMES

EXAMPLES	MORPHEME TYPE	WORD
ten-	bound	not a word
-ant	bound	not a word
tenant	two bound	one word
cosm-	bound	not a word
-ic	bound	not a word
cosmic	two bound	one word

FIGURE 1.10 ✿ BOUND BASE PARADIGM

BASE	BOUND MORPHEME	WORD
ten-	+ **-ant**	ten**ant**
ten-	+ **-able**[5]	ten**able**
ten-	+ **-acious**	ten**acious**
ten-	+ **-acity**	ten**acity**
ten-	+ **-ure**	ten**ure**

5 *Able* as a free morpheme has the meaning of "having the power, skill (to do something)"; *-able* as a suffix has the meaning "able to (durable) or capable of being."

Since we structure our sentences based on words and not on isolated morphemes, it is sufficient to say that bound morphemes simply require a second morpheme (free or bound) to form a word, to move a word from one category to another, or to extend grammatical meaning.

Affixes (prefixes and suffixes; derivational and inflectional)

Affix is an "umbrella term" for bound morphemes, which are dependent on a base/stem to form a word. They can be either prefixes (before) or suffixes (after), attached to a base/stem. They are very useful units for our language flexibility, because they allow us to do three things:

1. To create new words from pre-existing ones,

[PREFIX]	.	[BASE/STEM]		[NEW WORD]
un-	+	happy	=	unhappy

2. To move words from one word class to another by adding certain affixes,

[NOUN]		[SUFFIX]		[ADJECTIVE]
man	+	-ly	=	manly

3. To extend grammatical meaning.

[VERB]

[1ST/2ND PERSON SINGULAR]		[SUFFIX]		[3RD PERSON SINGULAR]
sing	+	-s	=	sings

Affixes are not placed indiscriminately on words; there are guidelines depending on the purpose of attachment. Often more than one morpheme affix will be attached as a prefix or suffix, or both.

PREFIXES

Prefixes are bound morphemes added to the beginning of a base/stem to create new words from pre-existing ones. Their meanings are usually those of English prepositions and adverbs, which generally make them more familiar to us. We classify all prefixes as *derivational* morphemes, a category which we shall cover shortly. English has approximately seventy-five prefix morphemes; Figure 1.11 following shows a representative list with their meanings and examples.

Many of these prefixes vary only slightly from one another in meaning, so we need to be careful when using them. Prefixes expressing the negative (*a-, in-, non-, un-*) are the most common. Knowing these slight variations is important for understanding the meaning of the word.

Some prefixes cause problems in that they are spelled and sound the same, but their meanings differ somewhat when attached to certain base/stems.

FIGURE 1.11 ✿ PREFIX MORPHEMES

PREFIXES	MEANINGS	EXAMPLES	
a-	in, into, on, at	**a**board	**a**sleep
a-	not	**a**sexual	**a**gnostic
ab-	away, from, down	**ab**dicate	**ab**duct
anti-	against, opposite	**anti**biotic	**anti**dote
co-	together, with	**co**operate	**co**exist
com-	with, together with	**com**bine	**com**pass
con-	together	**con**ceive	**con**cern
de-	away, from, off	**de**rail	**de**cline
dis-	separation	**dis**honest	**dis**joint
in-	no, not, without	**in**sufficient	**in**apt
intra-	within	**intra**mural	**intra**city
mal-	bad, wrong	**mal**content	**mal**treat
mis-	wrong(ly), no	**mis**behave	**mis**hap
non-	not	**non**active	**non**basic
ob-	toward, whole	**ob**ject	**ob**solete
post-	after in time	**post**mortem	**post**date
pre-	before in time	**pre**cede	**pre**clude
un-	not	**un**faithful	**un**happy

Consider, for example, the *ex-* prefix in Figure 1.12 below.

The *ex-* morpheme in each of the words has the same sound, but its meaning varies slightly. The *ex-* morpheme in *exalt* does not have the same meaning as the *ex-* morpheme in *exterminate*. The former means (to move upward), while the latter means (to do so thoroughly). The context is important, because its meaning varies slightly with the base morpheme to which it is attached.

Knowing the number and order of affixes added to a base/stem, either prefixes or suffixes, is very helpful in understanding the composition of words. Often only one prefix occurs, and it is a negative; however, many words have two prefixes as Figure 1.13 shows.

FIGURE 1.12 ✿ PREFIX MORPHEMES

EXAMPLES	**ex-** MEANS[6]	
exalt	upward	*to move upward*
excess	beyond	*to move beyond*
expel	from, out	*to move away from, out of*
ex-president	former	*the previous or former person*
exterminate	thoroughly	*to do so thoroughly*

FIGURE 1.13 ✿ PREFIXES ADDED TO A BASE/STEM

PREFIXES	PREFIXES	BASE/STEM
counter-	+ **re-**	form
multi-	+ **de-**	nomination-al
co-	+ **ad**	minister
out-	+ **de-**	sign
over-	+ **in-**	form
re-	+ **a-**	just
un-	+ **en-**	force-able

6 *Webster's New World Dictionary*, p. 212.

Unlike suffixes as we shall see, more than two prefixes is uncommon. The following example, *non-co-independent*, may be pushing the limits; however, there is a valuable exercise in seeking these out.

[PREFIX]		[PREFIX]		[PREFIX]		[BASE/STEM]
non-	+	co-	+	-in-	+	dependent

We can conclude, therefore, that one or two prefixes on a base/stem is not uncommon; more than two is most unlikely. As well, the negative prefix closes off the stem to further additions.

SUFFIXES

Suffixes are bound morphemes occurring after bases/stems; they are more complex than prefixes and also more numerous. The complexity grows out of the fact that suffixes can be added one to another, and unlike prefixes there are often more than two suffixes. Whereas all prefixes are derivational; suffixes can be either derivational or inflectional. The meanings of suffix morphemes are generally more distinctive than those for prefixes. Figure 1.14 shows a partial list of derivational suffix morphemes.

SUFFIXES
are bound morphemes occurring after bases or stems.

FIGURE 1.14 ✿ SUFFIX MORPHEMES

SUFFIX	MEANINGS	EXAMPLES	
-al	of, like	norm**al**	form**al**
-able	capable	dur**able**	love**able**
-(at)ion	act, condition, result	alter**ation**	audit**ion**
-er	one who does	play**er**	jok**er**
-ful	quality of	joy**ful**	help**ful**
-ic	like, do with	angel**ic**	volcan**ic**
-ive	nature of	creat**ive**	substant**ive**
-ize	cause to be (like)	steril**ize**	oxid**ize**
-less	without, not	value**less**	tire**less**
-ment	result, act	move**ment**	govern**ment**
-ness	state, quality	sad**ness**	new**ness**
-ous	full of	hazard**ous**	danger**ous**
-ship	state, skill	friend**ship**	leader**ship**
-(t)ion	act, state of	correc**tion**	ela**tion**
-ure	result	expos**ure**	compos**ure**
-y	little, like	kitt**y**	dirt**y**

The following example illustrates a base/stem with a series of three derivational morphemes; more than three is rather exceptional. However, with the addition of a final inflectional morpheme, a total of four suffixes is not uncommon.

FIGURE 1.15 ✿ SUFFIXES ADDED TO A BASE/STEM

BASE/STEM	SUFFIXES				NEW WORD
commerce	1	2	3	4	
	+ -ial				commercial
	+ -ial	+ -ize			commercialize
	+ -ial	+ -ize	+ -ation		commercialization
	+ -ial	+ -ize	+ -ation	+ s	commercializations

Again, the latter example may be pushing the limits; but its purpose is to show that after a series of derivational suffixes an inflectional suffix may be added.

Similar to prefixes, there are suffixes that vary in meaning although they may sound and be spelled the same. Figure 1.16 illustrates this.

All of the *-er* morphemes in Figure 1.16 vary in their meanings. The first four show a morpheme with slight variations of meanings, "*one who …*"; whereas the last *-er* morpheme has an entirely different meaning, which we shall discuss under *inflectional morphemes*.

7 *Webster's New World Dictionary*, p. 208.

FIGURE 1.16 ✿ SUFFIX PROBLEMS

EXAMPLES	-er- MEANING[7]
	DERIVATIONAL
play**er**	one who
New York**er**	one living in
spray**er**	one that
flick**er**	repeatedly
	INFLECTIONAL
great**er**	comparative

DERIVATIONAL

DERIVATIONAL AFFIXES are bound morphemes added to bases or stems to create new words from pre-existing ones, and sometimes to move a word from one category to another.

Derivation describes the common and productive process of forming new words by adding meaningful affixes to pre-existing word bases, and sometimes they move a word from one category to another. All prefixes and *most* suffixes are derivational morphemes. As prefixes they often close off words and seldom build beyond two morphemes; as suffixes they seldom close off a word and allow for other derivational and/or inflectional suffixes to be added.

An example of four derivational suffixes is found in the word *phonological*.

$$\underset{}{\text{phono} + \text{o}} \quad + \quad \overset{1}{\text{log}} \quad + \quad \overset{2}{\text{ic}} \quad + \quad \overset{3}{\text{al}}$$

The following figure shows examples of derivational prefixes and suffixes as they change word categories.

FIGURE 1.17 ✿ DERIVATIONAL AFFIXES

BASE	ORIGINAL CATEGORY	PREFIX + BASE	NEW WORD CATEGORY
fill	verb	**re**fill	verb/noun
city	noun	**inter**city	adjective
date	noun/verb	**post**date	verb
plain	adjective	**ex**plain	verb
found	verb	**pro**found	adjective
rail	noun	**de**rail	verb
sleep	noun/verb	**a**sleep	adjective
tempt	verb	**at**tempt	verb/noun

BASE	ORIGINAL CATEGORY	BASE + SUFFIX	NEW WORD CATEGORY
angel	noun	angel**ic**	adjective
correct	verb	correct**ion**	noun
improve	verb	improve**ment**	noun
sad	adjective	sad**ly**	adverb
sterile	adjective	steril**ize**	verb
together	adverb	together**ness**	noun
up	adverb	up**on**	preposition

However, the change in word category does not necessarily happen every time an affix is added; some categories overlap. The base *fill* does not have to move categories with the addition of *re-*, because *refill* can be used either as a verb or as a noun.

It is also helpful to remember that certain derivational suffixes help to identify a word category: *-ment*, *-ness*, and *-ion* identify nouns; *-ic* is typical of adjectives; *-ly* is typical of adverbs (although a number of adjectives end with it as well); and *-ize* is reflective of verbs.

INFLECTIONAL

Inflectional suffixes are bound morphemes occurring after a base/stem, producing different forms in the paradigm of the same word. We identify nine inflectional suffixes: three are attached to the category of nouns, four to the category of verbs, and two to the categories of adjectives and some adverbs. Inflectional morphemes differ from derivational morphemes in that they extend grammatical meaning; they do not create news words, nor change word category.

We have been using the phrase *lexical meaning* up to this point, and we now introduce its counterpart—*grammatical meaning*.

> **Lexical meaning** is the denotative or dictionary meaning that a speaker attaches to actual objects, events, actions etc.; for example: "*A box is a square or rectangular container with hard or stiff sides.*"[8]

> **Grammatical meaning** has to do with the relationships of words within a sentence; for example: *Box**es** (plural noun) **are** (plural verb) square or rectangular containers (plural noun) with hard or stiff sides (plural noun).*

The changes, singular to plural nouns and singular to a plural verb, illustrate grammatical relationships within this sentence. These changes from singular to plural do not create new words, nor do they change word categories; they simply extend the grammatical meaning from *singular* to *plural*.

Inflectional morphemes in English specialize in expressing grammatical meaning. Several of the primary categories or *parts of speech* are inflected to show relationships to other words within sentences: *nouns*, *verbs*, *adjectives*, and *adverbs*.

Some inflections in English are irregular in that they do not come at the end of words as suffixes, but occur in the middle of a word. These irregular forms are sometimes called *infixes*, which work inside the word instead of at its boundaries, to parallel prefixes and suffixes; however, they are not infixes as understood in other languages. The linguistic phrase for these changes is *morphological processes*. What goes on in this process is that one unit of grammatical meaning is actually replaced by another unit of grammatical meaning.

English has two types of these processes: umlaut [Greek um = *about* + laut = *sound*] or *mutation*, and ablaut [Greek ab- = *away* + laut = *sound*] or *gradation*. The first accounts for internal modifications taking place in irregular nouns; the

INFLECTIONAL AFFIXES are bound morphemes occurring after or within a base or stem, producing different forms in the paradigm of the same word.

8 *Collins Cobuild Learner's Dictionary* (Concise Edition). Harper Collins: 2001, p. 126.

second accounts for internal modifications taking place in irregular verbs. Both processes produce changes in grammatical meaning, and date back to the language of the Old English period. Figure 1.18 contrasts regular and irregular formations of noun plurality and verb tenses.

FIGURE 1.18 ✿ INTERNAL MODIFICATION OF NOUNS AND VERBS

	REGULAR	IRREGULAR
	Nouns	Umlaut
singular	table	foot
plural	table**s** [-s suffix]	f**ee**t [-ee- umlaut]
	Verbs	Ablaut
present	ask	sing
past	ask**ed** [-ed suffix]	s**a**ng [-a- ablaut]

NOUNS As Figure 1.19 shows, regular nouns are marked with three inflectional suffixes to extend grammatical meanings.

FIGURE 1.19 ✿ REGULAR NOUN INFLECTIONS

GRAMMATICAL MEANINGS	INFLECTIONS	EXAMPLES
1. Noun plural	**-s** or **-es**	girl**s** or church**es**
2. Noun singular possessive	**-'s**	girl**'s**
3. Noun plural possessive	**-s'**	girl**s'**

VERBS As Figure 1.20 shows, regular verbs are marked with four inflections to express grammatical meanings.

FIGURE 1.20 ✿ REGULAR VERB INFLECTIONS

GRAMMATICAL MEANINGS	INFLECTIONS	EXAMPLES
1. Present 3rd person singular	**-s**	walk**s**
2. Present participle	**-ing**	walk**ing**
3. Past tense	**-ed**	walk**ed**
3. Past participle	**-ed**	walk**ed**

Because inflections for the past tense and past participle are the same, it might appear that these could cause problems, and they do. However, there are guidelines for distinguishing between them; as we move into verb structures we shall see that the past participle will require a supporting auxiliary verb, and this distinguishes it from the past tense.

ADJECTIVES AND ADVERBS   Adjectives are inflected, using *-er* and *-est* to express the grammatical meanings of *comparative* and *superlative* degrees, respectively. The stem form is called the *positive* and is not inflected.

Adverbs are generally not inflected; instead, we mark them with different derivational suffixes: *-ly* (carefully), *-wise* (clockwise), and *-ward* (skyward).

Depending upon the syllabic structure of adjectives and adverbs, inflections *-er* and *-est* are replaced with *more* and *most*, respectively.

FIGURE 1.21 ✿ REGULAR ADJECTIVE AND ADVERB INFLECTIONS

GRAMMATICAL MEANINGS		INFLECTIONS	EXAMPLES
1. Positive	$\emptyset$[9]	great	[ADJECTIVE]
		fast	[ADVERB]
		careful	[ADVERB]
2. Comparative	**-er**	great**er**	[ADJECTIVE]
		fast**er**	[ADVERB]
	more	**more** grateful	[ADJECTIVE]
		more carefully	[ADVERB]
3. Superlative	**-est**	great**est**	[ADJECTIVE]
		fast**est**	[ADVERB]
	most	**most** grateful	[ADJECTIVE]
		most carefully	[ADVERB]

9 "ø" has the meaning of zero or no ending.

English follows the order of always adding derivational suffixes before an inflectional suffix to a base/stem. An earlier example illustrates this very well.

base/stem +   derivational suffixes   +   inflectional suffix
commerce   +   -ial
           +   -ial + -ize
           +   -ial + -ize + -ation   +   -s

Inflectional suffixes always close off a word; no other suffix may be added, neither a derivational nor another inflectional morpheme.

MORPHEME VARIANTS

Irregular noun inflections

English nouns have a number of inflectional variations as noted in Figure 1.22.

FIGURE 1.22 ✿ IRREGULAR NOUN UMLAUT INFLECTIONS

NOUNS (SINGULAR)	NOUNS (PLURAL)	MORPHEME (INFLECTIONS)	
go**oo**se wom**a**n	ge**ee**se wom**e**n	umlaut	-oo- → -ee- -a- → -e-
child ox	child**ren** ox**en**	plural	+ -(r)en
alumn**us** stimul**us**	alumn**i** stimul**i**	plural	-us → -i
dat**um** criteri**on**	dat**a** criteri**a**	plural	-um → -a -on → -a
alumn**a** formul**a**	alumn**ae** formul**ae**	plural	-a → -ae
deer fish	d**ee**r f**i**sh	plural	-ø[10]

English plurality consists of both regular and irregular inflections. For most nouns we simply add an *-s* or *-es* to the base/stem of the word. For irregular forms, if they are historical English forms, they have an umlaut change, an *-en* or *-(r)en* suffix or ø. All other suffix variations result from English word borrowing.

Irregular verb inflections

Certain verbs also have irregular inflections; these are also forms derived from the language of the Old or Middle English period. Words borrowed at a later time from other languages follow the regular inflection for English verbs.

Whereas an internal change within a noun is called an *umlaut*, an internal change within a verb is called an *ablaut*. There are many ablaut variations in English as can be seen in the following Figure 1.23.

FIGURE 1.23 ✿ IRREGULAR VERB ABLAUT INFLECTIONS

STEM	PAST TENSE	PAST PARTICIPLE	MORPHEME ABLAUT INFLECTIONS				
arise	arose	arisen	-i-	→	-o-	→	-i-
bind	bound	bound	-i-	→	-ou-		
bleed	bled	bled	-ee-	→	-e-		
come	came	came	-o-	→	-a-		
dig	dug	dug	-i-	→	-u-		
draw	drew	drawn	-a-	→	-e-	→	-a-
drink	drank	drunk	-i-	→	-a-	→	-u-
fly	flew	flown	-y-	→	-e-	→	-o-
hang	hung	hung	-a-	→	-u-		
sit	sat	sat	-i-	→	-a-		
shine	shone	shone	-i-	→	-o-	→	-o-

Vowel variations generally occur in the past tense and past participle of the base/stem. The examples presented here are only representative; the patterns become quite complex if we focus on all the ablaut patterns. Fortunately, we have learned these irregular forms as children acquiring our language, and so they generally do not cause us difficulties.

Overlapping with these ablaut variations are a number of irregular suffixes and some bases/stems which do not change for the past tense and past participle. Figure 1.24 illustrates these variations.

FIGURE 1.24 ✿ IRREGULAR VERB SUFFIX INFLECTIONS

STEM	PAST TENSE	PAST PARTICIPLE	MORPHEME SUFFIX INFLECTIONS				
arise	arose	arisen	-i-	→	-o-	→	-i- + -n
draw	drew	drawn	-a-	→	-e-	→	-a- + -n
know	knew	known	-o-	→	-e-	→	-o- + -n
beat	beat	beaten	+ -en				
bid	bid	bidden					
hear	heard	heard	+ -d				
lie	lied	lied					
dream	dreamt	dreamt	+ -t				
burn	burnt	burnt					
cut	cut	cut	ø				
let	let	let					

In Figure 1.24 we have three examples with an umlaut variation plus an -*n* suffix. Other examples show the addition of -*en*, -*d*, -*t* and ø inflections. Appendix B, *Irregular Verbs*, will list other irregular forms, for example, the verb *be* with variations of *was* and *been*; *bring* with *bought* and *bought*; *go* with *went* and *gone*.

FIGURE 1.25 ✿
INFLECTION PROBLEMS

EXAMPLES	-s MEANING
NOUN	
cat**s**	plural
cat**'s**	possessive singular
cat**s'**	possessive plural
VERB	
sing**s**	3rd person singular

We saw with the derivational prefix *ex-* and the derivational suffix *-er* that problems with meaning can occur. One of the more confusing morphemes in English is the inflectional suffix *-s*; it has four possible grammatical meanings, depending on its word category. Although all four examples are inflectional suffixes, their grammatical meanings are again different.

This is the benefit of analyzing words according to their morphemic status. We not only come to understand the word as a whole, but we also learn the individual parts that make up that word, and the variation of meanings attributed to particular morphemes. Variations of morphemes may seem confusing at first, but they are very helpful in understanding word formations in English.

MORPHEME ANALYSIS

The next important step in understanding morphemes is to break words down to identify each morpheme component. The process is a binary one, in that we make a division into two parts at each stage. The general pattern is to first remove the inflectional morpheme, of which there can only be one; inflectional morphemes do not accumulate. Next we remove the derivational morphemes, generally beginning at the extreme right; derivational suffixes do accumulate, so there often is more than one. We say *generally* here because often prefixes are removed before suffixes, but this is not a rule. It depends upon the meaning of the word: in other words, the lexical meaning must always be clearly understood. This process continues until only the base/stem morpheme is left. As each word is broken down into morphemes, we place a wedge under that part of the word in which we make the division to note the order of cuts.

FIGURE 1.26 ✿ MORPHEME ANALYSIS

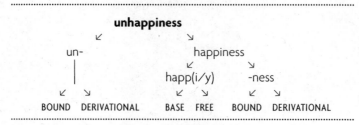

Here are slightly more difficult words broken down.

FIGURE 1.27 ✿ MORPHEME ANALYSIS

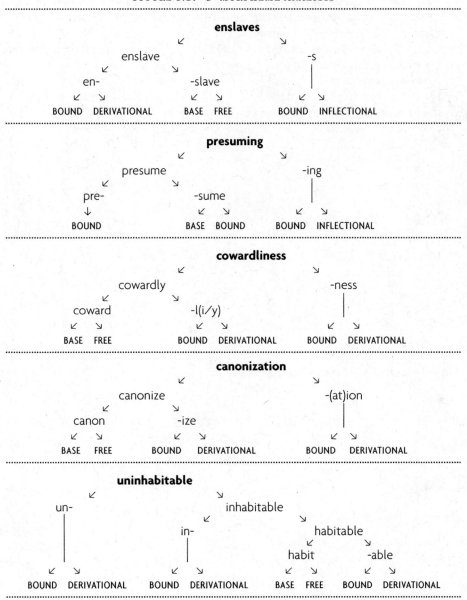

Unlike its Germanic cousins, English has lost most of its inflections (these were more common in Old English). There has been a process of compensating for this loss of inflection by fixing word order, which we shall see is very important to our sentence syntax.

From morphemes we create words, and by means of morphemes we also inflect words. In fact, morphemes form the basis for categorizing parts of speech. It is important to understand the make-up of words and the roles that morphemes carry out in expressing grammatical meanings. With our understanding of morphemes, we can now move on to word categories.

As we analyze and discuss the forms of the various word categories, we shall see again the importance of derivational and inflectional morphemes. In fact, word categories and morphemes are an integral part of each other; word categories cannot be fully understood without knowledge of morphemes.

2 WORDS
FORM CLASS

1 L. Bloomfield,
Language, 8th ed.
(London: Allen &
Unwin, 1962 [1933]).

2 R.R.K. Hartman and
F.C. Stork, *Dictionary of
Language and Linguistics*
(New York: John
Wiley and Sons, 1976),
p. 256.

WORDS

Native speakers have an intuitive understanding of the words they use and what those words mean. We look up words in dictionaries, read them on pages, and often discuss or argue about their particular variations of meanings. As a unit of language, however, the word is more difficult to define. One better known definition comes from Leonard Bloomfield, a linguist, who says that a word is a *minimum free form.*[1] Essentially this means that the word is the smallest unit that we can use alone to form an utterance, and it must consist of at least one free morpheme.[2] Hartman and Stork note that even if we accept this definition, there are words that are marginal: for example, *the, a, of,* etc. can hardly stand alone as utterances. To avoid ambiguity, let us define the concept of "word" in the context in which it is used. Since we are interested in the *word* as a lexical unit, we might define it as a *free standing form consisting of one or more morphemes of which one is a lexical base.*

WORDS
are free standing
forms consisting of
one or more
morphemes of which
one is a lexical base.

The form of words, *what a constituent IS,* is our first category of *grammatical* analysis; this is because words are the smallest units that we use to compose sentences. Although we began with morphemes, these units of themselves have no grammatical function; it is only at the word level and within sentence constituent relationships that we interpret them. We divide words into form (open) class or structure (closed) class categories; each group has common features which characterize its members.

Form class words, as noted in Figure 2.1, are *nouns, verbs, adjectives,*

FIGURE 2.1 ✿ FORM CLASS WORDS AND INFLECTIONS

↓ NOUNS	↓ VERBS	↓ ADJECTIVES	↓ ADVERBS
1. base ∅	base ∅	positive ∅	positive ∅
2. plurality **-s**	3rd person **singular -s**	comparative **-er/more**	comparative **-er/more**
3. singular possessive **-'s**	present participle **-ing**	superlative **-est/most**	superlative **-est/most**
4. plural possessive **-'s or -s'**	past tense **-ed/t**		
5. umlaut	past participle **-ed/t**		
6.	ablaut		

and *adverbs*, which readily admit new members by adding derivational affixes to already existing base/stems to change word category. Most borrowed foreign words follow these patterns.

NOUNS

NOUNS
are form class words generally completing the paradigm of inflections: *-s plurality, 's singular possessive* and *'s or s' plural possessive*.

Regular nouns

Words belonging to the noun category traditionally have been defined as words naming *persons*, *places*, *things*, or *concepts*. This is a rather general and somewhat vague description that often causes problems; it says nothing about the grammatical structure of this category of words. A more precise classification is to identify nouns according to their inflectional paradigm. Figure 2.2 identifies noun inflections.

FIGURE 2.2 ✿ NOUN INFLECTIONS

NOUNS	PLURAL -(e)s pl	SINGULAR POSSESSIVE -s sg ps	PLURAL POSSESSIVE -s pl ps
CODES ∅	{-s pl}	{-s sg ps}	{-s pl ps}
girl	girls	girl's	girls'
lady	ladies	lady's	ladies'
boy	boys	boy's	boys'
dog	dogs	dog's	dogs'

Examples to illustrate these are:

a. [SINGULAR]
"The defense **secretary** took a shot at members of Congress who said he had worked to kill the bill."

"As we talked with shelter providers, we also became involved in debates over responsibility of the **church** and of the state for care of the homeless."

b. [-S PLURAL]
"European **countries** had also made moves to head off certification."

"This group is open to all who are attempting to place harm reduction on the agenda of **churches**, **synagogues** and **mosques**."

c. [-S SINGULAR POSSESSIVE]
"People refer to that as a **Sophie's** choice situation."

d. [-S PLURAL POSSESSIVE]
"Ondaatje writings have continued to resonate with the **Modernists'** interest in myth."

Words that cause confusion when applying possessive inflections are those which end in *-s*. The guidelines for using the apostrophe are:

a. ['S IS ATTACHED TO SINGULAR NOUNS, EVEN IF THEY END IN AN -S]
"By all reports Virginia Feliz had been a happy 6-year-old before her **mother's** expulsion."

"**Bonds's** role in the steroids scandal could be determined as he starts taking aim at Hank Aaron's record of 755 home runs."

b. ['S IS ATTACHED TO IRREGULAR PLURAL NOUNS]
"High winds, driving snow and poor visibility forced cancellation of Thursday's final training for the first **women's** World Cup downhill race of the season."

c. ['S IS ATTACHED TO THE END OF COMPOUND NOUNS]
"He was convicted despite the fact the **22-year-old's** body was never found."

d. ['S IS ATTACHED TO THE SECOND NOUN WHEN JOINED TOGETHER BY A COORDINATING CONJUNCTION TO NOTE POSSESSION]
"On every side lay cultivated fields showing no sign of **war and war's** ravages."

e. [' ONLY IS ADDED TO PLURAL NOUNS ENDING IN -S]
"The **Ratignolles'** soirees musicales were widely known, and it was considered a privilege to be invited to them."

Most words categorized as nouns are inflected in this manner; however, there are always exceptions as we saw when discussing *umlaut* inflections, and these need to be identified.

Irregular nouns

Irregular noun inflections fall into one of four classes: *nouns with only a plural inflection, nouns expressing plurality with no inflection, nouns with irregular inflections,* and *nouns with foreign inflections.* Except for nouns noting inanimate objects, all irregular nouns have regular singular and plural possessives.

1. Nouns with only a plural inflection: Some nouns have only plural forms; there is no equivalent singular form. Figure 2.3 shows representative examples.

There may appear to be singular counterparts to some of these words, for example, cloth/clothes, glass/glasses, and new/news; however, it is the meaning of the word that counts. As noted when discussing morphemes, if the meaning changes when we break down the word it does not belong to the same lexical base.

a. [PLURAL]
"When he moved, a skeleton seemed to sway loose in his **clothes**."

FIGURE 2.3 ✿
NOUNS WITH ONLY A PLURAL INFLECTION

SINGULAR	PLURAL
cloth**es**	cloth**es**
(eye) glass**es**	glass**es**
good**s**	good**s**
headquarter**s**	headquarter**s**
meas**les**	meas**les**
new**s**	new**s**
oat**s**	oat**s**
plier**s**	plier**s**
scissor**s**	scissor**s**

"Here, maybe her **scissors** are in here—and her things."

"We conducted a survey to determine the accuracy of the clinical diagnosis of **measles** in Zimbabwe."

The plurality of these words may be confusing when we consider the broader relationships grammatically. English has *number* (singular and plural) agreement between its subject and predicate within a sentence: a singular subject goes with a singular predicate, and a plural subject goes with a plural predicate. Consider the following two examples:

a. [SINGULAR SUBJECT PLUS SINGULAR VERB]
Measles *is* a contagious disease.

b. [PLURAL SUBJECT PLUS PLURAL VERB]
Measles *are* all over the child's body.

The same form of the noun is used in both cases; yet the verb form changes from singular to plural depending upon the meaning expressed in the sentence. The first sentence expresses *measles* collectively as a single *disease*; whereas the second sentence expresses *measles* as separate spots. A similar problem arises in English with collective nouns: the committee *is* or *are* ...; the government *is* or *are* ....

Nouns in this group are not inflected for the possessive according to the regular paradigm; generally, *possessiveness* is attributed to animate beings and not to inanimate objects. Having said this, it must be noted that English contains many examples of the opposite. However, the rule is more applicable than the exception. Consider the following examples.

a. [ANIMATE]
"I have been held by some whose opinions I respect to have denied **men's responsibility** for their actions."

b. [INANIMATE]
"The expense of getting wool down to the **ship's side** would eat up the farmer's profits."

"The **clinic's director** made no bones about the underlying problem."

"After spending some months in a rather depressing Convalescent Home, I was given a **month's sick leave**."

In the first example, *men* is animate using the regular possessive inflection; the following examples, *ship*, *clinic*, and *month* are inanimate, but the regular inflection is still used. To attribute possessiveness to inanimate objects we generally use the *periphrastic possessive*, that is, a prepositional phrase (beginning with a preposition and followed by a noun). For the inanimate examples, we might expect the following:

> [INANIMATE]
> The expense of getting wool down to the **side of the ship** would eat up the farmer's profits.
>
> The **director of the clinic** made no bones about the underlying problem.
>
> After spending some months in a rather depressing Convalescent Home, I was given **sick leave for a month**.

This is obviously a transitional feature that is happening in English; language is constantly changing.

2. Nouns expressing plurality with no inflection: A second group of irregular nouns has no contrast between singular and plural forms. See Figure 2.4. They show only the existing[3] plural form. These nouns generally name animals.

Examples illustrating this category of nouns are:

> a. [SINGULAR]
> "Now and again **a fish** broke, or a great bird swooped down and slit the surface."
>
> b. [PLURAL]
> "When the **fish** were opened, I saw smaller **fish** taken out of their stomachs."

Occasionally, in spoken dialects[4] you will hear the regular plural for some of these forms:

> a. [PLURAL]
> "'Begob,'" said he, "'tis fine weather for **fishes**.'"

Seeing these words in the context of the whole phrase or sentence is necessary for distinguishing between singular and plural forms.

3. Nouns with irregular inflections: Some nouns have irregular plural forms; their singular and possessive forms, however, are regular. See Figure 2.5. These forms again date to the Old English period, when nouns were categorized as *weak* and *strong* declensions; this is evident by the umlaut forms *feet*, *mice*, and *women*; also the weak plural form *-(r)en*.

FIGURE 2.4 ✿
NOUNS EXPRESSING PLURALITY
WITH NO INFLECTION

SINGULAR	PLURAL	INFLECTION
buck	buck	
deer	deer	zero
fish	fish	ending
salmon	salmon	= ø
sheep	sheep	
trout	trout	

3 It is necessary to note change in grammatical meaning, and because there is no inflection we mark this plural as having a zero (written ø) ending.

4 A variety of language, differing in pronunciation, grammar and vocabulary from the standard language.

Here are some contrastive examples to illustrate these irregular plurals.

a. [SINGULAR]

"At one o'clock I was at the **foot** of the saddle."

"So saying, the energetic little **woman** twirled her hair into a button at the back of her head."

b. [PLURAL]

"He set his **feet** close together, heel to heel and toe to toe."

"For all **women** thought a wound the best decoration a brave soldier could wear."

FIGURE 2.5 ✿
NOUNS WITH IRREGULAR INFLECTIONS

SINGULAR	PLURAL	INFLECTIONS
brother	breth**ren**	-(r)en
ox	ox**en**	-en
foot	f**ee**t	-ee-
leaf	lea**ves**	-(v)es
mouse	m**i**ce	-i-
woman	wom**e**n	-e-

4. Nouns with foreign inflections: English has two sources of irregular word formations, those reflecting earlier formations of the language and those borrowed from foreign languages. We saw that earlier forms can be patterned and explained rather easily. Foreign words are not as easily grouped because they come from languages that have different formations. Some borrowed words often retain their foreign forms for a long time in the host language, while others undergo the process of fitting into regularly inflected paradigms more rapidly. During this process, two forms often exist simultaneously. The representative examples, shown in Figure 2.6, come from Latin and Greek.

FIGURE 2.6 ✿ NOUNS WITH FOREIGN INFLECTIONS

SINGULAR	PLURAL	INFLECTIONS
appendi**x**	appendi**ces**	-ces
	appendi**xes**[5]	-es
alumn**us**	alumn**i**	-i
alumn**a**	alumn**æ**	-æ
criteri**on**	criteri**a**	-a
dat**um**	dat**a**	-a
formul**a**	formul**æ**	-æ
	formul**as**	-s
hippopotam**us**	hippopotam**i**	-i
	hippopotam**uses**	-es
ind**ex**	indi**ces**	-ces
	inde**xes**[6]	-es
nucle**us**	nucle**i**	-i
stadi**um**	stadi**a**	-a
	stadi**ums**	-s
stimul**us**	stimul**i**	-i

The following examples illustrate current use of these forms.

a. [SINGULAR]

"The Jets will take the field at Giants **Stadium** with an 8-3 record."

b. [PLURAL]

"We are proud to present you the most comprehensive stadium database on the net, which currently contains more than 8,500 **stadiums** in over 214 countries."

5 "Appendices" is used to refer to supplementary sections at the end of books or reports, while "appendixes" refers to parts of the anatomy.

6 "Indexes" is used to refer to alphabetical lists at the end of books; "indices" is used elsewhere.

"This is the only guide to all the Greek Football **Stadia** and Basketball Arenas."

Although the forms listed in the last three sections do not follow the regular inflectional noun paradigm, they are quite regular in that they have singular and plural forms. As well, their possessives follow the regular inflectional noun paradigm. We categorize these foreign words as nouns because they function·as nouns, regardless of their forms. The paradigm in Figure 2.7 shows the regular possessive formations.

FIGURE 2.7 ✪ NOUNS WITH FOREIGN INFLECTIONS

NOUNS	-s pl	-s sg ps	-s pl ps
brother	brethren	brother**'s**	brethren**'s**
ox	oxen	ox**'s**	oxen**'s**
women	women	woman**'s**	women**'s**
sheep	sheep	sheep**'s**	sheep**'s**
salmon	salmon	salmon**'s**	salmon**'s**
alumnus	alumni	alumnus**'s**	alumni**'s**
alumna	alumnæ	alumna**'s**	alumnæ**'s**
hippopotamus	hippopotami	hippopotamus**'s**	hippopotami**'s**

Noun groups

We also categorize nouns according to characteristics other than inflections. Consider the breakdown of categories in Figure 2.8.

FIGURE 2.8 ✪ NOUN SUBCATEGORIES

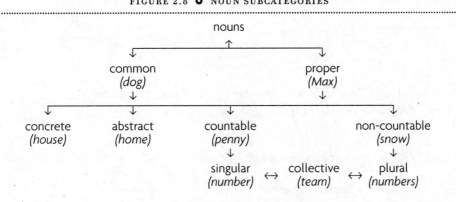

1. Common nouns designate a general class of objects or concepts; while proper nouns refer to specific persons, places, things, or concepts, as shown in Figure 2.9.

FIGURE 2.9 ✿ COMMON VERSUS PROPER NOUNS

COMMON	PROPER		
boy	Holmes	→	person
city	Edinburgh	→	place
car	Land Rover	→	thing
religion	Christianity	→	concept

Examples to illustrate these are:

a. [COMMON VERSUS PROPER PERSON]
"The **boy** returned with a telegram, which **Holmes** handed to me."

b. [COMMON VERSUS PROPER PLACE]
"I recognized the **city** of my dream as **Edinburgh**, where I had never been."

c. [PROPER VERSUS COMMON CONCEPT]
"**Christianity**, like most **religions**, is tied up with specific symbols or sacraments."

1.1. Common nouns are also *concrete* or *abstract*. Concrete nouns have material substance and abstract nouns refer to concepts, qualities and states, as noted in Figure 2.10.

FIGURE 2.10 ✿
CONCRETE VERSUS ABSTRACT NOUNS

CONCRETE	ABSTRACT
heart	heartiness
house	home
blood	bloodshed

Examples for contrastive pairs of concrete and abstract nouns are:

a. [CONCRETE]
"*Cardiology* is concerned with the **heart** and the cardiovascular system and their diseases."

"He sees the idea of 'safe injection rooms' as little better than crack **houses**."

b. [ABSTRACT]
"This mixture of **heartiness** and gravity seemed to sit well on him."

"Belgium is **home** to a number of high-quality museums and institutions."

1.2 Countable nouns occur as singular or plural in a countable number; *non-countable* nouns are not similarly counted.

Some examples to illustrate these are:

a. [COUNTABLE]
"I come from **a land** where they ban all kinds of literature as being subversive."

"I came to this country **three weeks** ago."

"Between 40 and **70 per cent** of the homeless in various American cities are mentally disabled."

b. [NON-COUNTABLE]
"Little **movement** on the bill was seen on Capitol Hill on Tuesday."

"The American military has intentionally used psychological and sometimes physical **coercion**."

"There is still little police **presence** amid the devastation in post-invasion Falluja."

FIGURE 2.11 ✿
COUNTABLE VERSUS
NON-COUNTABLE NOUNS

COUNTABLE	NON-COUNTABLE
land	movement
week	coercion
per cent	presence

1.3 Collective nouns refer to a group of persons, things, or ideas. They are inflected like regular nouns, but their usage often varies depending on whether we consider them to be singular or plural. Figure 2.12 lists a representative group of these nouns.

Illustrative examples for collective nouns, using singular and plural contrasts, are:

a. [COLLECTIVE SINGULAR]
"You are extinct—as **a** county **family**."

"Among these on-lookers were three young men of **a** superior **class**."

b. [COLLECTIVE PLURAL]
"The **family** have to change **their** name."

"In reality, there are two categories of new poor: **members** of the middle **class** and those who always were marginally poor."

FIGURE 2.12 ✿
COLLECTIVE
NOUNS

committee
majority
choir
minority
family
people
government
team
group
class

The key to quickly recognizing whether these collective nouns are being used in the singular or the plural is to check other words in the sentence for number agreement. Sentences using the collective noun as a singular unit are noted by the article *a* preceding the noun in the first two examples; those using the noun as a plural unit are noted by the plurality of an agreeing noun or pronoun, in this case, *their* and *members*.

Nouns are not restricted to a particular subcategory; that is, a single noun can occupy several of these categories. For example:

1. [common, concrete, and countable]   dogs

2. [proper, concrete, and collective]   American Government

3. [proper, abstract, and countable]   Christian faith

VERBS

Regular verbs

VERBS

are form class words having distinctions for a stem, a third person singular and a present participle. (Verbs also have past tense and participle forms that may not be distinctive.)

Verbs have been traditionally defined as *action words*. This definition, however, like the traditional definition for nouns, is rather vague. A more precise way of identifying words belonging to this category is again by inflection. Verbs are form class words having distinctions for a *base/stem*, a *third person singular*, and a *present participle*. (Verbs also have past tense and past participle forms that may not be distinctive).

Verbs are marked with four inflections beyond the base form, as shown in Figure 2.13.

FIGURE 2.13 ❂ VERB INFLECTIONS

VERBS	BASE	3rd PERSON SINGULAR	PRESENT PARTICIPLE	PAST TENSE	PAST PARTICIPLE
CODES	ø	(-s 3rd p sg)	(-ing pp)	(-ed pt)	(-ed ptp)
	look	looks	looking	looked	looked
	talk	talks	talking	talked	talked
	want	wants	wanting	wanted	wanted

Examples to illustrate verb inflections are:

a. [VERB BASE/PRESENT TENSE]
    "I **look** forward to building on her good work."

b. [3RD PERSON SINGULAR/PRESENT TENSE]
    "Yet that is what it **looks** like."

c. [PRESENT PARTICIPLE]
    "As a journalist, he was **looking** to find the truth, not just to have headlines."

d. [PAST TENSE]
"France's Carole Montillet-Carles won both downhills last year but **looked** average in training."

e. [PAST PARTICIPLE]
"It has not **been looked** at because it doesn't suit the coalition."

Some spelling conventions cause additional changes to the bases of verbs when they take on the various inflectional suffixes of the verb paradigm. Many of these were covered in our analysis of morphemes. Figure 2.14 shows five common spelling changes.

FIGURE 2.14 ❖ SPELLING CHANGES

BASE	PAST TENSE	CHANGES
slap	slapped	1. Doubling a final consonant
hope	hoped	2. Dropping the final *e*
carry	carried	3. Changing a final *y* to *i*
keep	kept	4. Loss of -*e*- and taking -*t* rather than -*ed*
dream	dreamt dreamed	5. Verbs taking -*t* and/or -*ed*

Doubling a final consonant on the base is also a frequent occurrence for a number of verbs when forming the present participle. Such verbs also double the final consonant of the base in past tense and past participle forms. See Figure 2.15.

Irregular verbs

Similar to irregular nouns, we also have irregular verbs, which also derive from the Old English period. At that time they were called *strong* and *weak* verbs respectively. Strong verbs formed their past tense and past participle with an *ablaut* or *vowel gradation* (a means of marking different functions of a word by varying the vowel sound in its base). Weak verbs formed their past tense and past participle with an inflectional suffix, that is, a {-*d*} or {-*t*} suffix. With the loss of inflections during the Middle English period, all new verbs took on the weak verb formation with an {-*ed*} or {-*t*} in past forms. This weak formation soon became the norm for what we now refer to as English regular verbs; strong verbs became irregular verbs.

Irregular verbs show differences in the past tense and past participle forms from regular verbs. Where an {-*ed*} inflectional suffix is added to regular verbs, ablaut variations occur in irregular ones. The following subcategories identify the major characteristics, and a more complete list of irregular verbs can be found in the appendix.

FIGURE 2.15 ❖ SPELLING CHANGES— DOUBLING CONSONANTS

BASE	PRESENT PARTICIPLE
begin	beginning
bet	betting
bid	bidding
cut	cutting
dig	digging
forget	forgetting
get	getting
sit	sitting
spin	spinning
spit	spitting
swim	swimming
win	winning

1. Figure 2.16 shows examples of ablaut occurring in the past tense and the past participle, with an inflectional *-(e)n* added to the past participle in the second group.

FIGURE 2.16 ✿ ABLAUT CHANGES IN PAST TENSE AND PAST PARTICIPLE

BASE	ø	(-s 3rd p sg)	(-ing pp)	(-ed pt)	(-ed ptp)
a.	begin	begins	beginning	began	begun
	drink	drinks	drinking	drank	drunk
	ring	rings	ringing	rang	rung
	sink	sinks	sinking	sang	sung
b.	arise	arises	arising	arose	arisen
	eat	eats	eating	ate	eaten
	fall	falls	falling	fell	fallen
	grow	grows	growing	grew	grown
	rise	rises	rising	rose	risen
	throw	throws	throwing	threw	thrown
	wake	wakes	waking	woke	woken

The base, 3rd person singular and the present participle are similar to regular verbs. Changes occur only in the past tense and in the past participle. In the first group there is a consistent change with an *-a-* in the past tense and a *-u-* in the past participle. In the second group there are various changes in the vowels of the past tense, but with the exception of *woken* the others return to the base form plus a suffix *-n*.

Examples to illustrate these are:

a. [VERB BASE/PRESENT TENSE]
"But its standings do not **begin** until one year before the Ryder Cup."

"All religious thought, utterance, and practice **grow** out of particular times and circumstances."

b. [3RD PERSON SINGULAR/PRESENT TENSE]
"The team is in contention for a playoff berth as it **begins** a potentially difficult December schedule."

"As the head **grows** clear the body will turn in the right direction."

c. [PRESENT PARTICIPLE]
"Women are **beginning** to replace men as the primary migrants."

"The stories in this book have been **growing** together for a long time."

d. [PAST TENSE]
"The British House of Commons Home Affairs Select Committee **began** an inquiry into organized crime in Britain."

"We were in the small southern Indiana town where I **grew** up."

e. [PAST PARTICIPLE]
"A series of critical news reports about questionable actions had **begun** to surface about Mr. Kerik."

"As a result, 'she **has grown** old beyond her 17 years,' her mother, told the court."

2. The past tense and the past participle frequently have identical forms in some verbs, ending with a {-t} or {-d} suffix, as shown in Figure 2.17.

FIGURE 2.17 ⚙ IDENTICAL PAST TENSE AND PAST PARTICIPLE

BASE ⌀	(3 p sg)	(-ing pp)	(-ed pt)	(-ed pt-p)
behold	beholds	beholding	**beheld**	**beheld**
feel	feels	feeling	**felt**	**felt**
get	gets	getting	**got**	**got**
sell	sells	selling	**sold**	**sold**

Examples to illustrate these are:

a. [PAST TENSE]
"But these contributions were not offered without serious and strongly **felt** domestic debate."

"His athletic passion did not dim as he **got** older."

b. [PAST PARTICIPLE]
"What Roddick did not explain at the time was that **he had** felt a twinge in his leg."

"You**'ve got** good business sense, I guess."

3. Figure 2.18 shows some other verbs having identical forms for the base, past tense, and past participle.

FIGURE 2.18 ⚙ IDENTICAL BASE, PAST TENSE AND PAST PARTICIPLE

BASE ⌀	(3 p sg)	(-ing pp)	(-ed pt)	(-ed pt-p)
bid	bids	bidding	**bid**	**bid**
cut	cuts	cutting	**cut**	**cut**
bet	bets	betting	**bet**	**bet**

Examples for these irregular verbs are not plentiful; the most frequently used verb is *cut*. However, here are representative examples for the others.

a. [PRESENT TENSE]
"I'll **bet** that I'd find her if she was above ground."

"It **cuts** across class and neighborhood."

b. [PRESENT PARTICIPLE]
"But it **is** simply **betting**."

"This crow **was** not **cutting** through the air with a wide sweep of wing."

c. [PAST TENSE]
"He **bet** basketball, baseball, football and ... hockey games."

"I **would** gladly **cut** out some forty or fifty pages if I could."

d. [PAST PARTICIPLE]
"He **has**n't **bet** on a single race."

"Exact casualty figures were hard to establish because many towns **were cut** off by landslides."

After searching a large corpus of random contemporary written text, it was surprising how few of these irregular verb forms occurred, particularly in the past tense and past participle forms. Those with three similar forms were most rare, and to provide examples it was necessary to search 19th century literary texts.

Finite vs. non-finite verbs

FINITE VERBS express tense and are marked for person and number; non-finite verbs express aspect and voice.

Finite verbs express *tense* and are marked for *person* and *number*; non-finite verbs express *aspect* and *voice*. The verb paradigm has three *finite* and two *non-finite* forms, as shown in Figure 2.19.

The base, third person singular and past tense are finite forms of verbs because they can be contrasted for tense (present and past), and marked for person (1st, 2nd, and 3rd) and number (singular and plural).

FIGURE 2.19 ✿ FINITE AND NON-FINITE VERBS

VERB PARADIGM	VERB FORMS	STATUS
base	drive	finite
3rd per sg	drives	
past tense	drove	
present participle	driving	non-finite
past participle	driven	

a. [1ST AND 2ND PERSON SINGULAR, AND 1ST, 2ND, AND 3RD PERSON PLURAL, PRESENT TENSE]
"This is in part because they **take** language itself so seriously."

b. [3RD PERSON, SINGULAR, PRESENT TENSE]
"She **takes** medication daily and faces an uncertain future."

c. [1ST, 2ND, AND 3RD PERSON, SINGULAR/PLURAL PAST TENSE]
"I **took** a similar course as a divinity student at Yale."

These three forms of the verb paradigm are independent in expressing their meaning.

The present and the past participle forms of verbs are non-finite, and require an additional helping verb to express tense, person and number.

a. [PRESENT PARTICIPLE]
"You ***are getting*** these returns precisely because you are taking on risk."

b. [PAST PARTICIPLE]
"The hugely successful Irish band U2 ***has taken*** a similar approach."

In the first participle example the verb *are* expresses the tense of the verb phrase; whereas, in the second participle example it is the verb *has*. Both participles need helping verbs to express tense. To further illustrate their dependency on helping verbs, consider the following structures.

a. [PRESENT PARTICIPLE]
*[7]You **getting** these returns precisely because you are taking on risk.

b. [PAST PARTICIPLE]
*The hugely successful Irish band U2 **taken** a similar approach.

7 The asterisk "*" means that the structure is ungrammatical.

Without the helping verbs the structures have no tense; participles do not convey tense, person, and number.

Infinitives, participles, and gerunds

Three forms of the verb paradigm are also used in other ways than expressing tense; they are generally called *verbals*.

INFINITIVES

Infinitives are base forms of verbs not limited by person, number, mood, or tense. They are also non-finite verbs, noting no inflections. They consist of at least two words and therefore are actually phrases by form. We generally recognize infinitives as the base of verbs preceded by the particle *to*.

Examples are:

a. [INFINITIVE]
"I had the opportunity **to ask** him about this apparent change."

b. [DOUBLE INFINITIVE]
"There were no real attempts **to stage or film** the work with a primarily dramatic intention in mind."

The only verb with an infinitive form different from the base as used in the present tense is the verb *be*. Here we use:

c. [*BE* INFINITIVE]
"You've mentioned that you never really intended the *Requiem* **to be** a theater piece as such."

PARTICIPLES (PRESENT AND PAST)

Besides being non-finite forms of the verb paradigm, the present participle ending in -*ing* and the past participle in its various forms are also used to qualify nouns and verbs.

Examples are:

a. [-*ING* PRESENT PARTICIPLE QUALIFYING A NOUN]
"He was Ottawa bureau chief for Global Television Network and in mid-stride of a **satisfying** career when cancer struck."

b. [-*ING* PRESENT PARTICIPLE QUALIFYING A VERB]
"He saw an old man **sitting** alone on the porch of his farmhouse."

c. [-*ED* PAST PARTICIPLE QUALIFYING A NOUN]
"In one, she said, an outgoing, academically **gifted** 12-year-old began failing classes."

d. [ABLAUT PAST PARTICIPLE QUALIFYING A NOUN]
"Out of the cramped sky of the upper-right-hand corner, irregular and **broken** lead strips serve to symbolize a halting emanation of angels."

GERUNDS

Gerunds are similar to present participles; they both have an *-ing* suffix. However, gerunds differ in that they are not qualifiers; they name actions, behaviours, or states. Gerunds are frequently called verbal nouns.

Examples are:

a. [GERUND AS VERBAL NOUN]
   "The Enniskillen **bombing** of November 1987 appears to have had a profound impact upon local politicians in Dungannon."

   "The temptations he warded off in the wilderness had to do with **smoking** and **drinking**."

Infinitives, participles, and gerunds will be later discussed more thoroughly as phrases, as well as in their various grammatical roles. The gerund and present participle, however, frequently appear as single words, and for that reason are introduced here. Because all three, *infinitives*, *participles*, and *gerunds* are grouped as verbals, all three were included.

Transitive, intransitive, and linking verbs

Verbs are also identified as *transitive*, *intransitive*, and *linking*. Each verb type has characteristics that guide us in our understanding of that verb category and its relationship to the other sentence constituents. Knowing the differences among these three types will help considerably in the analysis of grammatical functions.

TRANSITIVE VERBS

Transitive verbs take objects, that is, at least one noun or its substitute, functioning as an object(s). Under grammatical function we will identify these in their grammatical roles, as *direct* and *indirect* object(s). Verbs of this type do not require both objects, although both often occur. However, there has to be, at least, a direct object to identify the verb as transitive. Of the three types, transitive verbs are most common because we tend to attribute actions or descriptions to something more so than not. We illustrate this verb type with the following examples.

1. Transitive verbs with an object

a. [TRANSITIVE VERB + NOUN OBJECT]
   "Hackett even **devised** his own ***test*** for Pennington."

TRANSITIVE VERBS
take an object.

b. [TRANSITIVE VERB + PRONOUN OBJECT]
"The program director **tells** *us* that the level of violence has dropped drastically."

c. [TRANSITIVE VERB + GERUND OBJECT]
"John F. Burns contributed **reporting** from Baghdad, and Eric Schmitt and an Iraqi employee of The New York Times also contributed."

2. Transitive verb with two objects

a. [TRANSITIVE VERB + NOUN OBJECT + NOUN OBJECT]
"I can **give** your ***question*** a direct *answer* easily enough."

b. [TRANSITIVE VERB + PRONOUN OBJECT + NOUN OBJECT]
"So saying, **I threw** *him* his *pocket-book*, which he took up with a smile."

INTRANSITIVE VERBS

INTRANSITIVE VERBS do not require objects, but often take complements.

Intransitive verbs do not require objects; frequently, however, they take *complements* (words that identify or complete). Some intransitive verbs almost require a complement; otherwise the sentence seems incomplete.

1. Intransitive without a complement

a. [INTRANSITIVE VERB MINUS COMPLEMENT]
"Most of the centers envisioned **were never built**."

"And then the curious thing **happened**."

"The dog **knows**."

In these examples, the intransitive verbs stand alone and the meaning of the sentence is quite clear; for this reason they do not require a complement.

2. Intransitive verbs with complements

a. [INTRANSITIVE VERB + ADVERB COMPLEMENT]
"Everyone else was **staring *fixedly***, round-eyed, unblinking, certainly not ducking."

[INTRANSITIVE VERB + PREPOSITIONAL PHRASE COMPLEMENT]
"I even **sat *on my hands*** to be sure no one thought I was applauding."

If we leave off the complements here, the meanings of the sentences *seem* incomplete, even though the sentences are grammatically complete and correct.

a. [INTRANSITIVE VERB]
Everyone else was **staring** ...

I even **sat** ...

The tendency is to ask *staring at what?* and *sat where?* The phrases actually complete the meanings of the sentences: they are desired, if not necessary.

Problem: Many verbs can be used either transitively or intransitively, and this causes problems. To distinguish between them it is necessary to identify the constituents that follow the verb. Transitive verbs *must* take objects, and intransitive verbs *may take* complements. Consider the following contrastive examples:

a. [TRANSITIVE VERB]
"Carter **changed** *his mind* on decriminalizing 'soft' drugs."

"Offenders should **stop** *taking drugs and harming society.*"

"Bill Clinton has only slightly **improved** *the situation.*"

b. [INTRANSITIVE VERBS]
"Drieus's romantic notion of war soon **changed** on the battlefield of Charleroi."

"Near the end, Prime Minister Paul Martin **stopped** by the hospital to cheer on and cheer up Vienneau."

"The home-heating subsidy for the poor **will be improved** by more than 25 per cent."

The first group of examples use transitive verbs: these verbs are followed by noun objects. The second group use intransitive verbs, which are followed by complements.

Three contrastive verbs are of particular importance when discussing transitive and intransitive verbs: *lie/lay*, *sit/set*, and *rise/raise*. See Figure 2.20. Their meanings are often confused, with the result that their forms are also confused (particularly in dialect variations).

FIGURE 2.20 ✿ TRANSITIVE VS. INTRANSITIVE CONTRASTS

	BASE ø	(-s 3rd p sg)	(-ing pp)	(-ed pt)	(-ed ptp)
TRANSITIVE	lay	lays	laying	laid	laid
	set	sets	setting	set	set
	raise	raises	raising	raised	raised
INTRANSITIVE	lie	lies	lying	lay	lain
	sit	sits	sitting	sat	sat
	rise	rises	rising	rose	risen

8 *Merriam-Webster's
Dictionary of English
Usage.* Merriam-
Webster, 1994,
p. 587.

"Many people will use *lay* for *lie*, but certain others will judge you uncultured if you do. Decide for yourself what is best for you."[8] This statement from Merriam-Webster's Dictionary points out the confusion that overshadows all three verb contrasts. The following examples have been taken from current usage.

a. [TRANSITIVE VERBS]
"She might **lay *the child*** comfortably in his bed."

"The arts can **set**·us free, unlike our technological, image-making society, which seeks to control us."

"Understanding this helps **raise** the question of the use and limits of authority in the moral sphere."

b. [INTRANSITIVE VERBS]
"Some **lie** staring up at the ceiling."

"She did not **sit** there inwardly upbraiding her husband."

"One instrument in each pair will **rise** as its market index rises."

Here are a few examples where these transitive verbs function intransitively.

a. [INTRANSITIVE VERBS]
"'The dead hand of the present should not **lay** on the future,' I wrote in a recent harangue."

"*Superstar* never **set** out or intended to discuss anything at all like the resurrection."

"I **raised** up from his lap and peered across the tablecloth into father's face."

LINKING VERBS

LINKING VERBS
express states rather
than actions.

Linking or copulative verbs express **states** rather than **actions**. Their primary function is *to relate* the subject of a sentence to a complement that follows it. Both have the same *referent* (referring to the same person, place, or thing). *Be*, its variants (*am, are, is*), and *seem* are the most common linking verbs. These forms have little meaning apart from relating the sentence constituents, subject and complement. A few other verbs with the same joining function are categorized as expressing *existence* or *sensation*. Figure 2.21 shows a representative group of linking verbs.

Be can also be an auxiliary verb; all others except for *seem* can be transitive or intransitive action verbs.

a. [USED AS LINKING VERBS]
"Yet local authorities **are *important***, apart from the executive functions they undertake."

"The policy now is to do whatever council members **feel *fit*** to do."

"Once you let the person stay in the United States, it **becomes *extremely difficult*** in our society to make them go."

"Though a spokeswoman, Hanna German **remained *defiant and confident*.**"

"Houston **has grown *weary*** of addressing the matter."

"Sometimes it **sounds *better*** than when I was practicing four hours a day."

b. [USED AS TRANSITIVE VERBS]
"In the process, we **become *the very thing*** we hate."

"We will **continue *our discussions*** with the Americans."

"Waring told him, 'If you ever need a job, Bob, **look *me*** up.'"

"Finally, there **appeared *the group de resistance*.**"

c. [USED AS INTRANSITIVE VERBS]
"He and his aides said the protest should **continue *until the opposition-drafted electoral amendments become law*.**"

"Measles virus (MV) **remains *among the most potent global pathogens*,** killing more than 1 million children annually."

"Everywhere we were told that their numbers **were growing**, even in summer."

"This article **appeared *in the Christian Century*,** June 18–25, 1986."

To identify the verb type it is important to be able to identify sentence constituents following the verb.

FIGURE 2.21 ✿
LINKING VERBS

EXISTENCE

be: am, are, is, was, were

act
appear
become
continue
grow
prove
remain
seem
sit

SENSATION

feel
look
smell
sound
stay
taste

ADJECTIVES

ADJECTIVES
are form class words
completing the
paradigm of
inflections, *-er* (*or
more*) for the
comparative and *-est*
(*or most*) for the
superlative.

Adjectives are form class words completing the paradigm of inflections, *-er* for the comparative and *-est* for the superlative; the base form of adjectives is called the positive. These inflectional suffixes can be replaced with the words *more* or *most* respectively preceding the adjective for a few monosyllabic, some disyllabic and all polysyllabic adjectives.

Adjectives are classified in many ways: one such approach is to identify them as *descriptive* and *limiting*. Another is to categorize them as *short* and *long*. A third approach is to identify them by the number of syllables occurring in the word as monosyllabic, disyllabic, and polysyllabic adjectives. This method helps to distinguish between inflectional adjectives and those that take *more* or *most*.

Monosyllabic adjectives

Monosyllabic adjectives are generally inflected with *-er* and *-est* suffixes; exceptions to this rule are *right*, *wrong*, and *real*, which take *more* and *most*. Examples to illustrate these are shown in Figure 2.22. Some examples to illustrate these simple inflections are:

FIGURE 2.22 ✿ MONOSYLLABIC ADJECTIVE INFLECTIONS

ADJECTIVES	POSITIVE	COMPARATIVE	SUPERLATIVE
CODES	ø	(-er)	(-est)
MONOSYLLABIC	big	bigger	biggest
	long	longer	longest
	short	shorter	shortest

a. [POSITIVE]
"But now Christian rock is **big** and loud."

"Mr. Yushchenko has **long** insisted that he had been poisoned."

b. [COMPARATIVE *-ER*]
"It works less well if you have a **bigger**, very full soprano voice."

"There can no **longer** be any question of free discussion among theologians."

c. [SUPERLATIVE *-EST*]
"And for some reason, it's been the **biggest** European hit I've ever had."

"That's the **longest** speech you ever made in your life."

Sometimes *more/most* will be used to place emphasis upon an adjective. For example, we have:

a. [ADJECTIVES]
"'I demand the satisfaction due to a gentleman,' said the stranger, who had become **more calm**."

"But in hot climates people generally keep their rooms **more bare** than they do in colder ones."

Disyllabic adjectives

There is no simple rule for disyllabic adjectives; although most adjectives in this group take *more/ most*. Disyllabic adjectives can be further divided into three sub-groups for analysis; see Figure 2.23.

1. Disyllabic adjectives that generally take the inflections -er and -est.

FIGURE 2.23 ✿ DISYLLABIC ADJECTIVE INFLECTIONS

ADJECTIVES	POSITIVE	COMPARATIVE	SUPERLATIVE
CODES	ø	{-er}	{-est}
1.	narrow simple	narrower simpler	narrowest simplest
2.	easy happy	easier happier	easiest happiest
3.	frequent daunting	more frequent more daunting	most frequent most daunting

Adjectives following this pattern are disyllabic words whose second syllable is rather weak; technically they are disyllabic words, but more often they follow the monosyllabic pattern. Examples to illustrate this group are:

a. [POSITIVE]
"A period of relatively **narrow** and restrictive self-definition seems necessary."

"Behind their dark iconoclastic fervor is a **simple** love of music."

b. [COMPARATIVE -ER]
"And there is no part of the country where opinion is **narrower** than it is here."

"But other, **simpler** strategies may help you prepare for a softening of the market, they add."

c. [SUPERLATIVE -EST]
"The house with the **narrowest** front in the world has been sold in Scotland."

"The **simplest** explanation is always the most likely."

2. Disyllabic adjectives that *can* take -*er* and -*est*.

Adjectives following this pattern are disyllabic words whose second syllable stress is stronger; these are usually compared with -*er* and -*est*. Many adjectives in this group end in –*y*, for example: *angry, busy, empty, fancy, happy, heavy, hungry, lazy, lousy, merry, pretty, scary, sleepy,* and *ugly.* In speech, however, it is not uncommon for these adjectives to take *more* or *most.* Adjectives ending in –*ly* can go either way.

Examples for this group are:

a. [POSITIVE]
"Juggling art history and religion is not an **easy** task."

"There were days when she was very **happy** without knowing why."

b. [COMPARATIVE -*ER*]
"It's **easier** to get into Fort Knox than into most churches."

"I was on the whole **happier** with Polly Ann than I had been in the lonely cabin on the Yadkin."

c. [SUPERLATIVE -*EST*]
"It is the **easiest** thing in the world for a man to look as if he had a great secret in him."

"This was always the **happiest** moment of Dale's lonely days, as sunset was his saddest."

3. Disyllabic adjectives that take *more* or *most*.

Adjectives following this pattern are disyllabic words ending in –*ful,* –*less,* –*al,* –*ive,* and –*ous.* Those ending in –*ed* and –*ing* always take *more/most.* Examples to illustrate this group are:

a. [POSITIVE]
"On the nature of worship, one of Shaw's **frequent** themes, he makes three points."

"In Sudan, monitors find [their] tasks **daunting**."

b. [COMPARATIVE *MORE*]
"My visitors became more and **more frequent**."

"This task is much **more daunting** and frightening than propositional purity."

c. [SUPERLATIVE *MOST*]
"And, strange to say, it was not Dorothy whom he chose for his **most frequent** comrade."

"Andy Roddick is fitting right in this week as he prepares for the **most daunting** tennis task of his life."

Polysyllabic adjectives

As a general rule, adjectives in this group always take *more/most*, as shown in Figure 2.24.

FIGURE 2.24 ✿ POLYSYLLABIC ADJECTIVES

ADJECTIVES	POSITIVE	COMPARATIVE	SUPERLATIVE
CODES	ø	{more}	{most}
	beautiful	more beautiful	most beautiful
	important	more important	most important
	successful	more successful	most successful

Here are some examples:

a. [POSITIVE]
"Presently he was joined by a fashionably dressed and **beautiful** young woman."

"He said he wanted everyone to know how **important** their support was in his final battle."

"The results have been astonishingly **successful**."

b. [COMPARATIVE *MORE*]
"No angel in heaven could be **more beautiful** than she appeared."

"Punishing drug offenders became **more important** than getting them off drugs."

"We wouldn't be looking at the process if we had been **more successful**."

c. [SUPERLATIVE *MOST*]
"This has been the **most beautiful** day since February 4th."

"Being alive to music in religion is one of the **most important** elements of a sensitive Christian experience."

"*Cats* has been the **most successful** musical of all time."

A few spelling variations occur when inflectional suffixes are added to some words.

1. When an adjective ends in an -*e*, simply add an *r* to form the comparative and an -*st* to form the superlative; *late* becomes *later* and *latest* respectively.

2. When an adjective ends in a *consonant-vowel-consonant (CVC)*, double the last consonant; *big* becomes *bigger* and *biggest* respectively.

3. When an adjective ends in -*y*, the -*y* becomes an -*i*; *angry* becomes *angrier* and *angriest* respectively.

Irregular adjectives

Some words categorized as adjectives have irregular forms, as Figure 2.25 illustrates. Although some similarities occur in the comparative and superlative forms, they are distinctive in the positive forms.

FIGURE 2.25 ✿ IRREGULAR ADJECTIVE INFLECTIONS

ADJECTIVES	POSITIVE	COMPARATIVE	SUPERLATIVE
CODES	ø	(more)	(most)
	bad	worse	worst
	good	better	best
	far	farther	farther
		further	furthest
	little	less	least
	many	more	most
	much	more	most
	old	elder	eldest

These irregular adjectives are used in the following examples.

a. [POSITIVE]
"There are only two types of music—good music and **bad** music."

"The 1990s showed **little** improvement in the area of social commentary."

"The comparative **littler** and the superlative **littlest** are sometimes used in spoken language for meanings 1, 2, and 4, but otherwise the comparative and superlative forms of the adjective **little** are not used."[9]

b. [comparative *more*]
"She never would represent him as **worse** than he is."

"Jars of Clay has a **less** commercial sound that appeals to 'alternative rock' fans."

c. [SUPERLATIVE *MOST*]
"The **worst** U.S. loss in Ryder Cup history led to a shakeup in the qualification process."

"I had not the **least** doubt that he would do it."

ADVERBS

A dverbs are form class words used to describe actions; they are noted by derivational, rather than inflectional, suffixes: *-ly*, *-wise*, and *-ward*; see Figure 2.26. Unlike other form class words, adverbs are a mixed group, which makes them difficult to sort out. They provide information such as, *when, where,* and *how* something is happening; as well, they express *degree, frequency, manner, place, reason,* and *time,* among others. Adverbs can also be inflected for the comparative and superlative as adjectives are, but in a limited way.

1. Adverbs in -ly: The best-known adverb indicator is the derivational suffix *-ly*. This suffix means *like or characteristic of*, and is used to derive adverbs of manner from adjectives. However, it is not entirely reliable because *-ly* also appears with some nouns, for example, *folly, bully,* and also with some adjectives, *friendly, homely, lovely, ugly*. Confusion with these words will be clarified in how they function as sentence constituents.

Examples are:

a. {*-ly*}
"The obligation to judge **favorably** applies to our children too."

"I spent the time on the whole **happily** with this Dutchman, whose name was Hans Koppel."

"Why do new iMacs surf so **slowly**?"

9 Collins *COBUILD Learner's Dictionary Concise Edition.* HarperCollins: 2001: 644.

ADVERBS are form class words generally noted by the derivational suffixes *-ly, -wise,* and *-ward.*

FIGURE 2.26 ✿ ADVERBS

ADJECTIVES		ADVERBS
favorable		favorably
happy	**+ -ly**	happily
slow		slowly
NOUNS		
heaven		heavenward
length	**+ -ways**[10]	lengthways
side		sideways
side		sidewise
street	**+ -wise**	streetwise
time		timewise

10 The *Scribner-Bantam English Dictionary* (revd edn, 1991) lists *-ways* as an "adv suf" meaning in a specified way, direction, manner, or position.

2. Adverbs in -*wise*: This suffix has the meaning *in a specified direction, position, or manner*. In earlier periods of English, this usage was becoming less common; such usage, however, is now increasing. This derivational suffix is added to many nouns to create adverbs. Note that some adverb forms in *-wise* can also be adjectives in function.

Examples are:

a. {*-wise*}
"Indignant girls were tobogganing **sidewise** down the incline."

"We must become more **streetwise**."

"In a **timewise** solution the data points are considered as a discretized time series."

3. Adverbs in -*ward*: This suffix has the meaning *in a specific direction* and it is also added to nouns to create adverbs. In addition, *-ward* can be added to prepositions and other adverbs to express directions.

Examples are:

a. {*-ward*}
"Maryland coach's success has been a **westward** journey."

"Do not address the eternal question— 'Until when?' —only **heavenward** but also inward."

"After he took a knee to run out the clock, quarterback Chris Rix hoisted the ball **skyward**."

4. Adverbs in -*ways*: This word, at first, may not appear to be a suffix, although its being used as an adverb is not uncommon. Not all dictionaries even list it as a suffix; but those that cover suffixes thoroughly will show it.

Examples are:

a. {*-ways*}
"However, now with some positive **headways** being made, the outfit will start focusing on the examinations."

"The ball activates the muscles **lengthways**, sending the proper signals to the brain."

"European shares tracked **sideways** near recent highs early today."

Inflected adverbs

Adverbs, like adjectives, can also be inflected for the comparative and superlative by taking -*er* and -*est*, or *more* and *most* respectively. See Figure 2.27. Like adjectives, monosyllabic and some disyllabic adverbs form the comparative with -*er* and the superlative with -*est*; other adverbs form the comparative with *more* or *less*, and the superlative with *most* and *least* respectively.

FIGURE 2.27 ✪ ADVERB INFLECTIONS

ADVERBS	POSITIVE	COMPARATIVE	SUPERLATIVE
CODES	ø	(-er)	(-est)
	late	later	latest
	soon	sooner	soonest
	carefully	more carefully	most carefully
	often	more often	most often

Examples are:

a. [POSITIVE]
"After the attacks began **late** in the morning, American troops shut down three of the five bridges."

"The shelter may **soon** close for lack of funds."

"We take everything the Red Cross gives us and study it very **carefully** to look for ways to do our job better."

"In English we **often** distinguish the sciences and the humanities."

b. [COMPARATIVE -*ER*]
"**Later** he was General Secretary of the Board of Higher Education."

"A shuttle mission could be accomplished **sooner** and with a **higher** probability of success."

c. [COMPARATIVE *MORE*]
"Richard could not have planned **more carefully** than he did for these visits."

"Mr. Asakawa has been waking up a lot **more often**."

d. [SUPERLATIVE -*EST*]
"I intend to get through with it soon and trot home to you by the middle of August at the very **latest**."

"'With the least delay, the **soonest** I can arrive is 3 pm.'"

e. [SUPERLATIVE *MOST*]
"With this latter idea in my mind, I examined all the coffee-cups **most carefully**."

"The clock was the machine **most often** in view."

Irregular adverbs

Adverbs also have irregular forms; see Figure 2.28. Like irregular adjectives, positive forms are distinctive, while the comparative and superlatives are similar to one another. To illustrate irregular adjective inflections, consider the following examples.

FIGURE 2.28 ✿ IRREGULAR ADVERB INFLECTIONS

ADVERBS	POSITIVE	COMPARATIVE	SUPERLATIVE
CODES	ø	(-er)	(-est)
	badly	worse	worst
	far	farther	farthest
		further	furthest
	little	less	least
	much	more	most
	well	better	best

a. [POSITIVE]
"Jane suddenly realized that she had behaved **badly**."

"'I don't have peace because I'm not with my **little** girl,' she said in Spanish."

b. [COMPARATIVE]
"Economics as a discipline is not **worse** than others from a Buddhist or Christian point of view."

"National Beef officials estimated that **less** than 20 per cent of cattle is currently tracked by age."

c. [SUPERLATIVE]
"And his was that **worst** loneliness which would shrink from sympathy."

"And this teaching seemed to imply that we need not look elsewhere for any **further** data of revelation, **least** of all in the other religions."

Additional adverbs

Apart from the adverbs presented above, there are many others which belong to this category.

These words we identify as irregular adverbs because of the information they provide and the grammatical function they carry out. Although the headings for these adverbs vary in presentations, the following list is fairly complete, and expresses many aspects of the adverb and its complexity.

1. **Comparison:** *one is like or unlike another in someway.*

   As ... as, better ... than, less ... than, etc.

   "Sure, but perhaps they were **better than** we knew."

2. **Concession**: *a right or privilege given to someone.*

   nevertheless, still, yet, etc.

   "**Nevertheless**, she still continued to strive with him."

3. **Degree**: *one indicates the extent that something happens.*

   faster, higher, longer, quicker, etc.

   "For example, I want **faster** communications, easier travel, and more space and facilities in my home."

4. **Direction**: *the general line along which one is moving or pointing.*

   away, down, in, out, outside, up, etc.

   "A few candidates took themselves **out** of the running Friday."

5. **Duration**: *the time during which an event or state takes place.*

   always, as long as, while, until, etc.

   "**As long** as we are unfree—to that extent you are going to be unfree in this country."

6. **Frequency**: *the number of times an event happens during a particular period.*

   often, seldom, never, sometimes, etc.

   "They see us at church, you know, though we **seldom** meet them elsewhere."

7. **Intensifiers**: *to become greater in strength, amount or degree.*

   greater, slightly, too, very etc.

   "At first I thought the singing was on the tape, **too**, and that the vocalists were only lip-syncing the words."

8. **Manner**: *the way in which one does something.*

   badly, normally, favorably, humbly, etc.

   "He helps to keep our lives from being monotonous and gives a little comic relief where it is **badly** needed."

9. **Place**: *any point in space.*

   there, here, somewhere, upstairs, where, etc.

   "I am stranded **here** for tonight and will push on to Newport tomorrow."

10. **Probability**: *how likely something is to happen.*

    maybe, possibly, probably, etc.

    "If Unionists were in power we would **probably** be doing the exact same thing."

11. **Time**: *that which is measured in seconds, minutes, days, weeks, months or years.*

    now, today, frequently, monthly, yearly, etc.

    "**Today**, the artists have talent, the producers have money and the companies have experience."

❖ ❖ ❖

Knowing the forms of words and their categorical groups is basic to understanding how these words function grammatically as sentence constituents. At first, it may appear that there is a great deal of information to remember here. However, native speakers are already familiar with many of these words and know how they function in English, even if they may not know *why*.

The next chapter focuses on *Structure Class* words. These word categories are more diversified than *Form Class* words, particularly regarding word categories. With the exception of pronouns, these words are not inflected for grammatical meaning.

3   WORDS
STRUCTURE CLASS

Structure class is our second class of word analysis. These words are distinct from *form class* words in that they do not accept additions to their categories. For this reason, we called them *closed class* words.

We divide structure class words into five groups: *pronouns, determiners, auxiliaries, prepositions,* and *conjunctions*; each category is further divided as shown in Figure 3.1. The focus of this chapter continues on *Form*, considering in particular the question of *what a sentence constituent **IS***.

FIGURE 3.1 ✿ STRUCTURE CLASS WORDS

structure class words

pronouns	determiners	auxiliaries	prepositions	conjunctions
personal	possessive	primary	simple	coordinating
reflexive	relative	modal	-ing	subordinating
relative	interrogative	do	phrasal	conjunctions
interrogative	demonstrative			
demonstrative	indefinite			
reciprocal	articles			
indefinite	numbers			
	possessive			
	of names			

PRONOUNS

Pronouns are structure class words that substitute for words performing the noun functions. They are the most numerous and varied of this word category, and are subdivided into seven groups. Many personal pronouns can be inflected for *number, gender,* and *case* and some for *person*.

PRONOUNS
are structure class words that substitute for nouns.

[77]

Gender is a grammatical category noting *masculine*, *feminine*, and *neuter* genders. We call these "natural genders." This is a fairly general rule for Modern English, although some exceptions occur.

Number is a grammatical category referring to singular and plural forms. Singular refers to one person speaking or being spoken to; plural refers to more than one person speaking or spoken to.

Case is a grammatical category for inflected nouns, and mostly personal pronouns, showing their relationships to other sentence constituents. English has *subjective*, *objective*, and *possessive* cases. The subjective case applies when nouns/pronouns appear as subjects of finite verbs or as subjective complements of linking verbs. The objective case applies when nouns/pronouns appear as objects of finite verbs or as objects of prepositions. The possessive case applies when we wish to note ownership, generally by animate beings.

Person is a grammatical category that points out and takes note of the speaker. Generally we have both a speaker and a person being addressed. Often they are the same; other times they are not. The first person is *I* or *we*, the second person is *you*, and the third is *he*, *she*, *it*, or *they*.

Personal pronouns

PERSONAL PRONOUNS
name specific persons or things.

Personal pronouns name specific persons or things; they relate to us as persons. See Figure 3.2. Their current complexity dates back to the Old and Middle periods of the English language when it was highly inflected. These pronouns are distinctive in number (singular and plural), case (subjective, objective, and possessive), and person (first, second, third). Third person singular pronouns are also distinctive in gender (masculine, feminine and neuter).

FIGURE 3.2 ✿ SUBJECTIVE/OBJECTIVE PERSONAL PRONOUNS

	PERSON	SUBJECTIVE CASE	OBJECTIVE CASE
SINGULAR NUMBER	1st person	I	me
	2nd person	you	you
	3rd person		
	masculine	he	him
	feminine	she	her
	neuter	it	it
PLURAL NUMBER	1st person	we	us
	2nd person	you	you
	3rd person	they	them

SUBJECTIVE CASE

a. [1ST PERSON SINGULAR]
   "**I** headed to Toronto to broaden my academic horizons."

b. [2ND PERSON SINGULAR AND PLURAL]

"Now **you** will begin to see hospital life in earnest."

c. [3RD PERSON SINGULAR MASCULINE]
"**He** imagined himself on T.V., in an interview."

[3RD PERSON SINGULAR FEMININE]
"**She** would admire the honorable scar."

[3RD PERSON SINGULAR NEUTER]
"**It** may take only a few minutes if the problem is simple and straightforward."

d. [1ST PERSON PLURAL]
"**We** were able to focus the attention of the country on our issue."

e. [2ND PERSON PLURAL]
"**You** all don't understand what I'm saying."

f. [3RD PERSON PLURAL]
"But he said **they** were, 'constantly improving.'"

OBJECTIVE CASE

a. [1ST PERSON SINGULAR]
"'Now, pardon **me**, but I've got an appointment.'"

b. [2ND PERSON SINGULAR]
"'I should have given **you** six months' hard labour.'"

c. [3RD PERSON SINGULAR MASCULINE]
"The narrative would be tedious to **him** and painful to myself."

[3RD PERSON SINGULAR FEMININE]
"I gazed upon **her** with admiration."

[3RD PERSON SINGULAR NEUTER]
"They brought some maple syrup so we heated **it** outside on a camp stove."

d. [1ST PERSON PLURAL]
"Countries are helping **us** with the positioning of water purification units and medical supplies."

e. [2ND PERSON PLURAL]
"Let me tell **you** why there are these squatter camps."

f. [3RD PERSON PLURAL]
"I believe their reader advised **them** quite wisely."

POSSESSIVE CASE

Personal pronouns are also inflected for the possessive case. See Figure 3.3. Similarly inflected for gender and number, they also mark the distinction of *prenominal* (coming before a noun) or *substitutional* (substituting for a noun). Prenominal possessives are pronouns by form, since they replace a noun form; as we will see, they are adjective (modifiers) by function, since they describe the noun that follows.

FIGURE 3.3 ✿ POSSESSIVE PERSONAL PRONOUNS

	PERSON	PRENOMINAL	SUBSTITUTIONAL
SINGULAR NUMBER	1st person	my	mine
	2nd person	your	yours
	3rd person		
	masculine	his	his
	feminine	her	hers
	neuter	its	its
PLURAL NUMBER	1st person	our	ours
	2nd person	your	yours
	3rd person	their	theirs

Examples for possessive prenominal pronouns are:

a. [1ST PERSON SINGULAR]
"I'd sometimes borrow **my** father's car and drive aimlessly around town."

b. [2ND PERSON SINGULAR AND PLURAL]
"'Oh, I beg **your** pardon!' cried Alice hastily."

c. [3RD PERSON SINGULAR MASCULINE]
"Martin Luther King III asked the congregation to remember **his** father's legacy."

[3RD PERSON SINGULAR FEMININE]
"Once or twice she had peeped into the book **her** sister was reading."

[3RD PERSON SINGULAR NEUTER]
"And the Eaglet bent down **its** head to hide a smile."

d. [1ST PERSON PLURAL]
"The integrity of **our** game was beginning to come under fire."

e. [2ND PERSON PLURAL]
"Now, turn off those blasted machines and turn in **your** brown hymnals to Number 144."

f. [3RD PERSON PLURAL]
"I should frighten them out of **their** wits!"

For example, the possessive pronoun *my* signals that a noun will follow; as in *my book*; this phrase is then substituted with the possessive pronoun *mine*. The other substitutional pronouns follow similarly.

Examples for substitutional pronouns are:

a. [1ST PERSON SINGULAR]
"My father paused, and the hand he held to **mine** trembled."

b. [2ND PERSON SINGULAR]
"Would you consider allowing other works of **yours** to be filmed?"

c. [3RD PERSON SINGULAR MASCULINE]
"**His** is an extremely interesting case."

[3RD PERSON SINGULAR FEMININE]
"For this one evening, at least, the beauty of life was unmarred, and no cruel word of **hers** should spoil it."

d. [1ST PERSON PLURAL]
"Now at **ours** they had at the end of the bill 'French, music, and washing—extra.'"

e. [3RD PERSON PLURAL]
"And on the other hand the capitalist classes were allowed to call the best part of the cake **theirs**."

Reflexive/intensive pronouns

Reflexive or intensive pronouns rename or intensify a previous noun or pronoun in the sentence. See Figure 3.4. They usually refer to subjects or objects of sentences. The pronoun and the noun always have the same *referent*, that is, the person or thing to which the word names or refers. These pronouns are somewhat similar to personal pronouns in that they have number and person, but they do not have case.

FIGURE 3.4 ✿
REFLEXIVE/INTENSIVE PRONOUNS

	SINGULAR	PLURAL
1st person	myself	ourselves
2nd person	yourself	yourselves
3rd person		
masculine	himself	
feminine	herself	themselves
neuter	itself	
	oneself	

REFLEXIVE PRONOUNS refer back or intensify something.

Examples are:

a. [1ST PERSON SINGULAR]
"*I* do not think of **myself** as a hero."

b. [2ND PERSON SINGULAR]
"*You* [will] likely find **yourself** motivated."

c. [3RD PERSON SINGULAR MASCULINE]
"*He* ate lunch by **himself** every day."

[3RD PERSON SINGULAR FEMININE]
"Though *she* did recently purchase a massive home for **herself** and her family in her home state of North Carolina."

[3rd person singular neuter]
"*The room* **itself** was in lamentable confusion."

"The sudden sight of **oneself** as *one* appears in another's eyes is always a shock."

d. [1ST PERSON PLURAL]
"**We** are going to kill **ourselves** making land."

e. [2ND PERSON PLURAL]
"**You** taped **yourselves** wiping out on your own skateboards outside the studio."

f. [3RD PERSON PLURAL]
"**They** set **themselves** to cutting and uprooting the alders."

In each example the bold words refer back to the same person/people, or there is a sense of intensification focused on the subject of the sentence.

Relative pronouns

Relative pronouns relate or refer back to other words in the sentence. See Figure 3.5. Although they do this, they do not rename the referent as reflexive pronouns do. Three of the five relative pronouns have inflections for case, but not for gender or person; the other two have no such distinctions.

FIGURE 3.5 ✿ RELATIVE PRONOUNS

	PRONOUN	CASE
PERSONAL	who/that whom/that whose	subjective objective possessive
NON-PERSONAL	that which	

Examples are:

a. [PERSONAL SUBJECTIVE]
"The people **who** had turned out were the girl's own family."

b. [PERSONAL OBJECTIVE]
"His friends were those of his own blood or those **whom** he had known the longest."

c. [PERSONAL POSSESSIVE]
"Doctors **whose** primary professional focus is hospital medicine are called hospitalist."

d. [NON-PERSONAL]
"**That** is well recorded."

e. [NON-PERSONAL]
"The door, **which** was equipped with neither bell nor knocker, was blistered and disdained."

The relative pronoun *that* is frequently interchangeable with other relative pronouns. For example, in the sentence:

f. [PERSONAL SUBJECTIVE]
"I want to ask the name of the ***man* who** walked over the child."

The pronoun *who* can easily be replaced with *that*:

I want to ask the name of the ***man* that** walked over the child.

We also use relatives in particular ways.

Who and *Whom* refer only to humans:

a. [REFERENCE TO HUMANS]
"But he's still a devout socialist **who** blames the embargo for crippling Cuba's economy."

*But he's still a devout socialist **which** blames the embargo for crippling Cuba's economy.

Which refers to non-humans:

a. [REFERENCE TO NON-HUMANS]
"The result, *Requiem*, **which** premiered in New York in 1985, was immediately subject to both controversy and criticism."

*The result, *Requiem*, **who** premiered in New York in 1985, was immediately subject to both controversy and criticism.

That refers to both.

a. [REFERENCE TO HUMANS]
"This isn't the same **Conor Oberst that** you interviewed six years ago"

b. [REFERENCE TO NON-HUMANS]
"It also contained significant errors of *law* **that** were prejudicial to the appellant."

Interrogative pronouns

Interrogative pronouns are used to ask questions. These pronouns are *question-words* which produce information, in contrast to *yes/no* questions. Generally, they occur at the beginning of sentences, and they are similar in form to relative pronouns in that we inflect them for case. See Figure 3.6.

FIGURE 3.6 ✿
INTERROGATIVE PRONOUNS

	PRONOUN	CASE
PERSONAL	who whom whose	subjective objective possessive
NON-PERSONAL	which what	

Three of these interrogatives refer to person.

a. [SUBJECTIVE PERSONAL]
"**Who** is your all-time hero?"

b. [OBJECTIVE PERSONAL]
"And these days, **whom** do you spy on when you're not sure who the enemy is?"

c. [POSSESSIVE PERSONAL]
"**Whose** war is it now?"

Which refers to persons or things.

a. [PERSONAL]
"**Which** of the following Top Ten Great Canadians ranks highest in the category of genius?"

b. [NON-PERSONAL]
"Substance abuse recovery programs: **Which** one is right for you?"

What refers only to nonpersons.

a. [NON-PERSONAL]
"**What** are your immediate thoughts?"

Whose, which, and *what* may also occur directly before nouns, much like adjectives do.

For example:

a. [INTERROGATIVES BEFORE NOUNS]
"But recently Americans have begun to ask **whose *democracy*** is it?"

"**Which *cities*** are worst for asthma sufferers?"

"**What *hope*** does Omar Zakhilwal have for the people of Afghanistan?"

When you look at the pronouns in these examples, the question should arise: *how can you call these pronouns?* They are not replacing nouns; in fact, they are introducing nouns. They also belong to a category of words called *determiners*, which signals a forthcoming noun. These we will cover shortly.

Demonstrative pronouns

Demonstrative pronouns substitute for nouns and carry out the role of determiners. We use these pronouns to point out or to indicate persons or things specifically. Inflected for number, singular and plural, they have the feature of proximity and distance. See Figure 3.7.

FIGURE 3.7
DEMONSTRATIVE PRONOUNS

	SINGULAR	PLURAL
NEARBY	this	these
FAR AWAY	that	those

DEMONSTRATIVE PRONOUNS substitute for nouns and carry out the role of determiners.

Examples are:

a. [SINGULAR—NEARBY]
"**This** is Sotheby's fourth sale of wines from Massandra since 1990."

b. [PLURAL—NEARBY]
"Some of **these** are highly specialized and are often not considered subdisciplines of surgery."

c. [SINGULAR—FAR AWAY]
"**That** really freaks ol' Francine out."

d. [PLURAL—FAR AWAY]
"'**Those** looking for a job should see me before vespers.'"

Demonstratives, like interrogatives, can also occur directly before nouns. Once again, they are pronouns by form but they also belong to the category of *determiners*, which signals a forthcoming noun. Consider the following examples:

a. [SINGULAR—NEARBY]
"You were surprised **this *evening*** that we have so many of your photographs."

b. [PLURAL—NEARBY]
"It is in **these *food-rich waters*** that the islands' penguins are thought to forage."

c. [SINGULAR—FAR AWAY]
"But these early days in the city were not at all the happiest days of **that *period*** in Richard's life."

d. [PLURAL—FAR AWAY]
"Even within **those *limits***, their behavior is extensively affected by the nature of their environments."

Reciprocal pronouns

RECIPROCAL PRONOUNS refer to previously named nouns or pronouns.

Reciprocal pronouns refer to previously named nouns or pronouns. They express mutual relationships, and they are inflected for the possessive case only. See Figure 3.8.

The reciprocal pronoun *each other* refers to each of two; *one another* usually refers to three or more in number.

FIGURE 3.8
RECIPROCAL PRONOUNS

PRONOUNS	POSSESSIVES
each other	each other's
one another	one another's

Examples are:

a. [RECIPROCAL NON-POSSESSIVE]
"And it's easy to let the dogs hang out with **each other** and become friendly."

"They got up and walked about and changed places and seemed to know **one another** better than we do at home."

b. [RECIPROCAL POSSESSIVE]
"Players actually enjoy **each other's** company."

"The Ciccones fell into **one another's** arms."

Indefinite pronouns

Indefinite pronouns form a large class of words, identified as specifiers and *quantifiers*. They replace nouns or noun phrases, but they do not refer to a definite person or thing. They specifically point out or they refer to the presence or absence of quantity; see Figure 3.9.

INDEFINITE PRONOUNS

form a large class of words, often identified as specifiers, quantifiers.

FIGURE 3.9 ✿ INDEFINITE PRONOUNS

SPECIFIERS (SINGULAR)		QUANTIFIERS (PLURAL)		
another	no one	any	less	one
anyone	nobody	all	little	other
anybody	nothing	both	many (a)	several
anything	someone	enough	more	single
everyone	somebody	each	most	some
everybody	something	every	much	such (a)
everything		few	(n)either	

a. [SPECIFIERS/SINGULAR IN NUMBER]
"As a man, Neil evidently didn't care if **anyone** paid attention to him or not."

"Does it mean **nothing** to you that you are **everything** to me?"

"What I look for is **someone** who has a point of view that moves me."

"**No one** could have heard this low droning of the gathering clans."

b. [QUANTIFIERS/PLURAL IN NUMBER]
"Not **all** owners have squeaky clean image like Flames brass."

"The sound of **many** feet and voices made that usually quiet hour as noisy as noon."

"In they came, **some** on stretchers, **some** in men's arms, **some** feebly staggering along propped on rude crutches."

"Just **such a** glimpse, as through that opened door, is all we know of those we call our friends."

The concepts expressed by each of these pronouns are sufficiently vague to suggest that they are indefinite.

DETERMINERS

DETERMINERS
are structure class
words signalling a
forthcoming noun or
noun phrase.

Determiners are structure class words signaling a forthcoming noun or noun phrase. The term itself is a *catch-all* one covering many form and structure class words. This "umbrella" term prepares us for how they will later function grammatically. It is important to note, however, that the word "*determiners*" refers to the *classification* and not to the *form* of these words.

Pronouns as determiners

We identify the following pronouns as *determiners*.

1. **possessives**   my, your, his, her, its, our, your, their
2. **relatives**   whose, which, that
3. **interrogatives** whose, which, what
4. **demonstratives** this, that, these, those
5. **indefinite**   any, each, either, enough, much, no, some, (n)either

The following examples contrast the words in this category, first as pronouns and next as determiners:

  a. [POSSESSIVE PRONOUN]
  "Heathcliff kicked **his** to the same place."

  b. [POSSESSIVE PRONOUN DETERMINER]
  "Appeals judges ruled last week Milosevic could again lead **his own defence**."

Note that in the first example the possessive is used simply as a pronoun; whereas, in the second example it is used as a determiner to signal the noun *defence*.

  a. [RELATIVE PRONOUN]
  "We were told **that** because each council is so different in make-up there is no simple policy that can cover all districts."

  b. [RELATIVE PRONOUN DETERMINER]
  "The SDLP still control **that *meeting*** on every vote, and on every issue they operate a strong party whip."

In this pair of examples, the relative is used first as a pronoun and next as a determiner to signal the noun *meeting*.

  a. [INTERROGATIVE PRONOUN]
  "**What** does one do with a day that seems to stretch out infinitely before one?"

b. [INTERROGATIVE PRONOUN DETERMINER]
"**What *sort*** of hope could you imagine her treasuring for her own future?"

The contrast continues with the interrogative pronouns. In the first example, the *what* pronoun is used to ask a simple question; whereas, in the second example the *what* pronoun precedes the noun *sort*.

a. [DEMONSTRATIVE PRONOUN]
"They caution many people—especially **those** living in northern climates."

b. [DEMONSTRATIVE PRONOUN DETERMINER]
"I want him to excel, like **those *kids*** who form campus sketch troupes or win college-wide trivia contests."

In the first example the demonstrative *those* is used as a pronoun; however, in the second example *those* signals the noun *kids*.

a. [INDEFINITE PRONOUN]
"'It's log-cabin pattern,' she said, putting **several** of them together."

b. [INDEFINITE PRONOUN DETERMINER]
"There are **several *ways*** to measure unemployment."

Finally, for this group the indefinite pronouns show the same contrast. The first example has the indefinite *several* used as a pronoun; the second example has *several* preceding the noun *ways*.

Words as determiners

Other word groups are also identified as determiners.

articles:
definite	the
indefinite	a(n)

possessive of proper names: John's, London's, New York's

multipliers and fractions: double, twice, half, a third

numbers:
cardinal	one (1), two(2), three(3) etc.
ordinal	first, second, third

words such as: what a, such a

Examples to illustrate these word groups are:

a. [DEFINITE ARTICLE DETERMINER + NOUN]
"**The *science*** of medicine is **the *body*** of knowledge about body systems and diseases."

b. [INDEFINITE ARTICLE DETERMINER + NOUN]
"Medicine is **a *branch*** of health science concerned with restoring and maintaining health and wellness."

c. [POSSESSIVE OF PROPER NAMES DETERMINER]
"She seemed to be not only singing but doing a ventriloquist routine that mimicked **Doc Severinson's *trumpet*** as well."

"We had received our calls to **God's *church*** in the same era if not at the same school."

"**Ontario's *highest court*** has given the go-ahead for the first class-action lawsuit by former students of a native residential school."

d. [MULTIPLIERS AND FRACTIONS AS DETERMINERS]
"Fans will look at the box score and see eight players in **double *figures*** for only the second time in franchise history."

"Cato would like his teammates to choke on the Raptors' first-**half *numbers***: 60 points on 51.1 per cent shooting."

e. [NUMBERS: CARDINAL AND ORDINAL AS DETERMINERS]
"**One *player*** who didn't make the team but certainly would have if the new system had been in effect was Todd Hamilton."

"The **second *category*** concerns a person who has a mixed track record."

f. [WORDS SUCH AS ... DETERMINERS]
"David was unwavering in his understanding of **what a** converged media **company** means."

"One need not even agree with the premise of **such a *question*** to grant the importance of its being raised."

In the first example for this last category, we see the determiner "*what a*" separated from its noun "*company*" by two adjectives "*converged media*". If the noun is preceded by an adjective(s) and/or other nouns, the determiner precedes these modifiers. Here are a couple of particularly good examples.

a. [DETERMINER + ADJECTIVES + NOUN]
"But he was **a** *tight-fisted* **hand** at the grindstone, Scrooge, **a** *squeezing, wrenching, grasping, scraping, clutching, covetous old* **sinner**!"

"Holmes was silent, but **his** *little darting* **glances** showed me the interest which he took in **our** *curious* **companion**."

Sometimes when a determiner is not present, the sentence will produce an ambiguity. These are often seen in newspaper headlines. For example, we have:

a. [AMBIGUOUS]
"Hamas ready to accept Palestinian state"

This sentence has two possible meanings. Hamas are ready to accept the current state (conditions) of Palestine; or, Hamas are ready to accept a new Palestinian State. However, if we place a determiner before *Palestinian* we get:

b. [NOT AMBIGUOUS]
Hamas ready to accept **a** Palestinian state

It is really the absence of the determiner that causes the ambiguity; although a capital *s* on *state* would help.

Determiner positions

Determiners have been presented in a number of ways for understanding, and one of these is to subclass them according to the position they hold in relationship to one another.

1. **Determiner plus a pre-determiner**: Many of the above determiners can take another determiner preceding it. Those that generally occupy that pre-position are:

multipliers and fractions: double, twice, half, a third
words as: all, both, what a, such a

To illustrate these we have the following examples:

a. [PRE-DETERMINER + DETERMINER]
"It ordered a fine to the State of **double the** money embezzled."

"They took **all his** money and one of the children and stole his boat."

This is not to say that these pre-determiners are restricted to this position; it simply means that they often occur there. Here are the same pre-determiners occupying the determiner position.

a. [DETERMINER + NOUN]

"Its first album went **double** platinum with astonishing sales of over 2 million copies."

"At **all** events Robert proposed it, and there was not a dissenting voice."

2. **Determiner plus a post-determiner**: This same group of determiners can also take a second determiner after it. Those that usually follow a first determiner are:

numbers:
ordinal	first, second, third, fourth, etc.
cardinal	one, two, three, four etc.

indefinite: every, few, less, little, many (a), more, most, other, same, several, single, such (a)

Examples for this position are:

a. [DETERMINER + POST-DETERMINER]

"**The three** possible causes of misquotation must have had its share in the apparent blunder."

"She stood for **a few** moments helplessly staring at the glistening great rhubarb leaves near the door."

Again, this is not to suggest that these post–determiners are restricted to this position. Many determiners that occupy this position can occur with or without other determiners.

The following examples illustrate this.

a. [WITHOUT DETERMINERS]

"**Twenty** new gas-guzzling sport utility vehicle (SUV) models and light trucks may be rolling off assembly lines within five years."

"The couple made **several calls** but the transmissions bounced off different cellular telephone towers."

AUXILIARIES

AUXILIARIES are structure class words making distinctions for tense, aspect, and voice in verb phrases.

Auxiliaries are structure class words making distinctions for tense, aspect, and voice in verb phrases. Sometimes called *helping verbs*, they have no common forms. We mark them as *primary verbs*, *modals*, and the *stand-in verb*, *do*. We use them as adjuncts or secondary verbs to extend the grammatical meaning of lexical verbs. Primary verbs and the verb *do* also have full verbal paradigms, whereas modals do not. Modals do not occur independently from lexical verbs, unless an ellipsis (omission) occurs.

With auxiliaries we now return to the finite versus non-finite forms of verbs; auxiliaries are required with non-finite verbs. This is their role to mark non-finite verb forms for tense, aspect and voice, which non-finite verbs cannot express. Finite verbs mark these features on their own.

The most important statement to be made here is that when an auxiliary verb occurs with a non-finite form of a verb, the auxiliary is always the finite verb; if more than one auxiliary occurs, the first auxiliary is always the finite verb.

Primary auxiliaries

"Be" and "have" are lexical verbs, which also function as auxiliary verbs to mark tense, aspect, mood, and voice. Without doubt they are the most frequently used verbs in the English language, again dating back to the Old English period. As lexical verbs they *express a state* or *describe a person, thing, or event*, and they have a full verbal paradigm with both finite and non-finite forms. *Be* has more irregular forms, because it is a combination of two Old English verbs: *beom* and *eom*. When they occur together in a verb phrase, the order is *have + be*; forms of the latter verb are always closest to the head/lexical verb. *Be* is frequently called primary one and *have* as primary two to distinguish them. Figure 3.10 shows the full paradigm for these verbs.

PRIMARY AUXILIARIES
have and *be* are verbs used to mark tense, aspect, mood and voice.

FIGURE 3.10 ✿ PRIMARY AUXILIARIES *be* AND *have*

VERBS	BASE	3RD PERSON SINGULAR	PRESENT PARTICIPLE	PAST TENSE	PAST PARTICIPLE
CODES	ø finite	{-s 3rd p sg} finite	{-ing pp} non-finite	{-ed pt} finite	{-ed ptp} non-finite
	be/am/are	is	being	was/were	been
	have	has	having	had	had

Examples of the primary auxiliaries are:

a. [FINITE + NON-FINITE]
"He **is *waiting*** for me there, you know."

b. [FINITE + NON-FINITE + NON-FINITE]
"He **had *been playing*** softly when he came upon the boys."

c. [FINITE + NON-FINITE + NON-FINITE]
"David, on the lowest step, was very evidently not hearing a word of what **was *being said*.**"

In each of these examples, the primary auxiliary introduces a verb phrase, that is, a cohesive word group focusing on a head lexical verb (HV). Because the auxiliary occupies the first position, it becomes the finite verb and, therefore, the tense marker for that phrase. The final non-finite verb is the lexical verb in that it carries the meaning for the verb phrase, *head verb*. We say the *final non-finite verb* because as the third example shows, a verb phrase can have more than one non-finite form.

It is important to remember that the first auxiliary in the verb phrase is always the finite verb and tense marker of the verb. All other verbs within the phrase are then non-finite.

Modals

MODAL AUXILIARIES are adjunct verbs expressing such features as probability, possibility, and obligation.

Modal verbs are adjunct auxiliaries (helping verbs), expressing such features as ability, probability, possibility, and obligation etc. Unlike primary verbs, modals do not have full verbal paradigms. They lack the third person singular *-s*, the *-ing* present participle, and the past participle; they do have past tense correlatives or equivalent past forms. See Figure 3.11. You use the negative form *not* to make modals negative, even in the simple present and past tenses. You never follow a modal verb with *to*, with the exception of *ought to*.

FIGURE 3.11 ✿
MODAL AUXILIARIES

PRESENT TENSE	PAST TENSE
can	could
may	might
shall	should
will	would
must	[had to]
ought (to)	[ought to have + past participle]

Here are some examples to illustrate modals.

a. [PRESENT TENSE]
"Such energy, once it exists, **can** easily be forced into new channels."

"We **may** have borrowed other ideas from the Sumerians."

b. [PAST TENSE]
"We **could** not communicate information in speaking or writing."

"Of course, not all the artists pilloried by Hitler **would** have seen themselves as his natural enemies."

The last two modals in Figure 3.11, *must* and *ought (to)*, do not have past forms; however, their meaning of obligation can be expressed in the past with equivalent past tense forms that are components of other verbs.

To illustrate these, we have:

a. [PRESENT TENSE]

"The Source **must** be found again and reopened."

b. [PAST TENSE]

"By this time it was clear to me that I **had to do** with a case lying far outside of the common routine of life."

A verb phrase will take only one modal auxiliary at a time; although more than one primary auxiliary can occur within a single verb phrase.

Like primary verbs, modals when helping lexical verbs also follow a hierarchical order. Within the verb phrase they always occupy the initial position, and therefore become the finite verb, tense marker, for that verb phrase. Figure 3.12 illustrates this.

FIGURE 3.12 ✿ HIERARCHY OF AUXILIARIES

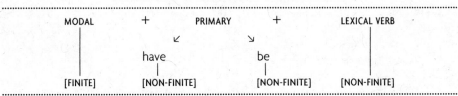

a. [FINITE-LEXICAL]

"A religion **needs** to get its sense of revealed truth under some control lest it fade off into indefiniteness."

b. [PRIMARY-FINITE] [LEXICAL-NON-FINITE]

"Everyone **is *waiting*** for the American secretary of state to arrive."

c. [MODAL-FINITE] [LEXICAL-NON-FINITE]

"A Christian **will** often ***insist*** that Jesus *alone* is savior and Lord."

d. [PRIMARY-FINITE] [PRIMARY-NON-FINITE] [LEXICAL-NON-FINITE]

"There **had *been fighting*** in the area and they had come across some people who were injured."

e. [MODAL-FINITE] [PRIMARY-NON-FINITE] [LEXICAL-NON-FINITE]

"As such, it **may *have been*** a tribute to van Gogh's father, who died a few months before."

d. [MODAL-FINITE] [PRIMARY-NON-FINITE] [PRIMARY-NON-FINITE] [LEXICAL-NON-FINITE]

"No horse **should have been ridden** down there."

ATTITUDE OR MOOD

An important characteristic of modal auxiliaries is that they express the *attitude* or *mood* of the speaker. We can identify seven different attitudes or moods; each is signalled by a modal. Note that some modals can express more than one mood/attitude.

1. **Ability**: "the power or capacity to do something."[1]

> *can, could*

> "Rich nations **can** halve world poverty within 10 years."

> "Weekend rain **could** cause more B.C. mud-slides."

2. **Condition**: "circumstances affecting the functioning or existence of something."

> *should, would*

> "The party with the largest number of seats **should** be allowed to form a majority."

> "It is believed it **would** kick in based on whether certain incentives are reached, according to a league source."

3. **Futurity**: "the future time."

> *shall, will*

> "I said to myself, in spite of everything I **shall** rise again."

> "Another day **will** do just as well."

4. **Obligation**: "an act or course of action to which a person is morally or legally bound."

> *should, must, ought to*

> "'Ah if you haven't why **should** I?' he asked."

> "When you have youngsters like me at dinner you **must** look for a little nonsense."

> "If schools fudge their grades, there **ought to be** a penalty."

1. *Oxford English Dictionary.* Ask Oxford.com. All definitions for the *attitude* or *mood* of the speaker are taken from this source.

5. **Permission**: "expressing a wish or hope."

   may, might

   "We **may** test our convictions to see whether they are reasonable and just."

   "'And who is Dinah, if I **might** venture to ask the question?' said the Lory."

6. **Possibility**: "the state or fact of being possible."

   may, might

   "A study finds alcohol **may** lessen inflammation."

   "Political leaders on both sides will be watching for disaffected members who **might** cross the floor and tip the balance of power."

7. **Probability**: "the extent to which something is probable."

   shall, will

   "I **shall** probably send you a letter."

   "Before them, too, **will** most likely be standing a soldier wrapped in his cloak, a dealer from the old-clothes mart."

8. **Volition**: "the faculty or power of using one's will."

   will

   "The issue **will** be resolved by Justice John Gomery, who is running the inquiry."

Other grammatical sources will include additional *moods*, for example, *intention*, *necessity*, and *certainty*; however, those given above are sufficient to cover the modals.

STAND-IN AUXILIARY DO

We often use the verb *do* as a *stand-in auxiliary*, much in the same way as we use primary and modal auxiliaries. Like primary verbs, it can function as an auxiliary or as a principal verb because it has a full verb inflectional paradigm; see Figure 3.13.

Do as an auxiliary verb:

a. [AUXILIARY VERB]
"Where **does** all the money **go**?"

"What we **do find** in abstraction, however, is a novel way of seeing."

"They **did** not **intend** to subordinate painting to a verbal sensibility."

Do as a lexical verb:

a. [LEXICAL VERB]
"But that the most acceptable service of God **is doing** good to man."

"When he **did** his analysis for his stories, there was no malice of any kind, he could be critical but fair."

"In face of violence, UN **has done** all it can technically for Iraqi elections."

FIGURE 3.13
STAND-IN AUXILIARY *do*

FORMS	DO
stem	do
present tense	does
present participle	doing
past tense	did
past participle	done

Because of the flexibility of this verb (it is also used to form questions, negatives, and for emphasis), it is important to pay close attention to how it is used. When it is used as an auxiliary, like the primary and modal verbs, it will occupy the initial position in the verb phrase, and there will always be a non-finite lexical verb to follow. When it is used as a lexical verb, it may be preceded by an auxiliary verb or simply stand alone.

PREPOSITIONS

PREPOSITIONS
are structure words
introducing a phrase
structure.

Prepositions are structure class words introducing a noun group as its object. They precede the object usually noting spatial, temporal, or logical relationships; other prepositions, however, have a number of different associations. They are a difficult group of words to classify, because of themselves they express little, if any, meaning. If we look up a preposition in a dictionary, we will find several variations of meaning for it.

The following examples illustrate some of the different associations.

1. **About**: shows a relationship with the subject matter of thought, speech, or feeling.

"It offers no theory whatever **about** the origin of the universe."

2. **At**: relates to a point on a numerical scale and also to rate.

> "Martin said Canada has no interest in creating a new arms race and has been **at** the forefront of the fight against nuclear proliferation."

3. **By**: relates to agent, means or measure.

> "No matter the pretext, democracy is never imposed at gunpoint **by** invading armies."

4. **In**: relates to a process or condition.

> "We're confident that **in** the near future we're going to be able to do this again."

Categorizing prepositions in this way is complicated since the focus is on meaning, and the meaning frequently varies with the context. As an alternative, we offer a simple three-way grouping based on their distinctive characteristics of form: *simple*, *-ing*, and *phrasal* prepositions.

Simple prepositions

These prepositions are probably the most frequently used, as you can see from the examples above, and therefore they are the better known ones; see Figure 3.14. Examples for these are frequently found, and often several to a sentence.

FIGURE 3.14 ✿ SIMPLE PREPOSITIONS

about	before	down	onto	upon
above	behind	for	opposite	with
after	below	from	out	within
along	beneath	in	outside	without
against	beside	inside	over	
among	between	into	through	
around	beyond	near	to	
as	by	of	under	
at	despite	on	until	

a. [SIMPLE PREPOSITIONS]
"The whistles rolled out **in** greeting a chorus cheerful **as** the April dawn."

"Anthrax is acknowledged as one **of** the most likely sources **of** a bioweapon **for** either a single criminal or terrorist group."

"A program to treat childhood asthma **in** Harlem has been successful **in** significantly reducing the need **for** emergency room visits **for** sick children."

"But a plant on the edge **of** a desert is said to struggle **for** life **against** the drought, though more properly it should be said to be dependent **on** the moisture."

"The city that will soon go **without** libraries produced one **of** America's brightest literary lights."

-ing prepositions

Prepositions ending in *-ing* are the most difficult group to identify because, at first, they look like present participles; their bases are verbs and they end in the *-ing* inflection; see Figure 3.15. However, upon closer examination, these same forms are used not in a verbal structure, but in a prepositional phrase structure. They will signal a forthcoming noun or its substitute. When this occurs we call them prepositions. It is in the role they carry out that distinguishes them.

FIGURE 3.15 ✿ *-ing* PREPOSITIONS

assuming	considering	including	regarding
barring	during	involving	succeeding
concerning	following	pending	

Examples to illustrates this group of prepositions are:

a. [*-ing* prepositions]
"Since then he has been the principle advisor to Bush on matters **concerning** the Middle East, India, Iran, Iraq, Turkey and Afghanistan."

"A handful of other states impose a range of penalties, **including** jail time, for such actions."

"A public meeting was held in December 2003 **regarding** the airport's environmental assessment, as required by the National Environmental Policy Act."

Phrasal prepositions

Phrasal prepositions may be the most complex of this structure class, because the phrase generally embeds other prepositions. This makes it look as though there is more than one prepositional phrase involved. For example, the prepositional phrase *by way of* looks like a combination of two prepositions (1) **by way**, and (2) **of** + *object*. Its structure, however, is as one phrasal preposition functioning in the same way as a single-word preposition. See Figure 3.16.

FIGURE 3.16 ✿ PHRASAL PREPOSITIONS

ahead of	in addition to	instead of
apart of	in advance of	on account of
as far as	in comparison with	on behalf of
because of	in lieu of	together with
by way of	in place of	up at
contrary to	in spite of	up to
due to	inside of	with regard to

The following examples illustrate this group.

a. [phrasal prepositions]
"A lot of the research stuff—the sales guys couldn't sell (it) because it was **ahead of** its time."

"It was doomed to be a failure **as far as** the principal person was concerned, but he approached the others with fussy importance."

"The brothers say Michael is doing well **in spite of** the intense media scrutiny."

Prepositional phrases, as we shall see later, carry out a number of grammatical functions, and for this reason it is important to know their various structures.

CONJUNCTIONS

Conjunctions *are structure class words which join sentence constituents and even sentences, identifying subordination, coordination, and conjunctiveness.* Coordinating and subordinating conjunctions are the better known ones; correlative conjunctions and conjunctive adverbs are probably the least known. As a form class category they have no common form; however, as we shall see later they do carry out a common grammatical function.

CONJUNCTIONS are structure class words identifying subordination, coordination, and conjunctiveness.

Coordinating conjunctions

Coordinating conjunctions join units of equal value: and, but, for, or, nor, yet.

Examples for these are:

a. [COORDINATING CONJUNCTIONS]
"Some of the contents of the annex were reported this week by *The Washington Post* **and** *The Los Angeles Times*."

"It found no evidence that senior Pentagon **or** White House officials pressured interrogators to use abusive tactics."

"I was greatly amused to behold an excellent caricature of my friend Joseph, rudely **yet** powerfully sketched."

Subordinating conjunctions

Subordinating conjunctions join units (especially clauses) where one depends upon another for its completed meaning, and in so doing they express particular meanings.

The following examples identify the various groups of these conjunctions.

1. **Concession**: although, even if, even, though, if, through, while

   "The party was shut out in 2000, **although** the Alliance won two seats."

2. **Condition**: as long as, if, in case, provided that, unless

   "**Unless** a provision of the Act specifies otherwise, the Act comes into force on the date of Royal Assent."

3. **Comparison**: as, as if, in case, provided that, unless

   "Bill Gates has talked glowingly about bringing music and media to the Xbox **as well as** connecting Xbox Live to MSN Messenger."

4. **Contingency**: if, once

   "Martin will bring back marijuana decriminalization **if** elected."

5. **Contrast**: whereas, while

   "**While** the two are ready to get together, they still have a long way to go to bridge the philosophical gap over controlling costs."

6. **Reason**: as long as, because, since

   "The doctor-patient relationship is important to the patient **because** the doctor has been given a monopoly on access to the prescription pad."

7. **Place**: where, wherever

   "Yet this is where the real challenge lies."

8. **Result**: so, so that

   "Food stamps, Medicaid and nutritional and social services have been cut, **so that** many people must dip into resources reserved for housing."

9. **Time**: after, as, as long as, before, now that, once, since, till, whenever, while

   "**Since** then she had fought steadily, with a certain lofty cheerfulness, for the life she so desired to save."

RELATIVE PRONOUNS

who (whom, whose), which, that

Examples for this group are:

a. [relative pronouns]
   "Suppliers **who** don't accede to Wal-Mart's 'everyday low price' mantra often find their products bounced from the chain's stores."

   "Most are victims of the nationwide policy of deinstitutionalization **that** has dominated the mental-health field since the mid '60s."

RELATIVE ADVERBS

when, where, why

Examples for this group are:

a. [RELATIVE ADVERBS]
   "His only suggestion is a 'Primary Health Care Summit' **where** experts can jaw."

   "She explained **why** she had not written you and also incidentally **why** she had written Childs."

INDEFINITE RELATIVE PRONOUNS

whoever (whomever, whosever), whichever, whatever

Examples for this group are:

a. [INDEFINITE RELATIVE PRONOUNS]
"Kegworthy, **whoever** he might have been, was wrapt in mystery."

"It seems he had slipped out to look for this drug or **whatever** it is."

CORRELATIVE CONJUNCTIONS

Correlative conjunctions connect both complete sentences and units within sentences.

both—and	either—or	whether—or
neither—nor	not only—but also	

Examples for this group are:

a. [CORRELATIVE CONJUNCTIONS]
"As a parent, I know it is **not only** my right, **but also** my responsibility to keep an eye on and protect my children."

"**Either** he went rabbiting in the woods, like a poacher, **or** he stayed in Nottingham all night instead of coming home."

CONJUNCTIVE ADVERBS

Conjunctive adverbs are not true conjunctions in the way that co-ordinating and subordinating conjunctions behave. They show logical relationships between two complete ideas, expressed in independent clauses or sentences. They are easy to recognize because they are generally preceded by a semi-colon, except for *so* and *therefore*. They show *comparison, contrast, cause-effect, sequence,* but they do so with adverb emphasis.

addition:	also, furthermore, in addition, moreover
apposition:	for example, namely, that is
concession:	at any rate, however, nevertheless
contrast:	instead, on the other hand, on the contrary
result:	as a result, consequently, therefore,
time:	in the meantime, meanwhile

Examples for this group are:

a. [ADDITION]
"According to Global Security.org, the complex is approximately 500 acres in size and, **in addition** to a palace, it contains elaborate pools, grounds and VIP residences."

b. [APPOSITION]
"The Hindu *Upanishads'* quest for union with the 'One' implies another, **namely**, the *mystical.*"

c. [CONCESSION]
"I had rejected it as absurd, **nevertheless** it persisted."

d. [CONTRAST]
"The correct moral position is to quit moralizing about drugs and **instead** to regard addicts with compassion."

e. [RESULT]
"A total of 45 percent of hung councils have, **therefore**, some form of coalition government."

f. [TIME]
"At Bergdorf's, meanwhile, sales climbed 15 percent for the three months ended in October."

Conjunctions are a very mixed group of words that play an important role in our grammatical system. They are numerous and therefore difficult to remember. Co-ordinating and relative conjunctions should cause few problems; the adverb conjunctions will come with usage.

WORD ANALYSIS

As with morphemes, to understand the structure of words, it is important that we are able to break them down into their bases and morphemic parts. As we do this, we should also label the individual parts. The following representative samples cover most of the word classes that we inflect.

1. **Nouns**

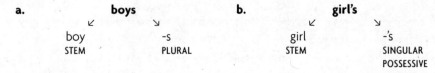

a.	**boys**		b.	**girl's**	
	boy	-s		girl	-'s
	STEM	PLURAL		STEM	SINGULAR POSSESSIVE

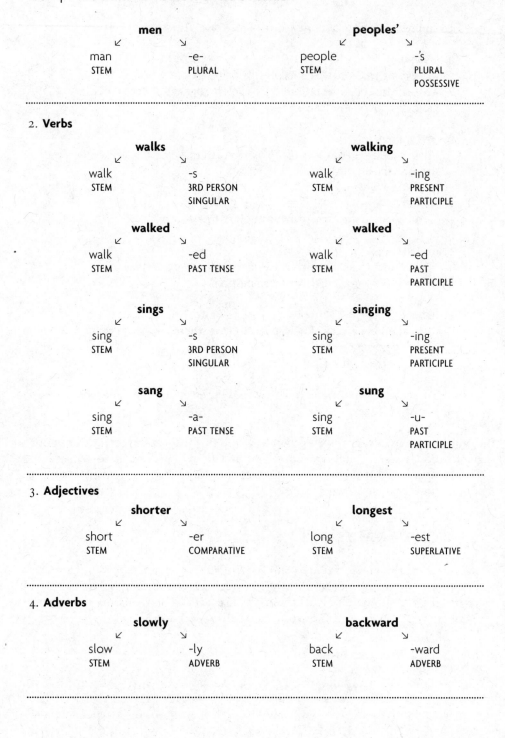

men
↙   ↘
man   -e-
STEM   PLURAL

peoples'
↙   ↘
people   -'s
STEM   PLURAL
POSSESSIVE

---

2. Verbs

walks
↙   ↘
walk   -s
STEM   3RD PERSON
SINGULAR

walking
↙   ↘
walk   -ing
STEM   PRESENT
PARTICIPLE

walked
↙   ↘
walk   -ed
STEM   PAST TENSE

walked
↙   ↘
walk   -ed
STEM   PAST
PARTICIPLE

sings
↙   ↘
sing   -s
STEM   3RD PERSON
SINGULAR

singing
↙   ↘
sing   -ing
STEM   PRESENT
PARTICIPLE

sang
↙   ↘
sing   -a-
STEM   PAST TENSE

sung
↙   ↘
sing   -u-
STEM   PAST
PARTICIPLE

---

3. Adjectives

shorter
↙   ↘
short   -er
STEM   COMPARATIVE

longest
↙   ↘
long   -est
STEM   SUPERLATIVE

---

4. Adverbs

slowly
↙   ↘
slow   -ly
STEM   ADVERB

backward
↙   ↘
back   -ward
STEM   ADVERB

---

5. **Personal Pronouns**

	I			**me**	
1ST PERSON SINGULAR		SUBJECTIVE	1ST PERSON SINGULAR		OBJECTIVE

	they			**them**	
3RD PERSON PLURAL		SUBJECTIVE	3RD PERSON PLURAL		OBJECTIVE

6. **Possessive Pronouns**

	my			**theirs**	
1ST PERSON SINGULAR		PRENOMINAL	3RD PERSON PLURAL		SUBSTITUTIONAL

7. **Relative Pronouns**

	who			**whom**	
SUBJECTIVE		PERSONAL	OBJECTIVE		PERSONAL

8. **Primary Auxiliaries**

	is			**were**	
be BASE		is 3RD PERSON SINGULAR	be BASE		were PAST

9. **Modal Auxiliaries**

	can			**might**	
can MODAL		PRESENT	might MODAL		PAST

✿ ✿ ✿

From words we create phrases, our next category for analysis. However, we are still concerned with *form* and so we will continue to identify basic structures. We shall now see that as sentence constituents, words and phrases are interchangeable. In fact, the names given to many words are the same as those given to many phrases. There is a good deal of overlap in the terminology here.

4   PHRASES

Phrases *are syntactic structures functioning as sentence constituents*. They do not contain finite verbs, and because of this their meanings cannot be inferred from the word groups of which they are constituted. Like words, phrases are single sentence constituents with relationships to other words and phrases within sentences. Although we now move from single words to word groups, we continue to focus on the *Form* of *What a constituent* **IS**.

All phrases are marked principally by a head word (HW), which identifies its structure. It is important to note the HW. Depending on the phrase structure, the HW can be any one of the nine phrase identifiers as noted in Figure 4.1, with the exception of the *absolute phrase*. This phrase can be represented by a number of structures having different HW identifiers. The location of a HW in a phrase varies, but frequently it occurs in the initial or final position.

PHRASES
are cohesive word groups forming full syntactic units within sentences.

FIGURE 4.1 ✿ PHRASES

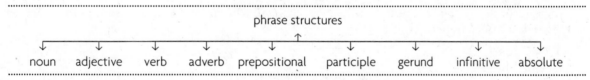

phrase structures

noun   adjective   verb   adverb   prepositional   participle   gerund   infinitive   absolute

NOUN PHRASE

Noun *phrases are syntactic structures with a head noun (HN) or its replacement as its focus*. Included in the noun phrase are all the pre-noun and post-noun qualifiers or describing constituents, which go to make up the phrase. The following examples illustrate this phrase:

NOUN PHRASES
are cohesive word groups focusing on a head noun or its replacement.

a. [NOUN PHRASES/HN]
"Just then **the *train*** jerked, and started slowly."

"**All its varied *expanse***" was bathed in the last bright glow of the sun."

"**The *door* of Scrooge's counting-house** was opened that he might keep his eye upon his clerk."

"**The *differences* of Mr Matthew's view from mine** are not of much importance."

"**Father Brown's *friend and companion*** was a young man with a stream of ideas and stories."

In the first example, the noun phrase is a simple structure of two words *the train*; the head noun is obviously *train*. The next example is more complex; it is a longer phrase, ending with the head noun *expanse*. All preceding words are qualifiers. Next we have a noun phrase where the head noun *door* occurs earlier in the phrase, because a qualifying phrase follows. The third example is much like the one that precedes it, where the head noun *difference* occurs earlier in the phrase with two qualifying phrases following it. The last example shows the noun phrase with a compound noun *friend and companion*, preceded by a determiner expressing the possessive of a proper name, *Father Brown's*. The various forms of these structures show how simple and yet how complex the noun phrase can be.

ADJECTIVE PHRASE

ADJECTIVE PHRASES are cohesive word groups describing or qualifying a noun or its replacement.

Adjective phrases are syntactic structures with a head adjective (HAdj) as its focus. They describe or qualify a noun or its replacement. The head adjective of the phrase is generally the last word, which may only be one in a series of qualifying words. Although these qualifying words usually precede the head adjective, they may also occur after it. The following examples illustrate adjective phrases in both positions.

a. [ADJECTIVES PRECEDING THE NOUN]
   "It was **cold, bleak, biting *weather***."

   "He's **an extraordinary looking *man***, and yet I really can name nothing out of the way."

   "In Beijing these days, one of the **fastest-growing *fortunes*** the world has ever seen is managed by fewer than **two dozen *traders***."

   "This was a **hearty, healthy, dapper, red-faced *gentleman***, with a shock of hair prematurely white, and a boisterous and decided manner."

b. [ADJECTIVES FOLLOWING THE NOUN]
   "It is the mark of a modest man to accept his friendly ***circle* ready-made** from the hands of opportunity."

"He became sensible of confused noises in the air; in coherent sounds of lamentations and regret; *wailings* **inexpressible sorrowful and self-accusatory**."

"This was a hearty, healthy, dapper, red-faced gentleman, with a shock of *hair* **prematurely white**, and a boisterous and decided manner."

"There were three strange wants at Wakefield: a *parson* **wanting pride**, *young men* **wanting wives** and *ale-houses* **wanting customers**."

Adjective phrases, like noun phrases, can be combinations of simple adjectives as illustrated above, or other words and phrases that can carry out the role of an adjective. This is evident in the last example, where we have a participle phrase carrying out the adjective role: *wanting pride*, *wanting wives*, and *wanting customers*.

There may be very little difference between a noun phrase and an adjective phrase in structures where the adjectives occur before the word it qualifies. Most noun phrases consist of a head noun plus one or more adjectives, or indeed an adjective phrase itself. Consider the examples in *a*, below.

a. [ADJECTIVE PHRASES]
"It was **cold, bleak, biting** *weather*."

"He's **an extraordinary looking** *man*, and yet I really can name nothing out of the way."

"In Beijing these days, one of the **fastest-growing** *fortunes* the world has ever seen is managed by fewer than **two dozen** *traders*."

"This was a **hearty, healthy, dapper, red-faced** *gentleman*, with a shock of hair prematurely white, and a boisterous and decided manner."

In each of these examples, if we include the italicized head nouns, we have noun phrases with embedded adjective phrases; without the head nouns, we have adjective phrases. The focus is always on the head word (HW).

VERB PHRASE

Verb phrases are syntactic structures functioning as sentence constituents with a head lexical verb (HV), finite or non-finite in form. The verb can be simple in structure or composed of a main lexical verb plus auxiliaries and/or verb qualifiers related syntactically to the verb. The following examples illustrate various compositions of verb phrases.

VERB PHRASES
are cohesive word groups focusing on a lexical verb.

a. [SIMPLE VERB PHRASES]
"The science of medicine **is** the body of knowledge about body systems and diseases."

"After van Gogh's 'conversion' to art, he **rejected** the religion of his parents."

"The Rothko Chapel, for instance, **will** never **offer** a suitable environment for Christian worship."

Each verb phrase focuses on a lexical head verb (HV). The first example has a single form of the verb *Be* in the present tense *is*; the next example has a simple past tense form of the verb *reject*; and, the third example has a simple future form of the verb *offer*. Although the third example consists of two verb forms, it is still considered simple for future tense.

b. [COMPLEX VERB PHRASES]
"The figures in *The Potato Eaters* **do** not **engage** each other in conversation."

"Pete Rose, baseball's career leader in hits, **was banned** from baseball in 1989 for betting on games."

"The budget **will be brought** down in late March."

Complex verb phrases consist of more than one verb form. The first example has a finite verb form *do*, identifying the tense as present, and a non-finite verb *engage*. The next example has a primary auxiliary *was*, indicating past tense, and a non-finite verb *banned*. The third example has a finite verb *will*, indicating future tense, and two non-finite verbs in *be* and *brought*.

Tense

TENSE
is the grammatical feature of verbs relating to time.

Tense is the grammatical feature of verbs relating to time. English verbs have distinctive forms for the *present* and *past* tenses; the so called future tense does not have a distinctive form, but it is expressed by an auxiliary modal plus a present tense form of the verb. This means that English has two distinctive tenses and a syntactic structure to express future time. Regardless of formation, we will identify three tenses.

PRESENT TENSE

The present tense is expressed by a combination of a personal pronoun plus a verb base; the base takes the inflectional -s suffix for the third person singular. See Figure 4.2. The present tense is used to express the following:

1. Habitual actions.

2. A present state.

3. General truths.

4. Historical present to relate most actions and states in literature, especially stage directions.

5. In most adverb clauses and in some noun clauses future time [future tense is usually not permitted in these kinds of dependent clauses].

FIGURE 4.2 ✿ PRESENT TENSE

	REGULAR VERB	IRREGULAR VERB
I	walk	sing
you	walk	sing
he/she/it	walk**s**	sing**s**
we	walk	sing
you	walk	sing
they	walk	sing

1. Habitual actions

"That always **seems** the difficulty to me."

"I **drill** with the volunteers twice a week, and lend a hand at the farms."

2. Present state

"She **works** in the Red Cross Hospital at Tadminster, seven miles away."

"This **draws** attention to the world view of the Enlightenment."

3. General truths

"But if the spiritual in art **is** not primarily a matter of content or representational or nonrepresentational technique, what is it?"

"In this paper he distinctly **recognises** the principle of natural selection, and this is the first recognition which has been indicated."

4. Historical present to relate actions and states in literature

"Thou didst well, for wisdom **cries** out in the streets and no man **regards** its."

"That sir which **serves** and **seeks** for gain,
And **follows** but for form,
Will pack when it **begins** to rain,
And **leave** thee in a storm."

5. Future time (tense)

"A third type of painting that you will **encounter** in a museum is a painting that is devoid of all subject matter as we normally understand it."

"Apparently most of us manage our crises intelligently, but funda-mentalists go off the deep end, expecting Armageddon **every time** the stock market drops."

PAST TENSE

The past tense, as we have seen, is marked by an *-(e)d* or *-t* inflectional suffix for regular verbs and frequently an ablaut for irregular verbs. See Figure 4.3. It marks the time of events and actions taking place before those of the present.

Verb *form* expresses *tense*; verb meaning expresses *time* of the action or state. English has three main uses for the past tense, which is to express:

FIGURE 4.3 ✿ PAST TENSE

	REGULAR VERB	IRREGULAR VERB
I	walk**ed**	sang
you	walk**ed**	sang
he/she/it	walk**ed**	sang
we	walk**ed**	sang
you	walk**ed**	sang
they	walk**ed**	sang

1. Action and states in past time.

2. Past truths no longer valid and habitual actions no longer occurring.

3. Tense sequence, although the state named may still be in effect.

1. Actions and states in past time

"Along the darkening road he **hurried** alone, with his eyes cast down."

"The yellow lights **went** climbing towards the sky."

2a. Past truths no longer valid

"In those days the world in general **was** more ignorant of good and evil by forty years than it is at present."

2b. Habitual actions no longer occurring

"Sometimes he **stayed** at home on Wednesday and Thursday evenings, or was only out for an hour."

3. To preserve tense sequence

"She **was** a most generous woman, and **possessed** a considerable fortune of her own."

"He **had married** two years ago, and **had taken** his wife to live at Styles."

FUTURE TIME (TENSE)

English forms the future tense by adding the modal auxiliaries, *shall* or *will*, to the present tense of a base verb; see Figure 4.4. This combination of a particular modal plus a present tense form of a verb conveys the meaning of future time. Examples to illustrate this concept of time are:

a. [FUTURE TENSE]
"We **shall go** to death as unresistingly as tired children go to bed."

"When you return, you too **will understand** the reason for my enthusiasm."

"We mourn the dead, but we, too, **will** soon **be** among them."

Apart from using the future tense, we also indicate future *intention* with some adverbs of time, and other time references consisting of adjectives and nouns. This is not an uncommon usage, and for this reason such structures are often thought of as being in the future tense, when they are actually in the present tense *with future intention*. The following examples will illustrate this:

a. [FUTURE INTENTION]
"The **future** is what I look to, for you."

FIGURE 4.4 ✿ FUTURE TENSE

	REGULAR VERB	IRREGULAR VERB
I	shall[1] walk	shall sing
you	will walk	will sing
he/she/it	will walk	will sing
we	shall walk	shall sing
you	will walk	will sing
they	will walk	will sing

1 In modern English, *will* is frequently used as the modal auxiliary in all persons to indicate the future tense. *Shall*, which was formerly the first person singular and plural form, is now typically reserved for emphasis or for stylistic purposes.

"**Tomorrow** we can discuss details."

"I needed all the time until the **next Saturday** to think the question through, to decide what should be done."

In our first example, the overall meaning of the sentence is to denote time in the future, and this is done by using the noun *future* to convey that intention. However, the verb form determines the tense of the structure, and in this case it is the simple present—*is*. The second example uses an adverb of time *tomorrow* to convey this notion; however, if we look at the finite verb in this structure the modal *can* is in the present tense, and therefore the verb tense is present. The third example uses the phrase *next Saturday*, an adjective plus noun to mark the future intention; the verb form is simple past. Regardless of the many ways in which we express future time in English, only those using *shall* and *will* are called the future tense.

Aspect

ASPECT
expresses grammatical meanings concerned with the continuity or distribution of events in time.

Aspect refers to the internal temporal constituency of an event, or the manner in which a verb's action is distributed through the time-space continuum. Tense, on the other hand, points out the location of an event in the continuum of events.[2]

Besides time distinctions made overtly in the verb tense, English can also make distinctions relating to the continuity or non-continuity of an action. Aspect is a grammatical category of the verb, noting not so much the location of an event in time (tense), but the duration and type of action that it expresses. It considers such features as: progressiveness, habituality, boundedness, duration, and instantaneousness.[3] English expresses four[4] aspects: *simple, progressive, perfect,* and *perfect progressive,* and within each we have *present, past,* and *future tense*s; see Figure 4.5.

2 Harrison, Richard K. *Journal of Planned Languages* (24th edition) 1996 B2002.

3 J.P. Kaplan, *English Grammar: Principles and Facts* (Englewood Cliffs, NJ: Prentice Hall, 1989), p. 177.

4 Some authors (e.g., S. Greenbaum) say that there are only two aspects: progressive and perfect. For our purposes, four aspects will be illustrated to give a more complete presentation on verb expansion.

FIGURE 4.5 ✿ ASPECTS

simple	simple present, past or future tense of lexical verb
progressive	be + present participle of lexical verb
perfect	have + past participle of lexical verb
perfect progressive	have + be + present participle of lexical verb

SIMPLE ASPECT

Verbs occurring in the simple present, simple past, or simple future tense express *simple aspect*.

1. **Present:** In the simple present tense the verb formation is [base or base + -*s*]; the action or event occurs now, or is habitual or timeless.

They **sing** very well.

PAST	PRESENT	FUTURE
	▼	

a. [SIMPLE PRESENT]
"It **gives** us the basis for several deductions."

2. **Past:** In the simple past tense the verb formation is [base + *-(e)d/t* or ablaut]; the action or event occurred at some single point in the past and is now completed.

They **sang** very well.

PAST	PRESENT	FUTURE
▼		

a. [SIMPLE PAST]
"It wasn't the man upstairs who **gave** us this schedule; it was the man below."

3. **Future:** In future tense the verb formation is [modal (shall/will) + base]; the action or event will occur at some point in the future.

They **will sing** very well.

PAST	PRESENT	FUTURE
		▼

a. [SIMPLE FUTURE]
"It **will give** me great pleasure to accept the invitation."

PROGRESSIVE ASPECT

Verbs noting progressive aspect express continuity of action or time of an event. They can also refer to habitual actions or general truths. The lexical verb is in the present participle form, with an *-ing* suffix, and has a form of the primary auxiliary verb *to be* to signal the tense. The lexical verb in its non-finite form remains unchanged for all three progressive aspects.

1. **Present progressive:** The verb formation in the present progressive is [be (present) + present participle]; it expresses an activity or event that is occurring now and continuing, and its duration is limited.

They **are singing** very well.

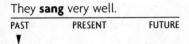

PAST	PRESENT	FUTURE
	⟶	

    a. [PRESENT PROGRESSIVE]
    "We **are going** through my mother's papers."

2. **Past progressive:** The verb formation in the past progressive is [be (past) + present participle]; it expresses an activity or event started at a particular point in the past and its action is of limited duration.

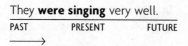

They **were singing** very well.

PAST	PRESENT	FUTURE

⟶

    a. [PAST PROGRESSIVE]
    "The terrorists told the civilians they **were going** to attack the Americans and to stay indoors."

3. **Future progressive:** The verb formation in the future progressive is [shall/will + be + present participle]; it expresses an activity or event that will begin in the future and continue into the future:

They **will be singing** very well.

PAST	PRESENT	FUTURE

        ⟶

    a. [FUTURE PROGRESSIVE]
    "This piece will of course do well because it **will be reaching** people in various cities."

PERFECT ASPECT

The perfect aspect describes an action either completed in the past or to be completed in the future. The lexical verb has the past participle form and is assisted with a form of the primary auxiliary *to have*, which signals the tense. The non-finite lexical verb remains unchanged for all three aspects.

1. **Present perfect:** The verb formation in the present perfect is [have + past participle]; it expresses an activity or event completed in the past but with some relationship to the present.

They **have sung** very well.

PAST	PRESENT	FUTURE

▼⟶▼

    a. [PRESENT PERFECT]
    "I **have talked** to the president about the whole question and the president says it does not imply the weaponization of space."

2. **Past perfect:** The verb formation in the past perfect is [had + past participle]; it expresses an activity or event completed before another action or event in the past.

> They **had sung** very well.
> PAST   PRESENT   FUTURE
> ▼

   a. [PAST PERFECT]
     "The defence **had pressed** for an acquittal, arguing that a fair retrial would be impossible."

3. **Future perfect:** The verb formation in the future perfect is [shall/will + have + past participle]; it expresses an activity begun, continued, and ended.

> They **will have sung** very well.
> PAST   PRESENT   FUTURE
>   ▼———→▼

   a. [FUTURE PERFECT]
     "No doubt errors **will have crept** in."

PERFECT PROGRESSIVE ASPECT

The perfect progressive aspect can also refer to habitual actions or general truths. It is formed with the lexical verb in the present participle form, and with both auxiliaries, *have* and *be*. The first auxiliary always carries the tense of the verb

1. **Present perfect progressive:** The verb formation in the present perfect progressive is [have + been + present participle]; it expresses an activity or event that began in the past and is continuing into the present.

> They **have been singing** very well.
> PAST   PRESENT   FUTURE
> ————————————→

   a. [PRESENT PERFECT PROGRESSIVE]
     "Lord and his Conservative government **have been feeling** the heat following a series of bad-news announcements."

2. **Past perfect progressive:** The verb formation in the past perfect progressive is [Had + been + present participle]; it expresses an activity or event that has continuing past action completed before another action (signaled by ▼) in the past.

They **had been singing** very well.

PAST   PRESENT   FUTURE

—▼→

a. [PAST PERFECT PROGRESSIVE]
"For several weeks I **had been observing** in him a growing habit of delay in answering even the most trivial of commonplace questions."

3. **Future perfect progressive:** the verb formation in the future perfect progressive is [Shall/will + have + been + present participle]; it expresses an activity or event that will begin before another action and still be in progress.

They **will have been singing** very well.

PAST   PRESENT   FUTURE

—▼→

a. [FUTURE PERFECT PROGRESSIVE]
I assure you, Sir Henry, that in a very few days the necessary arrangements **will have been coming forth**[5] and he will be on his way to South America.

5 The verb in this quotation is actually "made." I changed it to "coming forth" to have a suitable example for this aspect.

This presentation of aspect is often discussed under the heading of *verb expansion rules*, because essentially that is what occurs here. The verb phrase is expanded to express greater variations in meaning. If we take the number of modals that we can use with or without the possible variations of *have* and *be*, the result will give us quite a number of expanded verb phrases for each lexical verb. Of course, we do not cover all of these possibilities here.

Figure 4.6 summarizes the different aspects presented and is an excellent reference point for comparison.

FIGURE 4.6 ✿ TENSE AND ASPECT

TENSE	ASPECT	REGULAR VERB	IRREGULAR VERB
present	simple	we walk	we sing
past		we walked	we sang
future		we will walk	we will sing
present	progressive	we are walking	we are singing
past		we were walking	we were singing
future		we will be walking	we will be singing
present	perfect	we have walked	we have sung
past		we had walked	we had sung
future		we will have walked	we will have sung
present	perfect	we have been walking	we have been singing
past	progressive	we had been walking	we had been singing
future		we will have been walking	we will have been singing

ADVERB PHRASE

Adverb phrases are syntactic structures functioning as sentence constituents, with a head adverb (HAv) as its focus. They are similar to adjective phrases in that they may consist of one or more qualifying words.

ADVERB PHRASES
are cohesive word groups
focusing on adverbs as
their head word.

a. [ADVERB PHRASE]
"She watched **more keenly than ever**."

"The clock on the wall ticked **loudly and lazily**, as if it had time to spare."

"However, medicine often refers **more specifically** to matters dealt with by physicians and surgeons."

"But meanwhile the Semites have pushed **westward along the northern coast of Africa**."

Like adverb words, adverb phrases can cause confusion because of the flexibility of where they occur within sentences, and even in qualifying the whole sentence structure. The following examples clearly illustrate this.

a. [ADVERB PHRASE AT THE BEGINNING OF A SENTENCE]
"**Both musically and theologically** the *Requiem* is far removed from Lloyd Webber's earlier works."

b. [ADVERB PHRASE IN THE MIDDLE OF A SENTENCE]
"He had taken her hand **sympathizingly, forgivingly,** but his silence made me curious."

c. [ADVERB PHRASE AT THE END OF A SENTENCE]
"*Cats* is still doing so terribly well everywhere that I can't imagine anyone allowing it to become a movie **very quickly**."

Let us take the first example and show how that adverb phrase "**Both musically and theologically**" can be moved around without affecting the meaning of the sentence.

a. [ADVERB PHRASE AT THE BEGINNING OF A SENTENCE]
"**Both musically and theologically** the *Requiem* is far removed from Lloyd Webber's earlier works.'

b. [ADVERB PHRASE IN THE MIDDLE OF A SENTENCE]
The *Requiem* is far removed, **both musically and theologically**, from Lloyd Webber's earlier works.

C. [ADVERB PHRASE AT THE END OF A SENTENCE]
The *Requiem* is far removed from Lloyd Webber's earlier works, **both musically and theologically**.

As well, adverb phrases are sometimes embedded into other phrases. The following example shows an adverb phrase embedded into a verb phrase.

a. [ADVERB PHRASE EMBEDDED INTO VERB PHRASE]
"David, on the lowest step, *was* **very evidently not** *hearing* a word of what was being said."

Such flexibility can slow us down when identifying adverb phrases because its position does not always help us.

PARTICIPLE PHRASE

PARTICIPLE PHRASES
are cohesive word groups
consisting of non-finite
verb forms, present or past
participles, as head words.

*P*articiple phrases are syntactic structures functioning as sentence constituents with a head present participle (HPP) or a head past participle (HPTP) as its focus. The *head* participle, therefore, will be a non-finite verb form.

Present and past participles are non-finite verb forms expressing actions. The terms *present* and *past* are not very accurate when distinguishing them because non-finite forms do not show tense distinctions; they are not fixed in time. Instead, their distinction is one of aspect. As we saw, although participles frequently occur by themselves, they can also act as head words in participle phrases.

1. Present participle with *-ing* suffix:

a. [*-ING* (HPP) PRESENT PARTICIPLE]
"The **existing local government** *system* in Northern Ireland was established following the *Local Government (NI) Act* (1972)."

"Scrooge was a **squeezing, wrenching, grasping, scraping, clutching,** covetous old *sinner*."

2. Past participle with *-ed* suffix:

a. [*-ED* (HPTP) PAST PARTICIPLE]
"**The various specialized** *branches* of the science of medicine correspond to equally specialized medical professions dealing with particular organs or diseases."

"The owner of one scant young nose, **gnawed and mumbled by the
hungry cold** as bones are gnawed by dogs, stooped down at Scrooge's
keyhole to regale him with a Christmas carol."

3. Past participle with *-en* suffix:

a. [*-EN* (HPTP) PAST PARTICIPLE]
"In ancient Israel, among **the first chosen *people***, the kings and high
priests were anointed with oil."

"The value of Kiefer's work for Americans, however, lies in his ability to
stand on **his self-chosen Teutonic** foundations."

The present participle is more easily recognizable with its *-ing* suffix than the past
participle with its many varied regular and irregular forms, especially those with
ablaut changes.

GERUND PHRASE

*G*erund *phrases are syntactic structures functioning as sentence constituents, with a head
gerund (HG) as its focus.* These phrases express actions which are *complete*,
concrete, or *real*. Gerunds are based on verbs and, as we have discussed, they are
similar in form to participles and are called *verbals*. Figure 4.7 below identifies
representative verbs that belong to this category. There are a number of verb
combinations that belong to this group as well: *burst out, can't help, feel like, get
accustomed to, get through, give up, go on, fond of, leave off, keep on, tired of,* and *used to.*

GERUND PHRASES
are cohesive word
groups with a non-
finite *-ing* verb as its
head word.

FIGURE 4.7 ✿ VERBS TAKING GERUNDS

admit	deny	finish	postpone	stop
appreciate	detest	imagine	practice	suggest
avoid	dislike	keep	recall	understand
consider	enjoy	mind	regret	
delay	escape	miss	risk	

Present participles and gerunds look similar as words, and they also look
similar as phrases. Again, it is the *-ing* verbal form that causes this problem. To
clearly distinguish these, we need to consider their grammatical functions. A present participle functions as a non-finite form of a verb phrase, after verbs of
motion and position; it can be an adverb complement after these verbs; it can
qualify/modify as an adjective does. In contrast, gerunds like nouns have naming
roles and can occupy the place of nouns in many of their grammatical functions.
Unlike nouns, they do not name persons, places, things, or events; they name
actions, states, and behaviours.

a. [GERUND PHRASES]

"They looked at each other as with **the feeling of an occasion missed**."

"They are good folk, **struggling vigorously** against the temptations of sex and booze, **battling mightily** against the considerable forces that work to tear apart their families."

"When we were first rehearsing the *Requiem* in New York, I had a **very nice meeting** with a person from the 'Entertainment Tonight' television show."

Gerund phrases can begin with possessives, nouns, or pronouns, and when these are not present they can be easily added to help distinguish a gerund from a present participle. The following examples show gerund phrases beginning with possessives.

b. [GERUND PHRASES WITH POSSESSIVES]

"It was a long, long time before **Nick's breathing** told me that he was asleep."

"David changed our country's history through what **his reporting** revealed."

"He was struggling to support Virginia without **his wife's earnings** and was also being treated for depression."

Sometimes it is easier to understand a concept by proposing what it is not rather than saying what it is. The gerund falls into this category.

1. Words such as **evening**, **gosling**, **herring**, **morning**, **shilling**, **sterling**, and **thing** are not gerunds because the *-ing* is not a verbal suffix, but rather part of the base word.

"However, on Friday **morning** Israeli soldiers shot and killed an Islamic Jihad leader."

"The important **thing** is, the process is going now, it's moving."

2. Proper names, for example **Canning**, **Darling** and **Twining**, and the title **king** are not gerunds, because here again the *-ing* is not a verbal suffix but is part of the word base.

"In **Beijing** these days, one of the fastest-growing fortunes the world has ever seen is managed by fewer than two dozen traders."

"**Wuthering** Heights is the name of Mr. Heathcliff's dwelling."

3. Some nouns take an *-ing* suffix, such as **coupling**, **lodging**, **matting**, **stocking**, **clothing**, **flooring**, **grating**, **piping**, **siding**. These words are technically gerunds, but they have developed into common nouns with little relationship to the verbal forms.

> "Services, such as **housing**, education, roads and personal social services, are the responsibility of either government departments."

> "The judge put off a **ruling** on the matter pending further legal arguments."

> "Those **listings** led to asset freezes that dealt a strong blow to the group's finances."

INFINITIVE PHRASE

Infinitive phrases are syntactic structures functioning as sentence constituents, with a verb base (HI) as its head word. The verb base is preceded by the particle *to* and expresses actions or states of being. They are frequently used to express actions such as abstractions, futures, or that which is unreal. Like participles and gerunds, infinitives are verbals and are not marked for tense. Gerunds are used more frequently in English than are infinitives. Figure 4.8 identifies verbs taking infinitives.

INFINITIVE PHRASES are cohesive word groups consisting of the particle *to* plus a verb base as the head word.

FIGURE 4.8 ✿ VERBS TAKING INFINITIVES

agree	decide	intend	plan	refuse
be	fail	learn	prefer	remember
begin	hesitate	neglect	pretend	try
continue	hope	offer	promise	wait

Examples illustrating infinitives are:

a. [INFINITIVES]
"I want **to note** that a quite similar critique could be directed to many of the academic disciplines."

"**To understand** the world, they were convinced, one should focus on efficient causes."

"She seemed **to be** not only singing but doing a ventriloquist routine."

Although we tend to think of the infinitive phrase structure as consisting only of a particle plus a verb base, with or without other qualifiers, another variant of the infinitive phrase begins with *for* and is often followed by a personal noun or pronoun. Examples for these are:

a. [INFINITIVES WITH *FOR*]

"Physicians are generally eligible **for independent licensure to practice** primary care specialties at this point."

"Federal officials said they leave time **for parents to make arrangements** for their children, and refer them to a social service agency if necessary."

"I said all right; then the thing **for us to do** was to go for the magicians."

In general speech and writing, we tend to shorten infinitives to the particle plus verb base for general reference.

a. [INFINITIVE PHRASE]

"I said, all right; then the thing **for us to do** was to go for the magicians."

b. [HI/INFINITIVE PHRASE REDUCED]

"I said, all right; then the thing ... **to do** was to go for the magicians."

However, if the reference is specific to a person, thing or topic, it is necessary to include it.

a. [SPECIFIC NOUN + INFINITIVES PHRASE/HI]

"It was no new thing **for David to 'play'** the sunset."

"By the end of a fortnight David had brought his father's violin **for Joe to practice on.**"

"Whichever way it was, there was always sure to be something waiting at the end **for him and his violin to discover.**"

Because the reference is made specifically to *David*, *Joe*, and *him and his violin*, the infinitive phrase cannot be shortened without losing part of the meaning of the sentence.

PREPOSITIONAL PHRASE

PREPOSITIONAL PHRASES are cohesive word groups forming syntactic units, consisting of a preposition plus a noun or its replacement.

Prepositional phrases are syntactic structures functioning as sentence constituents, with a preposition as a head word (HPRP). The structure of a prepositional phrase is more significant than the preposition that introduces it, which generally has little meaning. Although the preposition is the head word in the phrase, it is the object of that preposition, a noun or its equivalent, that relates back to the sentence as a constituent. To understand the form of the prepositional phrase, however, it is necessary to consider its internal structure. Examples of prepositional phrase structures are:

a. [PREPOSITION + OBJECT OF THE PREPOSITION]

in	+	the forest
into	+	the room
during	+	the game
because of	+	the situation

Here are some prepositional phrases:

a. [HPRP + PREPOSITIONAL PHRASE OBJECTS]
"When the distinction was first established, the study **of society** was not far advanced."

"Of course, this simplifies matters **in several ways**."

"Passengers never see or feel what we do **on top *of a boxcar***, as the train speeds **through deserts and mountains**."

The first example shows a single prepositional phrase in a sentence; similarly, the second sentence shows a single preposition, but this one has a qualifier before the noun. So prepositional phrases can be extended and are not restricted to a preposition and a single object. The third example contains three prepositional phrases: a simple preposition plus its noun object; next a simple preposition plus a determiner before the noun object; finally, compound noun objects following a preposition. Recognizing and understanding prepositional phrase structures and later their grammatical functions is most important.

Prepositions and particles

A number of prepositions by form are used to create other phrase structures. Our first example of this was the preposition *to* joined with a verb base phrase (to + walk = to walk) to form an infinitive. In such cases we no longer refer to the word as a preposition, although that is what it is by *form*; we call it a *particle*. One might say that the term *particle* is more reflective of its *function* than its *form*. Other prepositions by form also function as particles in forming phrasal verbs. Figure 4.9 shows a representative list of phrasal verbs.

Some examples to illustrate these are:

a. [VERB PLUS ONE PARTICLE]
"She characterized the letter as a formality, and said that it did not **bring up** any problems."

FIGURE 4.9 ✿ PHRASAL VERBS

VERB	+	ONE PARTICLE
add		up
back		down
call		off
draw		up
eat		out
figure		out
get		across
hand		in

VERB	+	TWO PARTICLES
brush		up on
check		out of
drop		out of
face		up to
go		out with
jump		all over
watch		out for

"I'd go to Bonds and **figure out** what happened and persuade him to be part of the solution."

"The ruling appeared to stun the two men who, for now, **make up** the core of Ukrainian state power."

b. [VERB PLUS TWO PARTICLES]
"Her grandmother arrived at her school to take her and older sister Brittany home with her, because the girls' parents had **come down with** strep throat."

"'That's what you **get out of** the I.N.G.,' Colonel Gubler said."

"Cartwright had **come down with** me, and in his disguise as a country boy he was of great assistance to me."

Sometimes it is unclear whether we have a preposition or a particle, and this can cause problems in understanding the meaning expressed in the sentence. To make the distinction clear it is necessary to focus on the verb type. Consider the following contrived example.

a. [VERB PHRASE]
Max looked up the chimney.

Is the word *up* part of the verb as in *look + up*, or is it the head word for the prepositional phrase *up the chimney*? If it is a phrasal verb, then we have the following sentence structure:

b. [TRANSITIVE PHRASAL + OBJECT]
****Max looked up** the chimney.

In this case, *look up* is a transitive verb followed by a noun object. However, if *up* is a head word introducing a prepositional phrase, we have:

c. [INTRANSITIVE VERB + A PREPOSITIONAL PHRASE COMPLEMENT]
Max looked **up the chimney**.

The true test of any sentence is its meaning, and that may be difficult to establish. For the first example, we ask how can you *look up + the chimney*? You may *look up a number* in a telephone book, but not a *chimney*. You look up a *chimney sweeper*, but not *a chimney*. (There is no doubt that one could contrive a sentence where *looking up the chimney* would make sense; however, contextual information would have to be given.) For the second example, *Max* could be standing at the base of a tall chimney structure and *looked* in the direction of *up the chimney*.

As well, two word-verbs can often be split. For example, we can say:

a. [TRANSITIVE VERB + PARTICLE + OBJECT]
Max **looked up** the number.

b. [TRANSITIVE VERB + OBJECT + PARTICLE]
Max **looked** the number **up**.

However, we do not say:

a. [TRANSITIVE VERB + PARTICLE + OBJECT]
*Max **looked up** the chimney.

b. [TRANSITIVE VERB + OBJECT + PARTICLE]
*Max **looked** the chimney **up**.

Sentence meaning is not always the solution to this problem, because we can say:

a. [TRANSITIVE VERB + PARTICLE + OBJECT]
Barbara **looked up** the street.

b. [INTRANSITIVE VERB + PREPOSITIONAL PHRASE]
Barbara looked **up the street**.

In these examples, both meanings are possible. In the first example, *Barbara looked up the street on the map because she did not know where it was located*; in the second, *Barbara went out and looked in the direction up the street*. An ambiguity can occur.

The following prepositions in Figure 4.10 are those most frequently used as particles to help form phrasal verbs.

FIGURE 4.10 ✿ PARTICLES

about	down	on	through	with
across	in	out	to	
around	off	over	up	

These particles can occur with any number of verbs to form phrasal verbs.

ABSOLUTE PHRASE

Absolute (*or nominative absolute*) *phrases are syntactic structures functioning as a sentence constituent, not linked to the main clause syntactically or semantically by shared elements.* An absolute phrase relates conceptually to the sentence as a whole, rather than to specific constituents in the sentence. Within its own structure the absolute phrase consists of a *noun* (*phrase*) plus a *participle* (*phrase*),[6] or a noun phrase that includes a post-noun modifier(s). Generally, the modifier is an (-*ing*) present participle or an (-*en*/-*ed*) past participle; other times, it can be another noun phrase, a prepositional phrase, or even an adjective phrase. When the present

ABSOLUTE PHRASES
are cohesive word groups not linked to the main clause syntactically or semantically by shared elements.

6 It may simply be a noun and a participle, rather than phrases.

participle is not present it is understood to be the present participle of the verb BE, (*being*).

Unlike participle phrases, absolute phrases usually contain a word that has the grammatical function of a subject, but there is no finite verb to act as a predicate. They generally occur at the beginning of sentences, but sometimes we find them embedded or at the end of sentences. The choice depends upon emphasis and variety, and not on the meaning. As a structure it is therefore set aside from the rest of the sentence by one or more commas, or dashes. Examples to illustrate these are:

a. [ABSOLUTE PHRASE/NOUN PHRASE + PRESENT PARTICIPLE]
"Mr. Heathcliff followed, **his accidental merriment *expiring quickly in his habitual moroseness***."

"Dylan became the Christian music industry's and the religious press's new celebrity convert. Dylan, ***being* Dylan**, reacted predictably."

b. [ABSOLUTE PHRASE/NOUN PHRASE + PAST PARTICIPLE]
"At issue are papers provided to the inquiry by the Privy Council Office—among them **some memos *addressed*** directly to former prime minister Jean Chretien."

"I opened my mouth for a 'good-morning,' but closed it again, **the salutation *unachieved*.**"

Like participle phrases, absolute phrases can be active or passive, transitive or intransitive. Absolute phrases do not express tense.

Absolute phrases are of two kinds with different purposes and different effects.

1. Absolute phrases can explain *cause* or *condition*. Such phrases can be rewritten as subordinate clauses beginning with *if*, *because*, *when*, or *since*.

a. [CAUSE]
"'That's the judge,' she said to herself, '**because of his great wig**.'"

2. An absolute phrase can also add detail or focus to the idea in the main clause.

a. [INFINITIVE PHRASE]
"**To be sure**, it might be nothing but a good coat of tropical tanning."

Often the idea underlying the absolute phrase dominates the structure, when grammatically and structurally it is subordinate to the sentence.

By way of summary for this most complex of phrases:

1. Absolute phrases may contain participles or any other structures that follow BE.

2. Whenever a participle is not present, *being* is understood as part of the absolute phrase.

3. An absolute phrase consists of a subject and a participle phrase.

4. Like other participial phrases, the absolute phrase may be active or passive, transitive or intransitive, etc.

5. Absolute phrases do not have tense.

6. Just as adverbs may be found at the beginning or end of a sentence, absolute phrases may occur in either place. The choice depends upon emphasis and variety, not meaning.

PHRASE ANALYSIS

As with words and morphemes, it is important to be able to break phrases down into individual constituents. The phrase may be a constituent itself within the sentence, but of itself, it has constituents.

1. Noun phrase with pre-noun modifiers:

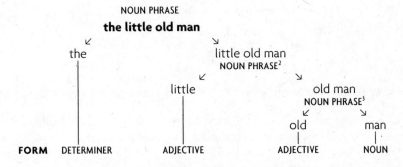

All words are simply identified by form. The first cut isolates *the*, a determiner; the second isolates *little*, an adjective; the third *old*, an adjective; the head word is *man*, a noun.

NP stands for the full noun phrase structure; NP^2 identifies a second noun within the NP; NP^3 identifies a third noun within NP^2. This order of cutting pre-noun modifiers is a simple binary analysis. Begin at the extreme left and cut one constituent at a time moving towards the HN at the extreme right. The maximum number of such modifying categories is five. Consider Figure 4.10.

FIGURE 4.10 ✿ PRE-NOUN MODIFIERS

pre-noun modifers

RESTRICTER	PRE-DETERMINER	DETERMINER	POST-DETERMINER	ADJECTIVES
especially	all	the	1, 2, 3...	little
even	both	her	first	old
just	half	Mary's	each	pretty

From the above examples, we can form any number of noun phrases, for example, "*especially all the first little school* **houses**." Although we identify five pre-noun categories, that is not to say that the longest noun phrase can only be six words (including the noun itself). On the contrary, several adjectives may precede the noun, as in: the *fragile little old* man. Here we have three modifying adjectives. Also, nouns can modify nouns, as in: *college student, school house*, etc.

While this figure identifies the pre-noun modifiers, it does not account for post-noun modifiers, which are generally phrases and clauses, as we shall see later. So the above example might also read, "*especially all the first little school houses in the rural districts of the country*." Here we have the addition of two post-noun prepositional phrase modifiers.

2. Verb phrase with auxiliary verbs:

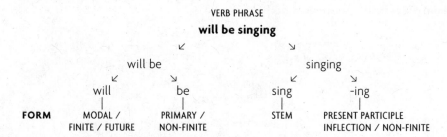

VERB PHRASE
will be singing

	will be		singing	
	will	be	sing	-ing
FORM	MODAL / FINITE / FUTURE	PRIMARY / NON-FINITE	STEM	PRESENT PARTICIPLE INFLECTION / NON-FINITE

Verb phrases are obviously different from noun phrases, but not that different. Head lexical verbs (HV) are generally found to the extreme right of the phrase. However, for verbs the inflectional endings have to be accounted for as well, because they frequently state aspect. In the above phrase we begin by first cutting the auxiliaries from the main verb. Next we divide auxiliaries into modal and primary auxiliaries; then we separate the base of the main verb and the inflectional suffix noting the aspect. Like noun phrases, verb phrases can also become quite complicated. For example, we might hear: *he may have been very willing to go.*

3. Prepositional phrase:

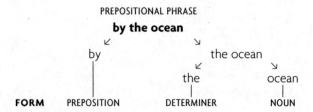

Prepositional phrases tend to be very simple. Generally they consist of a preposition, a modifier, and a noun or its substitute. Occasionally there may be more than one modifier. To break down a prepositional phrase, the cutting begins at the left with the preposition and moves to the right towards the noun object.

4. Participle phrase:

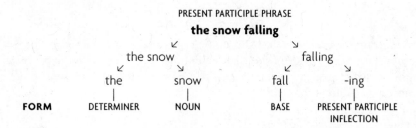

Participle phrases pose no more complexity than other phrase structures. In the above structure the noun phrase and the participle constitute the first cut; then the noun phrase is broken down further. To determine the grammatical function of the noun, it would be necessary to have a larger structure where it could be identified as a subject or object.

5. Gerund phrase:

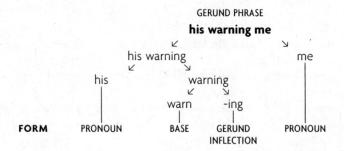

Gerund phrases are similar to participle phrases. The first cut separates the gerund and its modifier from all other constituents; next we separate the modifier and the gerund itself.

6. Infinitive phrase:

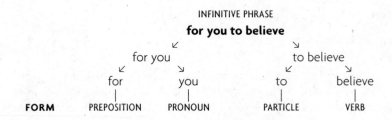

Infinitive phrases have essentially two components, the prepositional phrase and the actual infinitive.

✿　✿　✿

Before leaving phrase structures, we should first consider the phrase concept in its most important role—within the clause/sentence. All sentences have two essential phrase structures: a *noun phrase* and a *verb phrase*. We express these components in the following way:

$$S(entence) \ = \ N(oun) \ P(hrase) \ + \ V(erb) \ P(hrase)$$

These are grammatical functional roles, which we shall consider in more detail in chapters 6 and 7. However, it is important to introduce them here because the terminology overlaps: English has a noun phrase by *form*, and it also has a noun phrase by *function*; similarly it has a verb phrase by *form* and a verb phrase by *function*. As stated above, a noun or verb phrase by form is a cohesive word group; on the other hand, a noun or verb phrase by function is a *sentence constituent*. Either of these may or may not be a word group; one or the other may be a simple word. Examples to illustrate these are:

    a. [WORDS BY FORM/NOUN PHRASES BY FUNCTION]
    "**He** was a reporter who never let style trump substance."

    "**There** are millions of people who are illegally in the United States."

    "**David** was unwavering in his understanding of what a converged media company means."

Here we have a single word by form filling the position of a noun phrase; even as single words they are called noun phrases by function.

b. [NOUN PHRASES BY FORM/NOUN PHRASES BY FUNCTION]
"**Officials at the Department of Homeland Security** say they are simply enforcing laws adopted in 1996."

"**His impeccable print credentials** convinced many an ink-stained skeptic that there was more to television than teeth and hair."

"**His elderly father, James Baltovich, and brother Terry Chadwick,** greeted him as he emerged from the facility."

Noun phrases can become quite complex in structure, by including qualifiers and/or compounding the subject.

When analyzing a sentence, first identify the noun phrase (NP) and then the verb phrase (VP); both of which may contain other words or phrases that play further distinctive roles within the sentence. Because of this, the verb phrase may be further broken down into the single verb phrase and those elements that come after it. With elements occurring after the verb phrase, there is now a slightly more complicated sentence formula.

$$S(entence) \rightarrow N(oun)\ P(hrase) + V(erb)\ P(hrase) \pm N(oun)\ P(hrase)^2 \text{ or } C(omplement)$$

The best guide for identifying the following elements is to know the verb types. Transitive verbs always take objects, making up a third sentence component, a second noun phrase (NP^2). Intransitive verbs generally, but not always, take complements (C). Linking verbs must take complements (C), generally different from those occurring after intransitive verbs.

If a second structure follows, the verb phrase is further broken down as such:

$$S(entence) \rightarrow N(oun)\ P(hrase) + V(erb)\ P(hrase) \pm N(oun)\ P(hrase)^2 \text{ or } C(omplement)$$

$$S \rightarrow NP + VP \pm NP^2 \text{ or } C$$

$$VP \quad NP^2 \text{ or } C$$

$$NP^2 \quad C$$

and is further abbreviated as:

$$S \rightarrow NP + VP \pm NP^2/C$$

The $\pm$ symbol means "plus or minus" noting that other noun phrases or complements may or may not follow; however, they usually do. This formula is used throughout the text when analyzing grammatical functions and grammatical positions.

5   CLAUSES

INDEPENDENT CLAUSES

Independent clauses are subject and finite verb structures that stand alone with completed meaning. An independent clause or a simple sentence is the largest syntactic structure in our language system. Do not assume, however, that clauses and sentences are identical. While some sentences are simple in structure and are independent clauses, most sentences consist of more than one clause, usually a combination of, independent and/or dependent clauses. We also call independent clauses *main* or *matrix* clauses. Figure 5.1 identifies clausal types.

FIGURE 5.1 ✿ CLAUSES

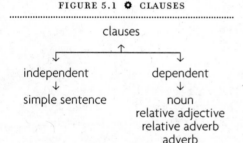

The basis of any clause is that it contains a noun phrase **NP** (*subject*) and a verb phrase **VP** (*predicate*). The subject can be expressed in a number of ways, but the verb phrase must always show tense. This is a distinguishing feature between phrases and clauses. Phrases frequently contain verb forms that are nonfinite; clauses must always contain a finite verb. The following are examples of independent clauses, because they have completed meaning as they stand.

1. [INDEPENDENT CLAUSES]

    S   →   NP   +   VP   ±   NP²/C

    a. [Sj   +   P   +   Do]
        "This   simplifies   matters in several ways."

    b. [Sj   +   P   +   Do]
        "Organisms   behave   purposefully."

    c. [Sj   +   P   +   C]
        "He   is   a retired minister."

CLAUSES
are independent and dependent structures, both generally consisting of a noun phrase and a finite verb phrase, that is, a subject and a predicate.

INDEPENDENT CLAUSES
are subject and finite verb structures that stand alone with completed meaning.

Understanding the meaning of these sentences is not difficult, because of structure and content. The first example contains a simple subject, predicate and direct object (after a transitive verb); the second contains a simple subject, predicate and complement (after an intransitive verb); the third contains a simple subject, predicate and complement (after a linking verb). It is generally the *completed* meaning of a structure that signals to us whether it is a sentence or not.

Perhaps the most common cause of sentence fragments is the use of a non-finite verb instead of a finite one. The ungrammaticality of "sentences" becomes clearer with present participles, that is, non-finite verbs being used for finite ones. If we take the last sentence of the preceding example and rewrite it, we have:

*He **being** a retired minister.

We can see how fragile independent structures can be. By changing the finite verb *is* to its non-finite form *being*, we create an ungrammatical structure.

A second example to illustrate this point can be found within the following structures:

a. [NON-FINITE VERB]
The reason **being** that she ***left*** town.

b. [NON-FINITE VERB]
The reason **being** she ***left*** town.

c. [FINITE VERB]
The reason **is** [that] she ***left*** town.

This is a common mistake carried over from spoken English, where the non-finite verb frequently replaces the finite verb. There are two verb forms here, but the second one is the finite verb *left* of the dependent clause. The independent clause has only a non-finite verb, and therefore has no tense marker. The occurrence of the finite verb in the dependent clause probably lessens the awkwardness of the structure, whereas the occurrence of two non-finite verbs reads a little more strangely.

DEPENDENT CLAUSES

DEPENDENT CLAUSES are subject and predicate (finite verb) structures needing a second clause structure for completed meaning.

Dependent clauses are subject and predicate (finite verb) structures needing a second clause structure for completed meaning. Although they contain a subject and a predicate, they rely on an independent or another dependent clause for completed meaning. The predicate of the dependent clause must also contain a finite verb, which can be a transitive, intransitive, or linking verb. Depending on the verb type, it may also take objects or a complement. As Figure 5.1 noted, we identify four types of dependent clauses: *noun*, *relative* (*adjective* and *adverb*), and *adverb*. Note that the relative clause can be further divided into two types: relative adjective and relative adverb.

The constituents of a dependent clause are the same as those of an independent clause. In analyzing these structures, constituents of the main clause will always appear above the structure in *upper-key* letters; constituents of the dependent clause will always appear below the structure in *lower-key* letters. This will enable us to distinguish between independent and dependent clause constituents within the same presentation.

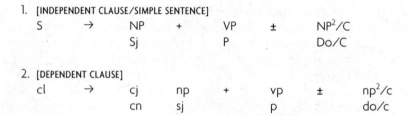

1. [INDEPENDENT CLAUSE/SIMPLE SENTENCE]

S	→	NP	+	VP	±	NP^2/C
		Sj		P		Do/C

2. [DEPENDENT CLAUSE]

cl	→	cj	np	+	vp	±	np^2/c
		cn	sj		p		do/c

The following are examples of dependent clauses.

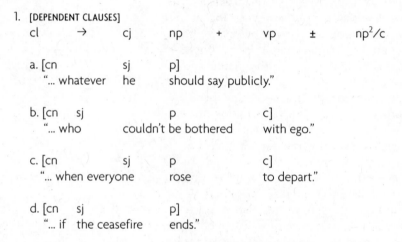

1. [DEPENDENT CLAUSES]

cl	→	cj	np	+	vp	±	np^2/c

    a. [cn   sj   p]
       "... whatever   he   should say publicly."

    b. [cn   sj   p   c]
       "... who   couldn't be bothered   with ego."

    c. [cn   sj   p   c]
       "... when everyone   rose   to depart."

    d. [cn   sj   p]
       "... if   the ceasefire   ends."

In the first sentence the conjunction is actually the object of the predicate. Obviously the meaning conveyed by the sentence is lost when we only have the dependent clause. Here are some sentences containing both independent and dependent clauses.

a. [INDEPENDENT/DEPENDENT CLAUSES]

    "Our whole economy is built on the basis of ever-increasing consumption, *which in turn adds endlessly to the stress upon the environment."*

    "Whatever else they may be (and they are other things besides), **Bowker claims that religions are, at the very least, systems for processing information."**

"**I saw few faces** *that looked familiar,* but **I recognized the hairdos, the polyester suits, the farm-shaped hands**."

"*Whenever a high note approached,* **the soprano surreptitiously hit the volume control on the tape deck** and **opened her mouth a little wider**."

The first two sentences highlight single independent clauses and single dependent clauses; the second two examples contain two independent clauses each, joined by coordinating conjunctions, and a single dependent clause. Dependent clauses most certainly add length to any sentence structure.

NOUN CLAUSES

NOUN CLAUSES are subject and predicate (finite verb) structures carrying out the grammatical functions attributed to a noun.

1 In the sense of *whether*.

Noun clauses are subject and predicate (finite verb) structures carrying out the grammatical functions attributed to a noun. They parallel noun words and noun phrases by *form*. The conjunction of a noun clause has a single grammatical function within the clause and that is to introduce it.

We connect noun clauses to independent or other dependent clauses with conjunctions, that is, the conjunction *that* and what we generally call *wh*-words. See Figure 5.2. The *wh*-words are a combination of pronouns—many of which also occur as relative and interrogative pronouns—and those ending in *-ever* are often called relative indefinite pronouns. Because of this overlap, confusion sometimes arises in recognizing the clause type. Generally, when we see *who, whom, whose,* and *which* we think of relative adjective clauses. The *that* conjunction can cause problems because it introduces both noun and relative adjectives clauses, and in both cases it can sometimes be deleted; the *wh-* conjunctions, however, cannot be deleted. Examples to illustrate noun clauses are:

FIGURE 5.2 ✿ NOUN CLAUSES

WH- WORDS		CONJUNCTIONS
who		that
whom		how
whose		if[1]
which	when	
what	why	
	where	
whether		
whoever		
whomever		
whosever		
whichever		
whatever		

S　　　→　　　NP　　+　　VP　　±　　NP²/c

1. [NOUN CLAUSES]
   [cn　　　sj　　　p　　　do/c]

   a. [cn　　　sj　　　p　　　do]
   "... that　　they　　have　a majority on the council."

b. [cn	sj	p	c]
"What	Roddick	did not explain at the time ..."	

c. [cn	sj	p	do]
"... ø	it	did not	matter"

d. [cn	sj	p	c]
"... whatever	else	is temporarily	in vogue."

If the noun clause occurs at the beginning of a sentence, the *that* conjunction must be present or we have no way of knowing which clause is the main one.

1. [NOUN CLAUSE]   [MAIN CLAUSE]

a. [cn	sj	p	c]	
"That	**she**	**was**	**by no means destitute**	*was obvious."*

b.	**"... she**	**was by no means destitute**	was obvious."

To distinguish one clause from the other, the pronoun *it* can generally be substituted for the noun clause.

c. **"It**   was obvious."

d. *That she was by no means destitute   **it**.

Here are some other noun clauses in the context of their independent clauses.

1. [MAIN CLAUSE]   [NOUN CLAUSE]

a. **"They acknowledge**   *that there are other ways of studying human beings."*

b. **"To begin with, ...**   *whoever else might benefit by Mrs. Inglethorp's death, ... her husband would benefit the most."*

c. **"'Naturally,' I went on, 'I'm going to warn you,**   *whether you like it or not.'"*

2. [NOUN CLAUSE]   [MAIN CLAUSE]

a. **"Whatever she did, too,**   *was done without conscious effort."*

b. **"What is of particular interest here, of course,**   *is the power sharing cohort."*

c. **"They've got to do**   *whatever he says."*

RELATIVE CLAUSES

RELATIVE CLAUSES
are subject and predicate
(finite verb) structures
carrying out the
grammatical functions
attributed to a modifier.

2 The antecedent (Latin
for "coming before") is
the noun or noun
replacement to which
the relative pronoun
relates.

*R*elative clauses are subject and predicate (finite verb) structures carrying out the gram- matical functions attributed to a modifier. By their very name, relative clauses (*adjective* and *adverb*) mean *to relate*, that is, to relate back to the antecedent.[2] The grammatical function of this relationship is called *modifier*; this is because it limits the person, place, thing, event, or action that it modifies. By *form* and *function* they parallel their counterparts, *adjectives* and *adverbs*, in the word and phrase cate- gories. Relative clauses are also *restrictive* or *nonrestrictive*, much in the same way as we saw with appositives.

Relative adjective clauses are introduced by the relative pronouns *who*, *whom*, *whose*, *which*, and *that*; they carry out the grammatical function of *connector*. Here are some examples of relative adjective dependent clauses.

S	$\rightarrow$	NP	+	VP	$\pm$	NP^2/C

1. [RELATIVE ADJECTIVE CLAUSES]

cl	$\rightarrow$	cj/np	+	vp	+	np^2/c

a. [cn/sj   p   do]
   "... **who**   had returned   home."

b. [cn   sj   p   do]
   "... **with whom** I   no longer had   anything in common."

c. [cn   sj   p]
   "... **whose**   individual names were known."

d. [cn/sj   p   do]
   "... **that**   breeds mostly   acquaintances."

e. [cn/sj   p   do]
   "**which**   has always intrigued   me."

To illustrate relative adjective clauses with their independent main clauses, we have:

1. [MAIN CLAUSE]	[RELATIVE ADJECTIVE CLAUSE]
a. "**As such, it may have been a tribute to van Gogh's father,**	*who died a few months before.*"
b. "**A god symbolized by a serpent is a god in**	*whom good and evil are equal principles.*"
c. "**They are a Band-Aid on wounds**	*whose source lies in the very structure of our society.*"

d. "**It exercises a dominant influence on the institutions**   *that support the global economy.*"

e. "**They required them to pay taxes in cash,** *which they could obtain only by wage labor.*"

RELATIVE ADVERB CLAUSES

Relative adverb clauses are subject and predicate (finite verb) structures carrying out the grammatical functions attributed to an adverb modifier. They are introduced by the relative adverbs *when, where,* and *why,* expressing such meanings as *time, place,* and *reason.* They differ from relative adjective clauses only with regard to the grammatical functions that the pronouns carry out within their own clauses. Similarly, these relatives carry out the grammatical function of *connector.* As sentence constituents they both modify or refer back to an antecedent in the independent clause, which is a noun or its replacement. Examples to illustrate relative adverb dependent clauses are:

S	→	NP	+	VP	±	NP²/C

1. [RELATIVE ADVERB CLAUSES]

cl→		sj/np	+	vp	+	do/c]

a.

[cn	sj	p	do]
"When	children	lose	a family member this way, ..."

b.

[cn	sj	p	c]
"Where	the child	is going to be ..."	

c.

[cn	sj	p	do]
"... why	they	call	him 'Cat.'"

Relative adverb clauses with their main clauses are as follows:

1. [MAIN CLAUSE]   [RELATIVE ADVERB CLAUSE]

a. "**Acrimony heightened in 1985** *when Sinn Fein councillors were elected to local authorities.*"

b. "**Yet this is** *where the real challenge lies.*"

c. "**Everyone knew** *why they were last on the program.*"

ADVERB CLAUSES

ADVERB CLAUSES
are subject and predicate
(finite verb) structures
carrying out the
grammatical functions
attributed to adverbs.

*A*dverb clauses are subject and predicate (finite verb) structures carrying out the grammatical functions attributed to adverbs. Adverb clauses are formed by adding a subordinating adverb conjunction to a noun phrase **NP** plus verb phrase **VP** structure. These adverbs denote time (*after, before, as soon as*, etc.), manner (*as, as if, like*, etc.), contrast or opposition (*although, whereas, while*, etc.), cause and effect (*because, in that, since*, etc.), condition (*in case, provided that, unless*, etc.), purpose (*so that, in order that*, etc.), and comparison (*more than, less than*, etc.). They modify words, phrases, and clauses of a verb/adverb composition.

Unlike relative adverb conjunctions, adverb conjunctions do not have grammatical functions within the clauses they introduce; in this respect they are similar to the conjunctions introducing noun clauses. Their only grammatical function is as a *connector* of the subordinate clause. Examples to illustrate adverb clauses are:

S	→	NP	+	VP	±	C

1. [ADVERB CLAUSES]

   [cn sj p ± do/c]

a. [cn sj p do]
   "... before we endorsed this policy."

b. [cn sj p]
   "As one critic wrote, ..."

c. [cn sj p c]
   "... because his son had died for America."

d. [cn sj p do]
   "... unless we keep   this wider religious world before us."

e. [cn sj p do]
   "... so that market forces can price it."

f. [cn sj p c]
   "more than ... they enrolled in 1996."

g. [cn sj p c]
   "Although the rule hasn't been made pubic ..."

Adverb clauses with their main clauses are:

1. [MAIN CLAUSE]   [ADVERB CLAUSE]

a. **"The feeling and intensity expressed in a piece of music may be remembered** *long after the sermon is forgotten."*

b. **"In the clubhouses, players could access piles of stimulants** *as if they were candy, according to the founder of the players union."*

c. **"At least 22 insurgents were killed,** *while 7 American soldiers suffered minor wounds, according to American commanders."*

d. **"Quebec dairy and beef farmers have suffered heavy financial losses since** *the United States closed its border to live Canadian cattle."*

e. **"I deliberated a moment whether, ... I would comply or otherwise."** *in case he invited me,*

f. **"He distributed all the sixty-four keys among the prisoners** *in order that they might free themselves."*

g. **"As soon as I got to the river side I liked it** *even less than I thought I should."*

✿   ✿   ✿

Summary of form words, phrases and clauses:

words	→	phrases	→	clauses
nouns		noun		independent
verbs		verb		dependent
adjectives		adjective		noun
adverbs		adverb		relative adjective
pronouns		participle		relative adverb
determiners		gerund		adverb
auxiliaries		infinitive		
prepositions		prepositional		
conjunctions		absolute		

function

6 MAJOR GRAMMATICAL FUNCTIONS

GRAMMATICAL FUNCTION

Grammatical function is our second category of analysis—form, *function*, and position—that is, *what a constituent **DOES***. Identifying words by *form* gives limited information about the characteristics of a word class. Identifying words by *grammatical function*, however, reveals the ongoing and often changing relationships sentence constituents have with one another. *Function is the role a constituent has within a sentence, along with its syntactic relationship to other constituents within that sentence.* Figure 6.1 identifies the four major grammatical functions.

FUNCTION
(grammatical function) is the role a constituent has within a sentence, along with its syntactic relationship to other constituents within that sentence.

FIGURE 6.1 ✿ MAJOR GRAMMATICAL FUNCTIONS

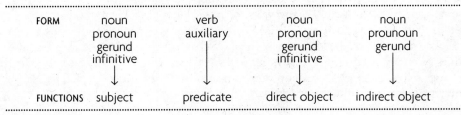

FORM	noun pronoun gerund infinitive	verb auxiliary	noun pronoun gerund infinitive	noun prounoun gerund
FUNCTIONS	subject	predicate	direct object	indirect object

Grammatical functions have been arbitrarily divided into *major* and *minor* functions, based on their importance in sentence structures. Major functions are more essential to sentence structures than are minor functions.

The basic components of all sentences, the noun phrase (NP) and the verb phrase (VP), are always expressed as the *subject* and the *predicate* respectively. When the predicate is a transitive verb, a direct object must follow and an indirect object may or may not follow.

We now make a major shift in the terminology that we shall use to describe grammatical *functions* as opposed to *forms*. When we discussed form categories, *what a constituent **IS***, we used terms such as noun, pronoun, verb, etc., and each time we used these terms we were referring to the *form of the constituent*. For example, a word classified as a *noun* means the *form* of that constituent. Now we move on to functional categories, *what a constituent **DOES***, and here we shall use new paralleling terms (subject, predicate, complement, etc.). Each time we use these terms, we shall refer to the grammatical functions of these constituents. A noun by form now becomes, for example, a subject by function, or a direct object by function.

Figure 6.2 summarizes the parallels between terms for grammatical form and grammatical function:

FIGURE 6.2 ✿ GRAMMATICAL FORM AND FUNCTION

	grammatical terms		
FORM	noun pronoun gerund infinitive	verb auxiliary	noun pronoun gerund infinitive	noun prounoun gerund
FUNCTION	subject	predicate	direct object	indirect object

SUBJECT

Subject has the grammatical meanings of that which performs, describes, identifies, or asserts. It is one of two essential grammatical functions needed in creating the sentence structure, and it always occupies the noun phrase (NP) component of sentences. By form it can be any word or phrase that has a *noun, pronoun, gerund,* or an *infinitive* as its head word (HW). A *noun clause* can also carry out this grammatical function, as we shall discuss later. Subjects are easy to identify because they generally occur at the beginning of sentences before the predicate. The first group of following examples notes the various form class categories that can carry out this grammatical function.

$$S \rightarrow \quad NP \quad + \quad VP \quad + \quad NP^2/C$$
$$Sj$$

a. [SUBJECT/PROPER NOUN]
  "**Mrs. Cressler** showed them to their rooms."

b. [SUBJECT/PRONOUN]
  "**We** will continue our discussions with the Americans."

c. [SUBJECT/NOUN PHRASE]
  "**The development of clinical medicine** shifted to the United Kingdom and the USA during the early 1900s."

d. [SUBJECT/GERUND]
  "**The brute's wailing and whining** died away on the desolate shore."

e. [SUBJECT/INFINITIVE PHRASE]
   "**To challenge the pursuit of global wealth** is not to oppose development."

Grammatical meaning: Meaning is the intention conveyed by a word or a word group. Lexical meaning, as we have seen, is the dictionary meaning of a word. Of themselves words always carry this lexical meaning in that category, but when we group words in special ways to form sentences we then create new *grammatical meanings* at another level.

Words grouped together randomly have little or no meaning on their own, unless it occurs accidentally. For example, each of the following words has lexical meaning at the word level, as is shown in a dictionary, but they convey no grammatical meaning as a group.

a. [WITHOUT GRAMMATICAL MEANING]
   Lights the leap him before the down hill purple.

However when a special order is given to these words, grammatical meaning is created because of the relationships they have to one another.

S → NP + VP + C
      Sj   P   C

a. [WITH GRAMMATICAL MEANING]
   "The purple lights leap down the hill before him."

Subjects can express one of five grammatical meanings:

1. To express the grammatical meaning of the subject performing an action, we use either a transitive or an intransitive verb.

S → NP + VP + NP^2/C
      Sj

a. [SUBJECT (PROPER NOUN)/TRANSITIVE VERB]
   "**Buddhism** holds that true life comes from the abandonment of all craving."

b. [SUBJECT (PRONOUN)/INTRANSITIVE VERB]
   "**She** dropped onto a couch next to her disabled father."

c. [SUBJECT (NOUN PHRASE)/INTRANSITIVE VERB]
   "**A body of research** has now emerged on the experiences of hung councils in Great Britain."

d. [SUBJECT (GERUND PHRASE)/TRANSITIVE VERB]
"**The Supreme Court's ruling** invalidated the Nov. 21 vote."

2. To express the grammatical meaning of the subject receiving an action, we similarly use either a transitive or an intransitive verb. This occurs when the verb is in the passive.

a. [SUBJECT (PROPER NOUN)/INTRANSITIVE VERB]
"So **Nora's hat** is gone but I am going to get another and save myself from sunstroke again."

b. [SUBJECT (PRONOUN)/TRANSITIVE VERB]
"'**I** don't have peace because I'm not with my little girl,' she said in Spanish."

c. [SUBJECT (NOUN PHRASE)/INTRANSITIVE VERB]
"**The child's fresh and rosy lip** was lowered."

d. [SUBJECT (INFINITIVE PHRASE)/TRANSITIVE VERB]
"**To be an artist** includes much."

e. [SUBJECT (NOUN PHRASE)/TRANSITIVE VERB (PASSIVE VOICE)]
"**Their country-place, Styles Court,** had been purchased by Mr. Cavendish early in their married."

3. To express the grammatical meaning of the subject as being the person or thing described, we use linking verbs. The subject and the adjective/complement have the same referent.

a. [SUBJECT (NOUN PHRASE)/LINKING VERB]
"**That lady** seemed at a loss to make a selection."

b. [SUBJECT (PRONOUN)/LINKING VERB]
"I don't remember what; —and **he** became so insulting and abusive that Robert gave him a thrashing on the spot."

c. [SUBJECT (GERUND)/LINKING VERB]
"**His coming** was in the nature of a welcome disturbance."

d. [SUBJECT (INFINITIVE)/LINKING VERB]
"**To watch his face** was like watching a darkening sky before a clap of thunder."

4. To express the grammatical meaning of the subject as being identified, we also use linking verbs. The subject and the noun/complement have the same referent.

a. [SUBJECT (PROPER NOUN)/LINKING VERB]
"**Jake Rogers** was the first man to reach the home of Tuscarora Hose Company Number Six."

b. [SUBJECT (PRONOUN)/LINKING VERB]
"**He** appeared to be in an absolute frenzy."

c. [SUBJECT (GERUND)/LINKING VERB]
"**Shaving** was not an easy task, for his hand continued to shake very much."

d. [SUBJECT (INFINITIVE PHRASE)/LINKING VERB]
"**To edge his way along the crowded paths of life,** warning all human sympathy to keep its distance, was what the knowing ones call 'nuts' to Scrooge."

5. To express the grammatical meaning of an assertion being made, we generally use the verb *be*. The assertion, however, does not have to be true. It is the grammatical meaning of the subject that is most important. The subject and following complement have the same referent.

a. [SUBJECT (NOUN)/VERB *BE*]
"**No eye** at all is better than an evil eye, dark master!"

b. [SUBJECT (GERUND)/VERB *BE*]
"**Horse-dealing** is only one of many human transactions carried on in this ingenious manner!"

c. [SUBJECT (INFINITIVE PHRASE)/VERB *BE*]
"**To know of a man that he is dead** should be enough!"

When discussing the subject, the phrase, *doer of the action* is often used. As shown here, only the first grammatical meaning expresses the *doer of an action*; all others are *receivers* of an action, a *description*, an *identity* or an *assertion*.

Extra-posed subjects

Subjects are sometimes extra-posed to a position after their predicates. When this occurs, the subject is replaced with one of two *expletives*, *it* or *there*. Expletives are *dummy* words that have *structural* rather than *grammatical* functions. We use them to replace the extra-posed subject or object; they can also shift stress within a sentence.

a. [EXTRA-POSED SUBJECT]
"It occurred to him **that the fact was fortunate.**"

$$S \rightarrow \underset{Sj}{NP} + VP + C$$

Noun clauses are the structures most frequently moved to the position after the predicate.

a. [SUBJECT PRECEDING THE PREDICATE]
   That the fact was fortunate occurred to him.

The subject moves to the position after the predicate.

$$S \rightarrow NP + VP + C + \underset{Sj}{NP}$$

a. [EXPLETIVE]   [COMPLEMENT]   [DELAYED SUBJECT]
   "It   **occurred** to him   that the fact was fortunate."

Sometimes it is necessary to extra-pose a subject to a position after the predicate to avoid an awkward sentence.

a. [EXTRA-POSED SUBJECT]
   "There is some rascally mystery here."
   "There ends the dream."

b. [SUBJECT PRECEDING THE PREDICATE]
   Some rascally mystery is here.
   The dream ends.

PREDICATE

PREDICATE
is the second of two essential grammatical functions of a sentence structure, having the grammatical meaning of asserting, describing, or identifying.

1 There are no absolutes in language analysis. In the literature an ellipsis is often used, that is, omitting the predicate in one sentence because it is understood in the context of another.

Predicate has the grammatical meaning of asserting, describing, or identifying; it occupies the verb phrase (VP) component of sentences. Predicates by form can be a single finite lexical verb, or a combination of auxiliary verbs including finite and non-finite forms. If it is a phrase combination, there will be a head verb (HV), which is always the lexical verb. As well, predicates can take objects, other verbals and/or complements. While we have sentences without visible subjects, for example, an imperative sentence that gives a command, we generally[1] do not have sentences without visible predicates.

Before analyzing predicate structures, it is necessary for us to return to our binary system of analysis where we first separated the NP from the VP. In that analysis we saw that the VP, providing that constituents follow it, is further divided into the VP²/P (predicate) and the other components. This usually results in a second NP^2 (noun phrase) or a C (complement). Let us review the structure as previously presented, but this time with examples:

$$S \rightarrow \quad NP \quad + \quad VP$$

$$VP^2 \pm NP^2$$
$$P$$

a. [PREDICATE (SIMPLE)/TRANSITIVE VERB]
"I **saw** the heart of time."

b. [PREDICATE (PHRASE)/TRANSITIVE VERB]
"The industrious rat **had built** his nest."

c. [PREDICATE (SIMPLE)/INTRANSITIVE VERB]
"Suddenly the steam **ceased** blowing off."

d. [PREDICATE (PHRASE)/INTRANSITIVE VERB]
"Now, for some space the revellers stood agape, unable to understand all that **had been done** in such haste."

e. [PREDICATE (SIMPLE)/LINKING VERB]
"Many critics **seem** frustrated by how difficult it is to categorize your works.

f. [PREDICATE (PHRASE)/LINKING VERB]
"Christianity historically **has not been** very clear about the intrinsic value of animals."

Once we have separated the three components, we turn our attention strictly to the verb phrase.

Grammatical meaning: Predicates indicate *actions* or denote *states*, and in so doing, they express time in *progress, completed,* or *recurrent.* They also denote speakers' attitude, for example, *promise, obligation,* and *prediction.* This latter information is expressed in part by auxiliary verbs and adverbs making up the verb phrase.

1. To express the grammatical meaning of a predicate asserting an action, we use transitive, intransitive or linking verbs.

$$S \rightarrow \quad NP \quad + \quad VP \quad + \quad NP^2/C$$
$$P$$

a. [PREDICATE/TRANSITIVE/SECOND NOUN PHRASE]
"Gradually the boy **lost** *himself in sweet fancies.*"

b. [PREDICATE/INTRANSITIVE/COMPLEMENT]
   "The clock on the wall **ticked** *loudly and lazily.*"

C. [PREDICATE/LINKING/COMPLEMENT]
   "The county attorney **seemed** *suddenly to remember his manners and think of his future.*"

2. To express the grammatical meaning of the predicate which describes, we use linking verbs.

a. [PREDICATE/LINKING/COMPLEMENT]
   "You **don't seem** *to know anything.*"
   "I **felt** *so lonesome* I most wished I was dead."

3. To express the grammatical meaning of the predicate which identifies, we also use linking verbs.

a. [PREDICATE/LINKING/COMPLEMENT]
   "I **became** *his zealous partisan,* and contributed all I could to raise a party in his favour."
   "He **had been** *one of the very best of Cossacks,* and had accomplished a great deal as a commander on naval expeditions."

SUBJECT-PREDICATE AGREEMENT

Since the two essential grammatical functions of a sentence are its subject and its predicate, it is reasonable to assume that there is a special relationship between them. The relationship that exists between two or more sentence constituents is called *agreement*. Subject-predicate agreement occurs when a third-person singular subject in the present tense takes the inflectional *-s* form of the verb. It also occurs when a plural subject takes the stem form of the verb.

a. [SUBJECT (SINGULAR NOUN)/PREDICATE (3RD PERSON SINGULAR PRESENT TENSE)]
   My foot **pains** terribly today.

b. [SUBJECT (PLURAL NOUN)/PREDICATE (PRESENT TENSE)]
   My feet **pain** terribly today.

This agreement of subject and predicate, however, is restricted to the present tense. In the past tense no indicators mark agreement between subject and predicate.

a. [SUBJECT (SINGULAR NOUN)/PREDICATE (PAST TENSE)]
   The boy **opened** the door.

b. [SUBJECT (PLURAL NOUN)/PREDICATE (PAST TENSE)]
   The boys **opened** the door.

The exception is the verb *be*, which shows agreement in both present and past forms. This is because *be* is highly inflected and has retained equivalents to its earlier forms.

a. [SUBJECT (SINGULAR NOUN)/PREDICATE (3RD PERSON SINGULAR PRESENT TENSE)]
The student **is** in class.

b. [SUBJECT (PLURAL NOUN)/PREDICATE (PRESENT TENSE)]
The students **are** in class.

c. [SUBJECT (SINGULAR NOUN)/PREDICATE (PAST TENSE)]
The student **was** in class.

d. [SUBJECT (SINGULAR NOUN)/PREDICATE (PAST TENSE)]
The students **were** in class.

The agreement of a subject and predicate can easily be confused when prepositional phrases occur between them.

a. [SUBJECT/PREDICATE AGREEMENT]
The **papers** on the desk **are** for exams.

b. [SUBJECT/PREDICATE NO AGREEMENT]
*The **papers** on the *desk is* for exams.

Both examples have plural subjects. The first shows number agreement between the subject and the predicate; the second shows number agreement between the object of the preposition and the predicate. The confusion occurs because the object of the preposition is closer to the predicate than to the subject. Therefore, the agreement is made between the object of the preposition and the predicate.

MOOD

Mood[2] *is the grammatical distinction in a verb form that can be expressed as a fact, a wish, a command or a statement.* English has three moods.

Indicative mood

Indicative mood states a fact or asks a question. This mood is marked by the inflectional *-s* indicating third person singular.

a. [STATEMENT]
"The Styles Case **has** now somewhat **subsided**."

MOOD

(mode) is the grammatical distinction in a verb form that expresses a fact, a condition contrary to fact, probability or possibility, or a command.

2 Do not confuse the mood of a verb with the mood or attitude of a speaker expressed by modal verbs.

b. [QUESTION]
"Why do Christians and members of other faiths stand guard so securely over their respective deposits of faith?"

Imperative mood

Imperative mood expresses a command or requires/forbids an action to be carried out. The subject is deleted and understood as the second person personal pronoun, *you*.

a. [IMPERATIVE]
"Take care! stand back! There is a rattlesnake in the old cellar."

"**[you]** Take care! **[you]** stand back! There is a rattlesnake in the old cellar."

"Spring it, kid! Don't look so serious!"

"**[you]** Spring it, kid! Don't **[you]** look so serious!"

A distinction must be made between the grammatical imperative and the meaning of the word, *command*. Not all commands are imperatives.

a. [INDICATIVE COMMAND]
"In this case, the Torah **commands** us to judge him favorably—to search for good."

"'Who are you? What are you doing here?' he **demanded** sharply."

b. [IMPERATIVE]
"Boy, boy, **stop** that!"

The first two examples are indirect commands, but they are not imperatives, whereas the third example is an imperative.

Subjunctive mood

Subjunctive mood does not state a fact. It expresses the hypothetical, doubtful, desirable, or obligatory. It is used to express condition contrary to fact, has present and past forms, and there is no inflection for the lexical verb.

The present subjunctive is formed from the stem of the verb. It is most distinctive in the verb *be* and the third person singular of other verbs, which lack the inflectional *-s*.

1. The present subjunctive is found in noun clauses beginning with *that*.

a. [INDICATIVE]
"He **is** weak, nobody denies it."

    b. [SUBJUNCTIVE]
    "The lawyer who had the hardihood to move **that he be** 'admonished' was solemnly informed that the court regarded the proposal with surprise."

2. The subjunctive is frequently used with the word *whether*, indicating choice or option.

    a. [SUBJUNCTIVE]
    "And that pretty girl—widow, I should like to know her history— **whether she be** a native of the country."

    "Let no one underrate the sustaining power of costume, **whether it take** the form of ballet-skirt or monk's frock."

3. The subjunctive follows certain verbs, for example: *recommend, suggest, demand, insist.*

    a. [INDICATIVE]
    "**He comes** in fifty minutes."

    b. [SUBJUNCTIVE]
    "The commission **recommended** in July that there **be** an intelligence director who would control the budgets of the C.I.A."

4. The subjunctive follows certain nouns, for example: *recommendation, suggestion, insistence.*

    a. [INDICATIVE]
    I know when he **goes**.

    b. [SUBJUNCTIVE]
    My **recommendation** is that he **go**.

5. The subjunctive follows certain adjectives, for example: *necessary, essential.*

    a. [INDICATIVE]
    She asked where he **was going**.

    b. [SUBJUNCTIVE]
    It is **essential** that she **come**.

In meaning, these uses are closer to the imperative.

6. The subjunctive is also used in certain set phrases, for example:

    a. [SUBJUNCTIVE]
    God **bless** you.

God **save** the Queen.

Come what may.

7. The past subjunctive has the same form as the past indicative, and is often used in conditional sentences.

a. [SUBJUNCTIVE]
If I **had** a lot of money I would be rich.

8. The verb *be* is expressed as *were* and not as *was*.

a. [SUBJUNCTIVE]
"For a moment the boy looked as if he **were** going to let them remain where they were."

b. [NON-SUBJUNCTIVE]
*For a moment the boy looked as if he **was** going to let them remain where they were.

It is clearly evident that the subjunctive is not popularly used in Modern English; the lack of examples in contemporary text is proof of this.

VOICE

VOICE
is a syntactic construction indicating particular relationships between the subject and object of the predicate.

Voice is a syntactic construction indicating particular relationships between the subject and object of the predicate. English has two voices, *active* and *passive*.

Active voice

We use the active voice to describe a verb category concerned with the relationship between the subject and the object; the action is expressed by transitive verbs.

$$S \rightarrow \quad NP \quad + \quad VP \quad + \quad NP^2$$
$$\quad\quad\quad Sj \quad + \quad P \quad + \quad Do$$

a. [ACTIVE VOICE]
"The shepherd's **dog barked** fiercely."

In this example the subject *dog* acts as the agent or performer of the action that the predicate describes *barked*. This relationship between the subject and the predicate is called an active relationship.

Passive voice

Passive or inactive voice is a feature of transitive sentences in which the grammatical subject of the predicate becomes the goal of the expressed action. *Passive* refers to the relationship between the subject and predicate. This means that passive structures do not occur with intransitive or linking verbs. Consider the following sentence transition:

$$S \rightarrow \quad NP \quad + \quad VP \quad + \quad NP^2$$
$$ Sj P Do$$

An example in the present tense is:

   a. [ACTIVE VOICE/PRESENT TENSE]
      "The practice of medicine **combines** both science and art."

[SUBJECT]	[PREDICATE]	[DIRECT OBJECT]
The practice of medicine	combines	both science and art.

[NEW SUBJECT]	[PASSIVE VOICE PREDICATE]	[AGENT]
both science and art	**is combined**	by the practice of medicine

   b. [PASSIVE VOICE/PRESENT TENSE]
      Both science and art is combined by the practice of medicine.

An example in the past tense is:

   a. [ACTIVE VOICE/PAST TENSE]
      "The Hebrew understanding of 'the land' certainly **implied** relations to nature."

[SUBJECT]	[PREDICATE]	[DIRECT OBJECT]
The Hebrew understanding of "the land"	certainly implied	relations to nature

[NEW SUBJECT]	[PASSIVE VOICE PREDICATE]	[AGENT]
relations to nature	**was certainly implied**	by the Hebrew understanding of "the land"

   b. [PASSIVE VOICE/PAST TENSE]
      Relations to nature is certainly implied by the Hebrew understanding of "the land."

Three changes occur:

1. The subject of the active structure becomes the agent of the passive structure.

2. The direct object of the active structure becomes the new subject of the passive structure.

3. The tense[3] of the predicate is retained in a form of the verb *be*; the lexical verb is replaced by its form in the past participle.

The agent of the passive structure forms a prepositional phrase, *by + agent—as object of the preposition*. We identify this structure as passive because the subject of the sentence is seen as passively undergoing the action of the verb. The importance of the performer of the action is not emphasized.

Two grammatical meanings have been shifted: ·

1. *The practice of medicine*, the performer of the action, is now the agent, expressed as object of the preposition, *by the practice of medicine*.

2. *Both science and art*, the undergoers, are now the subject of the passive sentence.

All transitions from active to passive are not as simple as the above examples. There are many features of active sentences that may have to be considered when structuring passive sentences.

1. Passive with deleted agents

$$S \rightarrow \quad \underset{Sj}{NP} \quad + \quad \underset{P}{VP} \quad + \quad \underset{Do}{NP^2}$$

a. [ACTIVE VOICE/PAST TENSE]
 "**Someone** wrote a column of figures on the verso totaling 2,199.78."

[SUBJECT]	[PREDICATE]	[DIRECT OBJECT]
Someone	wrote	a column of figures on the verso totaling 2,199.78.

[NEW SUBJECT]	[PASSIVE VOICE PREDICATE]	[AGENT]
a column of figures	was written	**(by someone)** on the verso totaling 2,199.78.

3 Examples to illustrate the passive voice are often given in the past tense, as in the second example above. Pay particular attention to passive transitions with the present tense because they tend to be overlooked.

b. [PASSIVE VOICE/PAST TENSE]
   A column of figures was written on the verso totaling 2,199.78.

In the above transition the subject, *someone,* is vague and as far as meaning is concerned, it does not add much to the passive transition. In such cases the subject/agent can be deleted. The *by phrase* is deleted; when returning to the active sentence simply replace the subject. Many indefinite words (*everyone, no one, all,* etc.) and the personal pronoun *they* fall into this category. It is only when the subject agent contributes meaningfulness to the sentence that it is necessary to keep it in the passive transition.

2. Passive with progressive aspect

S → NP + VP + NP²
   Sj   P   Do

a. [ACTIVE VOICE/PAST TENSE]
   "The government was surreptitiously setting this agenda."

[SUBJECT]	[PREDICATE]	[DIRECT OBJECT]
The government	was surreptitiously setting	this agenda.

[NEW SUBJECT]	[PASSIVE VOICE PREDICATE]	[AGENT]
This agenda	**was surreptitiously being set**	by the government.

b. [PASSIVE VOICE/PAST TENSE]
   This agenda was surreptitiously being set by the government.

When the progressive is used in the active voice, an extra step is required in the transition to the passive. The subject and object transitions are the same. However, the predicate must now show the progressive aspect. We use an appropriate form of the verb *be* with the past participle of the lexical verb as found in regular passives. The progressive aspect of the active predicate is now expressed in the present participle of the verb *be*. The progressive aspect has to be retained. Where there were only two verbs in the active predicate there are now three verbs in the passive predicate.

3. Passive with auxiliaries

i. The stem *be* occurs after a *modal.*

S → NP + VP + NP²
   Sj   P   Do

a. [ACTIVE VOICE/PRESENT TENSE]
"We **may** effectively **confront** the temptation to idolatry."

[SUBJECT]	[PREDICATE]	[DIRECT OBJECT]
We	may effectively confront	the temptation to idolatry.

↘ ↓ ↙

[NEW SUBJECT]	[PASSIVE VOICE PREDICATE]	[AGENT]
The temptation to idolatry	**may effectively be confronted**	by us.

b. [PASSIVE VOICE/PRESENT TENSE]
The temptation to idolatry may effectively be confronted by us.

In addition, the personal pronoun changes cases. The active sentence shows that the subject *we* is in the subjective case; the passive sentence must account for the case change and so the subjective *we* now becomes the objective *us*. The transition takes place because personal pronouns must reflect the function they hold. In this case, it is object of the preposition *by*.

The predicate of the active voice can frequently have an auxiliary verb. When this occurs the subject and object transitions are the same. The passive predicate is expressed as modal plus *be* plus the past participle of the lexical verb. We determine the form of the passive *be* by the preceding auxiliary.

ii. The present participle *being* occurs after *be*.

$$S \rightarrow \quad NP \quad + \quad VP \quad + \quad NP^2$$
$$Sj \qquad\qquad P \qquad\qquad Do$$

a. [ACTIVE VOICE/PAST TENSE/PROGRESSIVE ASPECT]
"I should be teaching your little micks all about the meaning of candles."

[SUBJECT]	[PREDICATE]	[DIRECT OBJECT]
I	should be teaching	your little micks all about the meaning of candles.

↘ ↓ ↙

[NEW SUBJECT]	[PASSIVE VOICE PREDICATE]	[AGENT]
your little micks all about the meaning of candles.	**should be being taught**	by me

b. [PASSIVE VOICE/PAST TENSE]
Your little micks should be being taught by me all about the meaning of candles.

iii. The past participle *been* occurs after *have*.

S → NP + VP + NP^2
    Sj   P   Do

a. [ACTIVE VOICE/PRESENT TENSE]
"Professor Owen admitted that natural selection **may have done** something in the formation of a new species."

[subject]	[predicate]	[direct object]
natural selection	may have done	something

↘ ↓ ↙

[new subject]	[passive voice predicate]	[agent]
something	**may have been done**	by natural selection

b. [PASSIVE VOICE/PRESENT TENSE]
Professor Owen admitted that something may have been done by natural selection in the formation of a new species.

Notice that both active and passive versions have the same meaning, including that provided by the auxiliaries. The aspect of the active structure is carried over to the passive structure.

4. Passive: past participles versus adjectives

In passive transitions the past participle can be confused with a predicate adjective. Passive sentences with deleted agents admit two separate readings.

S → NP + VP + NP^2
    Sj   P   Do

a. [ACTIVE VOICE/PAST TENSE]
"Quite satisfied, **he closed his door**, and locked himself in."

[SUBJECT]	[PREDICATE]	[DIRECT OBJECT]
he	closed	his door

↘ ↓ ↙

[NEW SUBJECT]	[PASSIVE VOICE PREDICATE]	[AGENT]
his door	**was closed**	by him

If we leave out *by him*, we have the meaning that someone closed the door; we can have a confused structure.

b. [PASSIVE VOICE]
his door **was closed**

c. [ADJECTIVE]
his door **was closed**

d. [ADJECTIVE]
his door **was green**

The active to passive transition is acceptable, but the passive can be confusing. Is the final sentence constituent a past participle or an adjective? There is really no way of knowing, unless we know the intent of the speaker. Any substitution of one adjective for another simply implies that it was an adjective in the first place.

5. Passive with *get*

English also has a passive in which the verb *get* replaces the verb *be*.

$$S \rightarrow NP + VP + NP^2$$
$$ Sj P Do$$

a. [ACTIVE VOICE/PRESENT TENSE]
"He brings mankind not rest but a sword."

[SUBJECT]	[PREDICATE]	[DIRECT OBJECT]
He	brings	mankind not rest but a sword.

[NEW SUBJECT]	[PASSIVE VOICE PREDICATE]	[AGENT]
mankind	**is brought**	by him not rest but a sword.
mankind	**gets brought**	by him not rest but a sword.

b. [PASSIVE VOICE/PRESENT TENSE]
Mankind gets brought by him not rest but a sword.

The meaning of *get* in the following examples is very close to that of *becomes*. This form of the passive is very useful in avoiding ambiguity.

a. The door **is** shut at 10:00 PM.

b. The door **got** shut at 10:00 PM.

In the first example two meanings are possible:

1. Some person shuts the door at 10:00 PM.

2. When we arrive at 10:00 PM, the door is shut, that is, not open.

The *get passive* specifies the first meaning only and therefore removes any possible ambiguity.

The *get passive* also has other meanings. Whenever we intend responsibility by the subject, a reflexive pronoun (herself, themselves, myself, etc.) is either expressed or understood.

a. Tom **got caught** in the tree.

b. Tom **got himself caught** in the tree.

In summary, we use the passive most frequently for the following reasons.

1. The subject/agent is unimportant, unknown, or not easily stated.

a. [ACTIVE]
   Someone hurt Mary in an accident.

b. [PASSIVE]
   Mary was hurt in an accident.

2. We wish to suppress the agent for objectivity.

a. [ACTIVE]
   We delete the by phrase in some passives.

b. [PASSIVE]
   The by phrase is deleted in some passives.

3. We emphasize the object/patient rather than the subject/agent.

a. [ACTIVE]
   The committee sent Mary as our representative.

b. [PASSIVE]
   Mary was sent as our representative.

4. We wish to avoid vague pronoun references.

a. [ACTIVE]
   You and I chose Tim as the best student.

b. [PASSIVE]

Tim was chosen as the best student.

5. The subject/agent is rather long.

a. [ACTIVE]

That everything might be ready on time gave **Tom** a reason to come.

b. [PASSIVE]

Tom was given a reason to come.

6. We wish to avoid the indefinite pronouns, *one* and *you*, where the context makes these words inappropriate.

a. [ACTIVE]

You answered the questions correctly.

b. [PASSIVE]

The questions were answered correctly.

Direct object

DIRECT OBJECT
is the person or thing that undergoes the action of transitive verbs. Its grammatical meaning is that which undergoes the action of the predicate, or is affected by it.

Direct objects are the persons or things that undergo the action of transitive verbs or is affected by it. They always follow transitive verbs, forming a second noun phrase NP^2, which is similar in structure in every way to the noun phrase NP. By form it can be any structure that has a *noun*, a *pronoun*, a *gerund* or *an infinitive* as a head word (HW). A noun clause can also carry out this function. The difference between subjects and direct objects is found in grammatical function and not in form. Direct objects have a high rate of occurrence because we frequently use transitive verbs as our predicates.

Grammatical meaning: Unlike the subject and the predicate, no general statement for grammatical meaning suffices for the direct object. It has many semantic and logical relationships. The description as presented is acceptable enough for most sentences; for others, it falls short, because the object neither receives the action nor is affected in any way by it. We can understand the direct object best by noting its position within the sentence structure.

$$S \rightarrow \quad NP \quad + \quad VP \quad + \quad NP^2$$
$$TV \qquad\qquad Do$$

a. [DIRECT OBJECT (PRONOUN)]

"His followers rarely accepted **him** uncritically."

b. [DIRECT OBJECT (NOUN PHRASE)]
"Procedural disputes between the British Government and Sinn Fein have stalled **the process**."

c. [DIRECT OBJECT (GERUND PHRASE)]
"After opening the forepeak hatch I heard **splashing in there**."

d. [DIRECT OBJECT (INFINITIVE PHRASE)]
"Vainly he sought, by tracing life backward in memory, **to reproduce the moment of his sin**."

EXTRA-POSED DIRECT OBJECT

Direct objects, similar to subjects, can also be extra-posed (sometimes called delayed object) and replaced with an expletive, *it* or *there*. The extra-posed object is frequently a noun clause beginning with *that*.

$$S \rightarrow \quad NP \quad + \quad VP \quad + \quad NP^2$$
$$TV \qquad\qquad Do$$

a. [EXTRA-POSED DIRECT OBJECT]
"I thought it right and necessary to **solicit his assistance for obtaining it**."

"The author wishes it to be understood that **Erewhon is pronounced as a word of three syllables**."

b. [DIRECT OBJECT NOT EXTRA-POSED]
I thought to solicit his assistance **for obtaining it** right and necessary.

The author wishes that Erewhon is pronounced as a **word of three syllables** to be understood.

Both extra-posed subjects and objects read as though they are less formal. This example taken from literature illustrates a very extended extra-posed object and proves the point of formality.

Indirect object

Indirect objects follow transitive verbs, placed between the predicate and the direct object. By form, they can be theoretically any structure that focuses on a *noun*, a *pronoun*, or a *gerund* as a head word (HW). It is similar in every way to other noun phrases. The indirect object differs from the direct object in its grammatical function and not in its form.

INDIRECT OBJECT is the second of two objects that follows transitive verbs. Its grammatical meaning is *to* or *for whom the action is performed*.

The indirect object is very restrictive in its composition. Words and short phrases are common, while longer structures, such as, longer phrases and clauses are very rare. An alternative structure, coming after the direct object as a prepositional phrase, occurs quite frequently.

The sentence formula used so far changes with the addition of the indirect object. It is rewritten as:

$$S \rightarrow \quad NP \quad + \quad VP \quad + \quad NP^2 \quad + \quad NP^3$$
$$ Sj P Ido Do$$

NP^2 now becomes the indirect object, and the direct object moves to be a third noun phrase NP^3.

Grammatical meaning: The grammatical meaning for the indirect object is quite clear in that it is *to* or *for whom* an action is carried out. It has no variations like the subject or predicate and it is much more precise than the direct object.

We identify a small class of transitive verbs that frequently take indirect objects. Figure 6.3 shows representative examples:

FIGURE 6.3 ✿ TRANSITIVE VERBS FREQUENTLY TAKING INDIRECT OBJECTS

bake	build	give	pass	send	throw
bring	cook	make	pitch	teach	toss

Although indirect objects usually name humans or animals, a few verbs also take inanimate indirect objects. The following examples illustrate indirect objects after transitive verbs.

$$S \rightarrow \quad NP \quad + \quad VP \quad + \quad NP^2 \quad + \quad NP^3$$
$$ TV Ido Do$$

a. [INDIRECT OBJECT (PROPER NOUN)]
   "Polly, give **Mis' McChesney** some salt."

b. [INDIRECT OBJECT (PRONOUN)]
   "The butler brought **me** my coffee into the library."

c. [INDIRECT OBJECT (NOUN PHRASE)]
   "Poirot seized his hat, gave **his moustache** a ferocious twist and, ...,
   motioned me to precede him down the stairs."

Indirect objects do not occur as frequently as direct objects, possibly because we can also convey their meanings by prepositional phrases occurring after the direct object.

$$S \rightarrow \quad NP \quad + \quad VP \quad + \quad NP^2$$

Sj	P	Do	OP

a. [OBJECT OF PREOPSITION (PRONOUN)]
"His wife is as lovely as he is but I can't give it **to you** all now."

b. [OBJECT OF PREOPSITION (PROPER NOUN)]
"I would forward it **to Sir Charles Lyell**, who sent it **to the Linnean Society**."

c. [OBJECT OF PREOPSITION (NOUN PHRASE)]
"Both alternatives envisage a greater role **for local government**."

In these sentences the indirect object is replaced by a prepositional phrase occurring after the direct object. Therefore, the structure is no longer an indirect object, although essentially the same meaning is retained.

Here are the features of the indirect object:

1. Indirect objects usually name humans or animals; a few verbs may take inanimate indirect objects.

2. A small class of transitive verbs takes indirect objects, for example: *throw, toss, send, pitch, give*, and such verbs as: *bake, make, cook, build, pass*, and *bring*.

3. Verbs taking both a direct and an indirect object have the word order of: Sj + P + Ido + Do.

4. A sentence is sometimes incomplete without an indirect object.

5. Direct objects as nouns have the choice of expressing the beneficiary of the action as an indirect object or as the object of a preposition.

The roles of the major grammatical functions are not difficult to understand. Grammatical meanings pose the greatest difficulty here: this difficulty lies not so much in understanding them, but in remembering them. The subject is the most complex with five possible meanings, followed by the predicate, with three. Only the direct object might present some problem in this category; the indirect object is very clear.

The subject is also the most varied in the forms of words and phrases that can carry out this function. The predicate is slightly complicated by the use of mood and voice. Subject and predicate relationships should be given particular note here, while direct and indirect objects should cause no problems.

From here, we move on to the minor grammatical functions. Although no more difficult than the major functions, they are more varied and will require more attention because of the detail. Consider the following parallels between form and function:

FORMS	FUNCTIONS
1. **noun**	subject direct object indirect object
2. **pronoun**	subject direct object indirect object
3. **noun phrase**	subject direct object indirect object
4. **verb**	predicate

7 MINOR GRAMMATICAL FUNCTIONS

GRAMMATICAL FUNCTION CONTINUED

Minor grammatical functions are not essential constituents in sentence structures, although we seldom have sentences without many of them. There is really nothing *minor* about them as far as the syntax of our language is concerned; they are more varied than major functions.

As noted in Figure 7.1 below, we identify five minor functions: *object* refers specifically to the object of prepositions; *modifiers* are adjectives, adverbs, and prepositional phrases; *apposition* is a noun form and follows immediately after the noun or pronoun to which it refers; *complements* can be a range of form class words; finally, *connectors*, a mixed group of form class words, are conjunctions by form.

FIGURE 7.1 ✿ MINOR GRAMMATICAL FUNCTIONS

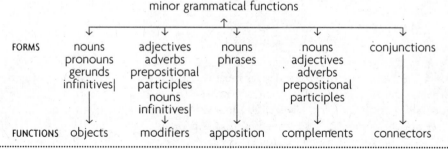

OBJECTS OF PREPOSITIONS

An object of a preposition has the grammatical meaning of that which relates to a noun or its replacement. We generally think of the prepositional phrase as a single sentence constituent carrying out the particular grammatical function of modifier. However, within its structure there is another grammatical function called the

OBJECT
of preposition has the grammatical meaning of that which *relates to a noun* or its replacement.

object of the preposition. The signal word here is a *preposition*, which notes that a noun or its replacement is forthcoming; that noun or replacement in turn becomes the *object* of the preposition. Objects of prepositions can be a word, a phrase, or even a clause.

PREPOSITION		OBJECT	PREPOSITIONAL PHRASE
by	+	[NOUN]	by war
with	+	[PRONOUN]	with him
on	+	[PHRASE]	on this sandy and false foundation
to	+	[CLAUSE]	to whom we wish to be just

The following examples illustrate objects of the prepositions:

a. [OBJECT OF PREPOSITION (NOUNS)]
   "The physical examination is the examination of the patient **from *head to toe*** looking **for *signs* of *disease***."

b. [OBJECT OF PREPOSITION (NOUN PHRASES)]
   "**After *a sustained campaign*** of opposition, unionist councils drifted back to *normal business*."

c. [OBJECT OF PREPOSITION (NOUN CLAUSE)]
   "And I very much enjoy writing for the sound of the Latin language, which obviously has something **in *that it has endured as long as it has***."

Prepositional phrases are frequent sentence constituents, which is evident from the number of occurrences in the sentences above.

MODIFIERS

MODIFIER
gives grammatical or lexical information about another word in the sentence. It has the grammatical meaning *that it modifies, limits or adds to the meaning* of a word.

Modifiers *give grammatical or lexical information about another word in the sentence.* This term has the grammatical meaning *that it modifies, limits or adds to the meaning* of a word, phrase, or clause. English has essentially two types of modifiers: *adjective* and *adverb*. However, prepositional phrases and some nouns also carry out this function. The adjective modifiers qualify *nouns, pronouns,* and other *adjectives*; the adverb modifiers qualify *predicates, adjectives,* other *adverbs,* or even *complete sentences.* Although they both have different focuses, they carry out the same grammatical function.

ADJECTIVE MODIFIERS
occupy either a pre- or post-position modifying nouns, pronouns, and other adjectives.

Adjective modifiers

Adjective modifiers occupy either a pre- or post-position modifying nouns, pronouns, and other adjectives. Initially, one associates adjective modifiers with nouns because that is where they are found most frequently. These modifiers can be as simple in structure as an adjective word, as complex as an adjective, participle, or prepositional phrase, or as complex as a relative adjective clause. Most sentences generally contain adjective modifiers.

1. Adjective modifiers of noun

    a. [MODIFIER/ADJECTIVES (PRE-NOUN)]
     "The **little** church on a hill had the **mossy *greyness*** of a rock seen through a **ragged *screen*** of leaves."

    b. [MODIFIER/ADJECTIVE PHRASE (PRE-NOUN)]
     "**His watchful and attentive *manner*** never varied."

     "Clergymen, judges, statesmen,—the **wisest, calmest, holiest *persons*** of their day,—stood in the inner circle round about the gallows."

    c. [MODIFIER/ADJECTIVE PHRASE (POST-NOUN)]
     "And under the sinister splendour of that sky the ***sea*, blue and profound**, remained still, without a stir, without a ripple, without a wrinkle—viscous, stagnant, dead."

     "Cynthia Murdoch was a fresh-looking young ***creature*, full of life and vigour**."

These next examples illustrate other form class words and phrases functioning as adjective modifiers in pre- and post-noun positions.

    a. [MODIFIER (ADJECTIVE)/PRESENT PARTICIPLE (PRE-NOUN)]
     "Biochemistry is the study of the chemistry taking place in **living *organisms***."

    b. [MODIFIER (ADJECTIVE)/PAST PARTICIPLE (PRE-NOUN)]
     "I remember seeing this with huge **mixed *emotions***."

    c. [MODIFIER (ADJECTIVE)/PRESENT PARTICIPLE PHRASE (PRE-NOUN)]
     "The **existing local *government*** system in Northern Ireland was established following the *Local Government (NI) Act* (1972)."

    d. [MODIFIER (ADJECTIVE)/PAST PARTICIPLE PHRASE (PRE-NOUN)]
     "The **most highly developed *systems*** of medicine outside of the Western or Hippocratic tradition are the Ayurvedic schools of India and traditional Chinese medicine."

    e. [MODIFIER (ADJECTIVE)/PREPOSITIONAL PHRASE (POST-NOUN)]
     "The cornerstone, the ***bedrock* of immigration law** is family unity."

  f. [MODIFIER (ADJECTIVE)/PRESENT PARTICIPLE (POST-NOUN)]
   "The **hungry *student* running about the streets of Kief** forced every
   one to be on his guard."

  g. [MODIFIER (ADJECTIVE)/PAST PARTICIPLE (POST-NOUN)]
   "***Men* deprived of house and home** grew brave there."

  h. [MODIFIER (ADJECTIVE)/RELATIVE CLAUSE (POST-NOUN)]
   "His government was hoping for an ***election* which reflect 'the true
   will' of the Ukrainian people**."

2. Adjective modifiers of adjectives

Adjective modifiers also modify other adjectives. One might expect this, since
adjectives modifying other adjectives generally make adjective phrases.

  a. [ADJECTIVE MODIFYING ADJECTIVE]
   "Van Gogh pursued his art with his **former religious *zeal*** and mission."

  b. [PRESENT PARTICIPLE MODIFYING ADJECTIVE]
   "This **wandering forest *life*** of his did not indicate that he did not care
   for the villagers."

  c. [PRESENT PARTICIPLE MODIFYING ADJECTIVE]
   "But we could have borne all this, had not a **fortune-telling gypsy
   *woman*** come to raise us into perfect sublimity."

We restrict the number of adjective modifiers only by the awkwardness of the
phrase structure. Having more than three adjectives generally creates this problem. However, literary style being what it is does not limit some authors.
Consider the following example:

  a. [MULTIPLE ADJECTIVE MODIFIERS]
   "About a mile up the river there was an island—it's a very **small, prettily
   wooded, sandy-beached little *place***, but it seemed big enough in
   those days."

3. Compound nouns vs. adjective modifiers

Compound nouns can often be mistaken for a combination of an adjective modifier plus noun. This occurs because we sometimes spell compound nouns as separate words. The meaning of a compound noun is often more restricted than that
of an adjective modifier plus structure.

  a. [COMPOUND NOUN]
   We saw a **blackbird**.
   We saw a **black** bird.

b. [MODIFIER + NOUN]
We saw an **attractive** bird.
We saw a **fancy** bird.

If we can substitute another adjective modifier for the first constituent, then it is a modifier plus noun; if not, it is a compound noun. The real test is found in the next example.

a. [ADJECTIVE MODIFIER]
They are hôt dógs.   = The dogs are hot

b. [COMPOUND NOUN]
They are hót dogs.   = They are edible (sausages)

In the first example *hot* is an adjective modifying *dogs*; in the second example *hot dogs* is a compound noun. To distinguish one from the other, we must move to the level of stress (*supresegmentals*). In speech we place a secondary stress on the root syllable of the first word, to signal a modifier plus noun structure; whereas we place a primary stress on the root syllable of the first word to signal a compound noun structure.

PRONOUNS BY FORM, ADJECTIVES BY FUNCTION

The possessive, demonstrative, relative, interrogative, and indefinite pronouns also function as adjective modifiers. By form they are pronouns, but by function they can be adjective modifiers because they signal a forthcoming noun or its replacement, and they limit the word they modify in some way. See Figures 7.2 to 7.6. To illustrate these different pronoun groups in their functional roles as adjectives, we have the following examples.

Possessive adjectives

a. [POSSESSIVE PRONOUN → POSSESSIVE ADJECTIVE]
"I just saw his head bobbing, and I dashed **my boat-hook** in the water."

"By the 1940s and '50s painters cut **their bonds** to nature altogether and began exploring the spiritual resonance of pure form."

Demonstrative adjectives

a. [DEMONSTRATIVE PRONOUN → DEMONSTRATIVE ADJECTIVE]
"**This house** of dust was the house I lived in."

"In **those days** triumphalism was not a reproach."

**FIGURE 7.2
POSSESSIVE
ADJECTIVES**

1ST PERSON
SG	PL
my	our

2ND PERSON
SG	PL
your	your

3RD PERSON
SG	PL
his	
her	their
its	

**FIGURE 7.3
DEMONSTRATIVE
ADJECTIVES**

SG	PL
this	these
that	those

FIGURE 7.4
RELATIVE
ADJECTIVES

....

which
whose

....

Relative adjectives

a. [RELATIVE PRONOUN → RELATIVE ADJECTIVE]
"**Which *Bible*** do you read?"

"Judge Thomas L. Ambro wrote, the schools are entitled not to associate with groups **whose *policies*** they oppose."

FIGURE 7.5
INTERROGATIVE
ADJECTIVES

....

which
whose
what

....

Interrogative adjectives

a. [INTERROGATIVE PRONOUN → INTERROGATIVE ADJECTIVE]
"It was unclear **what *changes*** Admiral Church might incorporate into his final version."

"Where, in **what land** or in **what planet**, was that optical absurdity moving now?"

Indefinite adjectives

a. [INDEFINITE PRONOUN → INDEFINITE ADJECTIVE]
"In **every *election*** for the last 4 terms the SDLP have increased their seats by one."

"Miss Howard, in particular, took **no pains** to conceal her feelings."

"But **whichever way** Lydgate began to incline, there was something to make him wince."

"**Several** tributaries cut across, but made no real boundary line."

FIGURE 7.6 ✿ INDEFINITE ADJECTIVES

SINGULAR	SINGULAR AND PLURAL		PLURAL
a, an	all	whatever	all
another	any	whatsoever	both
each	no	which	few
either	other	whichever	many
every	such		other
neither	what		several

ADVERB MODIFIERS

Adverb modifiers may occur before or after the word(s) they modify; they refer to circumstances such as *how*, *when*, or *why*. As adverb modifiers they function to modify words, phrases, or clauses associated with the predicate, other adverbs, adjectives, and even complete sentences. These modifiers can be as simple in structure as an adverb word, or as complex as an adverb, participle, or prepositional phrase, or more complex as a relative adverb or adverb clause. As modifiers they express *comparison, concession, condition, contrast, degree, direction, duration, frequency, intensity, manner, place, reason*, and *time*. While adverbs can modify adjectives, adjectives cannot modify adverbs.

ADVERB MODIFIERS occupy pre- or post-modifying positions, referring to circumstances such as *how*, *why*, or *when*.

1. Adverb modifiers of predicates

Adverb modifiers frequently modify predicates.

    a. [ADVERB MODIFIER]
    "I do **honestly *believe*** that many of them are sincere about achieving better relations."

    b. [ADVERB PHRASE MODIFIER]
    "Nature has **very evidently *given*** him up."

    c. [ADVERB RELATIVE CLAUSE MODIFIER]
    "That sense of uncertainty only ***deepens* when she thinks of her older sister's delayed reaction to the outbreak**."

2. Adverb modifiers of adverbs

Adverb modifiers also modify or intensify other adverbs.

    a. [ADVERB MODIFYING ADVERB]
    "Somebody changed the sign to read, **rather *hair-raisingly***, 'Drive carefully, Natives very cross here.'"

    b. [ADVERB PHRASE MODIFYING ADVERB]
    "It is **very easy *indeed*** to step from that persuasion to the belief that God has no use for them."

    c. [ADVERB CLAUSE MODIFYING ADVERB]
    "The IRA has not disbanded nor scaled down its operations and has not ceased planning terrorist attacks to be carried ***out* if the ceasefire ends**."

3. Adverb modifiers of adjectives

Adverb modifiers even modify or intensify adjectives.

a. [ADVERB MODIFYING ADJECTIVE]
"It all welled up from my memories of hot, humid nights in the small, **dimly *lit*** churches of my youth."

b. [ADVERB PHRASE MODIFYING ADJECTIVE]
"Tertiary care medical services are provided by specialist hospitals or regional centers equipped with diagnostic and treatment facilities **not generally *available*** at local hospitals."

4. Adverb modifiers of sentences

Adverb modifiers are often used to modify complete sentences, and are generally set off from the sentence by a comma(s). Their function is to modify the whole sentence, rather than a particular constituent within that sentence. They are moveable and can appear at the beginning, the middle, or the end of sentences. They are quite flexible in the structure that they modify.

a. [ADVERB MODIFYING SENTENCE]
"Through the woods there ran at intervals long lines of broken rock, covered with moss—the ruins, **evidently**, of ancient stone fences."

b. [ADVERB PHRASE MODIFYING SENTENCE]
"**Plainly, and very simply**, I love you with all my heart."

c. [ADVERB PREPOSITIONAL PHRASE MODIFYING SENTENCE]
"**During the preparations for the wedding**, I need not describe the busy importance of my wife, nor the sly looks of my daughters."

[ADVERB PRESENT PARTICIPLE PHRASE MODIFYING SENTENCE]
"At sunset hour the forest was still, lonely, sweet with tang of fir and spruce, **blazing in gold and red and green**."

d. [ADVERB INFINITIVE PHRASE MODIFYING SENTENCE]
"The tawny sibyl no sooner appeared than my girls came running to me for a shilling apiece, **to cross her hand with silver**."

e. [ADVERB CLAUSE MODIFYING SENTENCE]
"I have chosen to emphasize the theoretical one, **although I will also indicate how theory works out in practice**."

ADVERB NOUNS

A noun and an adverb combination may seem strange at first; however, a few nouns can occupy an adverb position and carry out the grammatical function of complement. When they function in this way, we call them *adverb nouns*. For example:

S	→	NP	+	VP	+	C
		Sj		P		PREPOSITIONAL PHRASES
				ITV		for **four years**

a. [SUBJECT/PREDICATE/PREPOSITIONAL PHRASES]
   Mark studied **for four years** for his doctoral degree.

The noun phrase *four years* is an object of the preposition *for*, which is a typical grammatical function for nouns. The prepositional phrase *for four years* is now an adverb complement after the intransitive verb studied. *Years* is a noun because it can be inflected for plurality; yet, if we delete the preposition *for*, we have the resulting structure.

S	→	NP	+	VP	+	C
		Sj		P		AV NOUN
				TV?		**four years**

a. [SUBJECT/PREDICATE/ADVERBIAL NOUN]
   Mark studied **four years** for his doctoral degree.

Both sentences carry the same meaning; however, the syntactic structure differs. Because *four years* is an adjective plus noun, one assumes that the predicate must be a transitive verb with a direct object. In fact, the predicate *studied* is still being used intransitively, although it can be used transitively as well. In the second example, we are not studying *four years* as we might study a *book*. The noun phrase **four years** is actually an adverb complement noting a length of time. The noun phrase can be substituted with a number of adverbs of *time*.

S	→	NP	+	VP	+	C
		Sj		P		AV NOUN
				ITV		**four years**
						yesterday
						last week
						in September

Consider the following examples:

S	→	NP	+	VP	+	C
		Sj		P		AV NOUN

a. [ADVERB NOUN]
"Lieutenant-Colonel Potogonkin **has lived** with me **seven years**, seven years already."

In this example, *seven years* is actually an adverb noun denoting a length of time, and it is a complement to the predicate *has lived*. Here is another example.

"They were very black and very frizzled, and had been bought at a reduced price from a travelling salesman **some ten years before**."

In view of this, consider the next example:

$$S \quad \rightarrow \qquad NP \qquad + \qquad VP \qquad + \qquad NP^2$$
$$ Sj P Do$$

b. [SUBJECT   TV-PREDICATE DIRECT OBJECT]
 Bernard   *studied*   **English language**.

In this example, we use the verb *studied* transitively, followed by a noun phrase, *English language*, as its direct object. In the above examples, we cannot replace the adverb complement with the pronouns, *it*, *them*, or *what*. This would be the case if it were a direct object. This switch can take place in the *b* example, however.

Bernard *studied* **what**?
Bernard *studied* **it**.

Again, we must always remember to note the category of analysis that we are considering. Form and function are different categories of analysis, and a word by form may not necessarily suggest its grammatical function, as in the case of the adverb noun.

PREPOSITIONAL PHRASE MODIFIERS

PREPOSITIONAL PHRASE MODIFIERS can also occupy adjective and adverb post-modifying positions.

Prepositional phrases are themselves sentence constituents and we use them frequently as adjective and as adverb modifiers, occurring after the sentence constituent they modify.

1. Prepositional phrase modifying a noun

a. [PREPOSITIONAL PHRASE/ADJECTIVE MODIFIER OF NOUN SUBJECT]
"His most notable **service** in **home politics** was his reform of the postal system."

b. [PREPOSITIONAL PHRASE/ADJECTIVE MODIFIER OF NOUN SUBJECTIVE COMPLEMENT]
"It was an **attempt** to make the God of Nature accessible and the God of the Heart invincible."

2. Prepositional phrase modifying an adjective

a. [PREPOSITIONAL PHRASE/ADJECTIVE MODIFIER OF OBJECT OF PREPOSITION]
"The writer is chary of **assertion or denial** in these matters."

b. [PREPOSITIONAL PHRASE/ADJECTIVE MODIFIER OF ADJECTIVE SUBJECTIVE COMPLEMENT]
"He was also **much** of a politician; too much, perhaps, for his station."

PREPOSITIONAL PHRASES AS ADVERB MODIFIERS

1. Prepositional phrase modifying a verb

a. [PREPOSITIONAL PHRASE/ADVERB MODIFIER OF PREDICATE]
"The reality of religion he believes **deals** wholly and exclusively **with the God of the Heart**."

"David **was unwavering** in his understanding of what a converged media company means."

2. Prepositional phrase modifying an adverb

a. [PREPOSITIONAL PHRASE/ADVERB MODIFIER OF ADVERB]
"Being a heavy stick the dog has held it **tightly** by the middle, and the marks of his teeth are very plainly visible."

"Vienneau wrote **extensively** about the Supreme Court, and the increasingly complex issues it faced."

3. Prepositional phrase modifying a sentence

a. [PREPOSITIONAL PHRASE ADVERB MODIFIER OF A SENTENCE]
"**By much trampling**, we had made it a mere quagmire."

"**In Baghdad**, several dozen black-clad militants stormed a police station just after dawn."

APPOSITION

The grammatical meaning for the appositive is essentially *that which renames*. It is a referent to the noun it qualifies, and it can replace the noun phrase carrying out the same grammatical function. Appositives are optional sentence constituents because they can be left out without affecting the syntax of the sentence. They have several qualifications: *post-modification*, *additional information*, or *description* by way of identification. As well, they can be restrictive or nonre-

APPOSITION
is essentially *that which renames*. It is a referent to the noun it qualifies.

strictive regarding the information they rename. Restrictive appositives add essential information; non-restrictive appositives add non-essential information.

1. Restrictive appositive (no commas)

a. [RESTRICTIVE APPOSITIVE]
"Was I not rescued from the wreck of the ***ship* Morrow**?"

"The scene was once the haunt of radicals—**antiestablishment Jesus freaks** whose passionate piety sometimes covered a multitude of theological and musical sins."

"Thus in the course of years he was known successively in Bombay, in Calcutta, in Rangoon, in Penang, in Batavia—and in each of these halting-places was just Jim **the water-clerk**."

"The SDLP's 1993 local government elections' manifesto '**Progress through Partnership**' highlighted the rewards of 'partnership' government."

2. Non-restrictive appositive (commas)

a. [NON-RESTRICTIVE APPOSITIVE]
"To Jim that gossiping crowd, **viewed as seamen**, seemed at first more unsubstantial than so many shadows."

"An ***Arab*, the leader of that pious voyage**, came last."

"John Michael Talbot, **a Roman Catholic**, and Michael Card, **a Baptist**, write soft, reflective pieces informed by years of theological and liturgical study."

"Its best song, '**Jesus Freak**,' is now a standard of modern rock."

"It opened recently in London and is called *Phantom of the Opera*, **a gothic tale** *which has always intrigued me, and which I felt cried out for scoring*."

This last example is a very interesting one, because the appositive *a gothic tale* is followed by compound relative adjective clauses.

Although appositives generally follow the nouns that they qualify, occasionally we have examples where the appositive is somewhat removed from its noun. Such is the case for some clausal structures or intervening modifying phrases.

[NON-RESTRICTIVE APPOSITIVE]
"The thing that I hope does come through theologically even now is the great *climax* of the whole first act, **the song 'Gethsemane**.'"

COMPLEMENTS

Complement has the grammatical meaning of that which *identifies* or *completes*. It is a catch-all expression for a single grammatical function. While the grammatical function is the same, the grammatical positions in which this function takes place vary.

We have three types of complements in Modern English: *subjective* complement, *adverb* complement, and *objective* complement. Only the subjective complement is further divided into *predicate noun* and *predicate adjective*.

Subjective complements

A subjective complement has the grammatical meaning of *that which follows a linking verb* and has the same referent as the subject. The relationship of subjective complement to linking verbs is similar to that of the direct object to transitive verbs; one requires the other. Once the verb is identified, we know that the grammatical function is limited. Linking verbs require a following subjective complement, which can be a predicate noun or a predicate adjective, or an adverb complement.

PREDICATE NOUNS

S	→	NP	+	VP	+	C
		Sj		LV		P-n

a. [SUBJECTIVE COMPLEMENT/PREDICATE NOUN]
"'He *is* a good **creature**, and more sensible than any one would imagine,' said Dorothea, inconsiderately."

b. [SUBJECTIVE COMPLEMENT/PREDICATE NOUN PHRASE]
"But he is liked and respected in the place and *is* **a skilled and devoted surgeon**."

c. [SUBJECTIVE COMPLEMENT/PREDICATE PRONOUN]
"In fact, they *are* all **yours**, dear."

d. [SUBJECTIVE COMPLEMENT/GERUND]
"Still, there *was* **no knowing** when the dormant faculty might wake and smite the lyre."

COMPLEMENT

has the grammatical meaning of that which *identifies* or *completes*.

SUBJECTIVE COMPLEMENT

has the grammatical meaning of *that which follows a linking verb* and has the same referent as the subject.

e. [SUBJECTIVE COMPLEMENT/INFINITIVE]
"His eyes, roaming about the line of the horizon, **seemed** *to gaze* hungrily into the unattainable."

f. [SUBJECTIVE COMPLEMENT/NOUN CLAUSE]
"It seems **Canadians are a lot like the Whos of Whoville.**"

All of these examples have linking verbs. Each predicate carries out the act of linking the subject of the sentence to the predicate noun that follows it. The predicate noun refers back to the subject, hence its name, *subjective complement*.

Predicate nouns are sometimes confused with direct objects. Both occur in a similar position after the predicate. Two features, however, distinguish them. Subjective complements occur only after *linking verbs* and *must* refer back to the subject. Direct objects occur only after *transitive verbs* and they *do not* refer back to the subject.

$$S \rightarrow \quad NP \quad + \quad VP \quad + \quad C$$
$$ Sj LV SC/\textit{p-n}$$

a. [SUBJECTIVE COMPLEMENT/PREDICATE NOUN]
Dr. Roger Butler is **my physician**.

My physician and *Dr. Roger Butler* are the same person.

$$S \rightarrow \quad NP \quad + \quad VP \quad + \quad NP^2$$
$$ Sj TV Do$$

b. [DIRECT OBJECT]
Dr. Roger Butler examined **the patient**.
The patient and *Dr. Roger Butler* are not the same person.

In the first example, the subject and subjective complement/predicate noun have the same referent. In the second example, the subject and the direct object do not have the same referent.

PREDICATE ADJECTIVES

$$S \rightarrow \quad NP \quad + \quad VP \quad + \quad C$$
$$ Sj LV SC/\textit{p-aj}$$

a. [SUBJECTIVE COMPLEMENT/PREDICATE ADJECTIVE]
"Islam began when Muhammad **became** *sensitive* to the dehumanizing implications of the idolatry of popular religious practice."

b.   [SUBJECTIVE COMPLEMENT/PREDICATE ADJECTIVE PHRASE]
     "In fact, to suppose that every period in history or every person is just
     as transparent to mystery as any other ***seems* quite implausible**."

c.   [SUBJECTIVE COMPLEMENT/PREPOSITIONAL PHRASE]
     "Hyde is gone to his account; and it only ***remains* for us** to find the
     body of your master."

d.   [SUBJECTIVE COMPLEMENT/PAST PARTICIPLE PHRASE]
     "At that time few of us ***felt* terribly threatened** by the highly
     authoritarian and obediential motifs of *Humani generis*."

The subjective complement in each of the above sentences is carried out by a
different form class word or phrase. However, they all have the same grammatical function of a subjective complement/predicate adjective. Again, the adjective
refers back to the subject.

ADVERB COMPLEMENTS

Adverb complements have the grammatical meaning of one that *completes*.
They occur in two positions, after intransitive verbs and after linking verbs.
They occur after linking verbs much like the subjective complement, but they do
not qualify the subject in the same way.

ADVERB COMPLEMENTS have the grammatical meaning of an adverb or adverb phrase which *completes*.

1. Adverb complements after linking verbs

S	→	NP	+	VP	+	C
		Sj		LV		Av

a.   [LINKING VERB/ADVERB]
     "Bettis rattled off four consecutive games with at least 100 rushing yards
     when Staley ***was* out** with a sore hamstring."

     "Total sales ***were* up** almost 12 per cent to $4.1 billion."

b.   [LINKING VERB/ADVERB PHRASE]
     "Nobody but I could have seized that chance or seen that it ***was* then
     or never**."

     "Whatever was the cause, the effect was dejection and a sense of
     impending evil; this ***was* especially so** in Dr. Mannering's study."

2. Adverb complements after Intransitive verbs

Adverb complements also occur after intransitive verbs and do so quite frequently. In fact, many intransitive verbs seem to require a complement to complete the meaning of the predicate.

S →   NP   +   VP   +   C
           Sj   ITV   Av

a. [INTRANSITIVE/ADVERB COMPLEMENT]
"I do not speak **wildly**."
"I do not speak ..."

"Quite a few have arrived **independently** at positions similar to his."
"Quite a few have arrived ..."

b. [INTRANSITIVE VERB/ADVERB PHRASE COMPLEMENT]
"To Hepzibah's blunt observation, therefore, Phoebe replied, **as frankly, and more cheerfully**."
"To Hepzibah's blunt observation, therefore, Phoebe replied ..."

"The medical encounter is documented **in a medical record**."
"The medical encounter is documented ..."

All words, phrases, or clauses that can function as adverbs can occur as adverb complements. A word of caution is necessary here, because adverb complements can easily be confused for direct objects. They follow immediately after the predicate much in the same way as direct objects. Being able to identify the verb type is the key here: transitive verbs *must* take objects which are nouns or their replacements; intransitive verbs *may* take adverb complements.

3. Prepositional phrase as adverb complements

We have seen in our discussion of modifiers that prepositional phrases can function similarly as adjective and adverb modifiers; therefore, they can be adverb complements, as well. When prepositional phrases function as adverb complements, they *must* occur after linking verbs but they *may* also occur after intransitive verbs.

S →   NP   +   VP   +   C
           Sj   LV   OP

a. [PREPOSITIONAL PHRASE/ADVERB COMPLEMENT AFTER A LINKING VERB]
"Sometimes he ***stayed* at home** on Wednesday and Thursday evenings, or was only out for an hour."

S	→	NP	+	VP	+	C
		Sj		ITV		OP

a. [PREPOSITIONAL PHRASE/ADVERB COMPLEMENT AFTER INTRANSITIVE VERB]
"He **succeeded** **in protecting the acre or two of earth**."

The prepositional phrase is a very versatile structure and one to which you should pay close attention. Here is a summary of its roles:

AS A MODIFIER   post–adjective
                  post–adverb

AS A COMPLEMENT   adverb

COMPLEMENT VS. MODIFIER

Adverb complements and adverb modifiers often appear to overlap. When is an adverb a complement and when is it a modifier? Are these distinctive terms? To answer these questions, we return to the basic sentence structure and the types of verbs that we use.

S	→	NP	+	VP
		Sj		P

In the following example, the transitive verb takes a direct object *a great deal of attention* plus an adverb modifier *to teleology*.

a. [TRANSITIVE VERB + DIRECT OBJECT + ADVERB MODIFIER]

	TV	+	NP2	+	Av M
Medieval thinkers,	influenced by Aristotle gave		a great deal of attention		**to teleology**.

The next example shows an intransitive verb taking an adverb complement *in and out*.

b. [INTRANSITIVE VERB + COMPLEMENT]

	ITV	+	Av C
"Madam Lebrum	was bustling		**in and out**."

This third example has a linking verb with a following subjective complement/predicate adjective.

c. [LINKING VERB + SUBJECTIVE COMPLEMENT/PAJ]

	LV	+	Aj C
"Her mind	was		**theoretic**."

Transitive verbs take following objects and adverb modifiers; intransitive and linking verbs take following complements. We saw that the grammatical meaning for an adverb modifier is one that *modifies*, *limits*, or adds to the meaning; the grammatical meaning for a complement is that which *identifies* or *completes*. This, however, does not mean that adverb modifiers cannot occur in another part of the sentence structure using intransitive and linking verbs.

1. Adverb modifiers follow transitive verbs.

2. Adverb complements follow intransitive and linking verbs.

3. Adverb modifiers may also modify adjectives, other adverbs and whole sentence structures.

OBJECTIVE COMPLEMENTS

OBJECTIVE COMPLEMENT

has the grammatical meaning of *that which describes or identifies* a direct object.

Objective complements have the grammatical meaning of that which *describes or identifies a direct object*. They follow direct objects, after certain transitive verbs; they can be nouns or adjectives. Unlike subjective complements, they are not distinguished as predicate nouns and predicate adjectives, although both nouns and adjectives can be objective complements.

$$S \rightarrow \quad NP \quad + \quad VP \quad + \quad NP^2 \quad + \quad NP^2$$
$$ Sj TV Do OC$$

a. [OBJECTIVE COMPLEMENT/NOUN]
"To my intense surprise, Cynthia burst out laughing, and called **me a 'funny dear.'**"

The direct object of the transitive verb *called* is *me*; a *'funny dear'* is the noun objective complement. Both have the same referent and can carry out the same grammatical function.

b. [OBJECTIVE COMPLEMENT/NOUN PHRASE]
"His brother Roger calls **it a turbulent time** when David assumed a parental role, helping look after his younger brother."

"One of Baltovich's lawyers, James Lockyer, said he was disappointed the Appeal Court didn't declare **Baltovich an innocent man**."

c. [OBJECTIVE COMPLEMENT/ADJECTIVE]
"Dr. Bauerstein considered **it advisable**."

"Some officials have argued that it should make **its concerns public** or at least aggressively confront the Bush administration."

d. [OBJECTIVE COMPLEMENT/ADJECTIVE PHRASE]
"I had thought to find **him elated with victory**."

"For sure it makes **me more confident**."

Not all transitive verbs allow their direct objects to take objective complements. Figure 7.7 shows a representative list of those verbs that do.

FIGURE 7.7 ✿ TRANSITIVE VERBS TAKING OBJECTIVE COMPLEMENTS

appoint	declare	get	like	paint	think
call	elect	have	make	prefer	want
consider	find	keep	name	take	

CONNECTORS

Connectors are the structure class subcategories: *coordinating conjunctions, correlative conjunctions*, and *subordinating conjunctions*. They have the grammatical meaning of *that which connects*.

1. Coordinating conjunctions join units of equal value.

    a. [COORDINATING CONNECTOR OF NOUN SUBJECT]
    "A **weasel or** a **mouse** that gets its own living is more interesting."

    b. [COORDINATING CONNECTOR OF PREDICATES]
    "Medicine as it is **practiced** now is rooted in various traditions, **but developed** mainly in the late 18th and early 19th century."

    c. [COORDINATING CONNECTOR OF PHRASES]
    "Under this Act 26 local government districts have three basic roles an executive role, **a representative role** and **a consultative role**."

    c. [COORDINATING CONNECTOR OF CLAUSES]
    "*White Crucifixion* depicts a world of unleashed terror within **which no saving voice can be heard** nor **any redeeming signs perceived**."

    d. [COORDINATING CONNECTOR OF SENTENCES]
    "**The day** we are commemorating **seems far away**, **yet** actually **it did not begin in history** and has never come to an end."

2. Subordinating conjunctions join units where one depends on another for its completed meaning.

    a. [SUBORDINATING CONNECTOR IN A NOUN CLAUSE]
    "Did I affirm **that *the stumbling block to his faith was the cornerstone of mine***."

CONNECTORS
are form class conjunctions, used to note subordination, coordination, and conjunctiveness; they have the grammatical meaning of *that which connects.*

b. [SUBORDINATING CONNECTOR IN A RELATIVE ADJECTIVE CLAUSE]
"She wore a loose robe of cream white, with flowing sleeves, **which left the arms bare to the shoulder**."

c. [SUBORDINATING CONNECTOR IN A RELATIVE ADVERB CLAUSE]
"The shock of it endured **when *all the world should have slept***."

d. [SUBORDINATING CONNECTOR FOR AN ADVERB CLAUSE]
"As I believe that our domestic animals were originally chosen by uncivilised man **because they were useful and bred readily under confinement**."

3. Correlative conjunctions connect both complete sentences and units within sentences.

a. [CORRELATIVE CONNECTOR OF WORDS]
"If **neither *Ferentz* nor *Mariucci*** emerges, Notre Dame will most probably sift through a hodgepodge of candidates."

b. [CORRELATIVE CONNECTOR OF PHRASES]
"**Both *the sciences* and *the humanities*** are further divided into narrower *Wissenschaften*, or academic disciplines."

c. [CORRELATIVE CONNECTOR OF CLAUSES]
"The honour of being a journalist is **that you are not only able to observe the times you live in, but influence them**."

d. [CORRELATIVE CONNECTOR OF SENTENCES]
"**Both** critiques are important, **and** a Buddhist or Christian perspective can inform either one."

4. Conjunctive adverbs are not true linking devices themselves. They show comparison, contrast, cause-effect, sequence, but they do so with adverb emphasis.

a. [CONJUNCTIVE ADVERB CONNECTOR]
"She is of a good height, her voice is deep and manly; **moreover**, remember, she and Inglethorp are cousins."

"As always he noted that the California Building across the way was three stories lower, **therefore** three stories less beautiful, than his own Reeves Building."

"He mounted and sped on his way; **while** Tess stood and waited."

"Goodwin has brought a beneficial melodic flair to the band; **for example**, his use of cascading synthesizers in an ode to faithful perseverance and struggle, 'I Still Believe.'"

5. The preposition, meaning to *place before*, carries out the grammatical function of *connector*, that is, it connects a preceding word to a noun or its replacement to form a phrase.

a. [PREPOSITION CONNECTOR]
"**In** the meanwhile he glowed with the ambition to leave it in his newly acquired splendour."

"I was told by the village doctor, about the only person with whom he held any relations, that **during** his retirement he had devoted himself to a single line of study."

Grammatical functions are the most important part of our grammar, because they are the core of the syntax of our language. We need to fully understand grammatical functions if we are to grasp the various relationships among sentence constituents.

We now move on to the grammatical functions of clauses as sentence constituents. As well, we will examine how clauses can interchange with words and phrases in many, but not all, functions. Consider now the parallels between structures by form and structures by function.

FORMS	FUNCTIONS
I. **nouns**	subjects
	direct objects
	indirect objects
	objects of prepositions
	subjective complements
	objective complements
	appositions
2. **pronouns**	subjects
	direct objects
	indirect objects
	objects of prepositions
	subjective complements
	objective complements
	connectors

3. **noun phrases**

subjects
direct objects
indirect objects
objects of prepositions
subjective complements
objective complements
appositions

4. **gerunds**

subjects
direct objects
indirect objects
objects of prepositions
subjective complements
objective complements

5. **infinitives**

subjects
direct objects
modifiers
adverb complements

6. **verbs and auxiliaries**

predicates

7. **adjectives**
adjective phrases

modifiers
subjective complements
objective complements

8. **participles**
participle phrases
prepositional phrases
relative adjective clauses

modifiers
subjective complements

9. **adverbs**
adverb phrases
participles
participle phrases
prepositional phrases
relative adverb clauses
adverb clauses

modifiers
adverb complements

10. **absolute phrases**

modifiers

11. **determiners**

modifiers

12. **conjunctions**

connectors

8 FUNCTIONS
CLAUSES

GRAMMATICAL FUNCTION OF CLAUSES

Because of their structural complexity, the grammatical functions of clauses are better dealt with separately from the grammatical functions of words and phrases. Relative clauses, in particular, require special consideration because of the dual role that their connectors have within the structure. However like words and phrases, clauses are no more or less sentence constituents.

As noted in Chapter 5, there are four types of clauses: *noun, relative adjective, relative adverb*, and *adverb*, carrying out a variety of grammatical functions; see Figure 8.1. The functions for the noun category, for example, are: *subject, direct object, indirect object, object of preposition, subjective complement, objective complement*, and *appositive*. Potentially, noun clauses can carry out all of these functions; however, as we shall see, some of them do not occur. Words, phrases, and clauses by *form* for each category are interchangeable regarding their respective grammatical functions.

FIGURE 8.1 ✿ GRAMMATICAL FUNCTION OF CLAUSES

....

grammatical function of clauses

FORMS	noun	relative adjective	relative adverb	adverb
FUNCTIONS	subject direct object indirect object object of preposition subjective complement objective complement appositive	complement modifier	complement modifier	complement modifier

....

NOUN CLAUSES

In the following examples, the noun clause is a single sentence constituent carrying out many of the grammatical functions that noun words or phrases do.

1. Noun clause as subject of a predicate

$$S \rightarrow \quad NP \quad + \quad VP \quad + \quad NP^2/C$$
$$\quad\quad\quad Sj$$

a. [NOUN CLAUSE AS SUBJECT]
"It left him doubtful **that the artillery had been as relentless as on the nights before**."

"**Whatever she did**, too, was done without conscious effort."

Note that in the first example the noun clause is an extra-posed subject, coming after the predicate. Let us illustrate the second example further by replacing the noun clause with a word and then a phrase to show that they are interchangeable.

a. [PRONOUN AS SUBJECT]
It, too, was done without conscious effort.

b. [NOUN AS SUBJECT]
Work, too, was done without conscious effort.

c. [NOUN PHRASE AS SUBJECT]
Walking all the way home, too, was done without conscious effort.

While the form of the sentence constituent changes, the grammatical function remains the same.

2. Noun clause as direct object

$$S \rightarrow \quad NP \quad + \quad VP \quad + \quad NP^2$$
$$\quad\quad\quad\quad\quad\quad TV \quad\quad\quad Do$$

a. [NOUN CLAUSE AS DIRECT OBJECT]
"I discovered **that he was most violently attached to the contrary opinion**."

"He was prouder than ever to be an American, and only another true American could understand **what he meant**."

3. Noun clause as an indirect object

$$S \rightarrow \quad NP \quad + \quad VP \quad + \quad NP^2 \quad + \quad NP^3$$
$$\quad\quad\quad\quad\quad\quad\quad\quad\quad Ido$$

a. [NOUN CLAUSE AS AN INDIRECT OBJECT]
The school gave **whatever he did** support.
The company gave **whomever they liked** the contract.

Here are two contrived examples to illustrate that a noun clause can function as an indirect object. They read awkwardly and for that reason finding examples is rare. They are more likely to appear as the following structures, which is a general occurrence for expressing the same meaning as that of the indirect object.

b. [NOUN CLAUSES AS OBJECT OF THE PREPOSITIONS]
The school gave support **to whatever he did**.

The company gave the contract **to whomever they liked**.

4. Noun clause as object of the preposition

S → NP + VP + C
OP

a. [NOUN CLAUSE AS OBJECT OF THE PREPOSITION]
"It really had nothing to do **with what I was doing before**."

"I'd talk to him **about whatever he should say publicly**, admit whatever he did and let the court of opinion deal with most of it."

5. Noun clause as subjective complement

S → NP + VP + C
LV SC/p-n

a. [NOUN CLAUSE AS SUBJECTIVE COMPLEMENT]
"In the former case, the argument is **that a gradual return of local government functions could be conditional on councils adopting power sharing**."

"As it is, it **seems that the clever prophecy** that was made by my cynical former partner Tim Rice **has actually come to pass**."

6. Noun clause as an appositive

Appositives, as noted, can be restrictive (essential information) or non-restrictive (non-essential information). Non-restrictive appositives are separated from their referents by a comma(s).

a. [RESTRICTIVE APPOSITIVE]
"I seriously considered the **possibility** that it might soon be on the first."

"A man who half starves himself, and goes the length in family prayers, and so on, that you do, believes in his **religion** whatever it may be."

b. [NON-RESTRICTIVE APPOSITIVE]
"She still had the letter, or **whatever it was**, in her hand?"

"This 'framework of peace,' **as it was described**, included the assertion that the ultimate decision on governing Northern Ireland would be made by the majority of its citizens."

7. Complements of noun or adjectives

Complements of nouns or adjective are restricted to a small group of English words derived from verbs and taking a noun clause. Figure 8.2 lists representative examples. First consider the verb group.

FIGURE 8.2 ✿ COMPLEMENTS OF NOUNS OR ADJECTIVES

VERBS		NOUN		ADJECTIVE
a. I assert...	→	my assertion...	→	assertive
b. I believe	→	my belief	→	believable
c. I contend...	→	my contention...	→	contentious
d. I fear...	→	my fear...	→	fearful
e. I hope...	→	my hope...	→	hopeful
f. I suspect...	→	my suspicion...	→	suspicious

$$S \rightarrow NP + VP + NP^2$$
$$Sj \quad P \quad Do$$

a. [NOUN CLAUSE AS DIRECT OBJECT]
"Now, Bonds, a slugger who is so dedicated to his body and so calculated with his career, must **hope that already wary fans will believe he took steroids unknowingly**."

"He does not **fear that you will let yourself die of hunger**."

In these examples, the predicates *hope* and *fear* take following noun clauses which function as direct objects.

If these predicates were the nouns, *hope* and *fear*, then the grammatical function of the noun clauses would change from direct objects of predicates to complements of nouns.

$$S \rightarrow NP + VP + C$$
$$Sj \quad P \quad Do$$

a. [NOUN CLAUSE AS COMPLEMENT OF A NOUN]
"It had been our **hope that we would be able to have a combination of increases** that mainly were Iraqi troops' increases."

"I wish you had sincerity enough to tell me whether Catherine would suffer greatly from his loss; the **fear that she would restrain me**."

In these examples, the noun clauses follow nouns and are complements of these nouns. The question may arise, how do these complements differ from appositives? In Chapter 7 where we discussed appositives, we noted that they are optional, that is, they can be left out without affecting the syntax of the sentence; complements cannot be left out. Consider the following examples without the complements.

> "Those who violate federal drug laws should never **believe** that drug trafficking from outside our borders puts them beyond the reach of justice."

> "Those who violate federal drug laws should never **believe** ..."

Similarly, we can have these same words functioning as adjectives, taking noun clauses as complements of adjectives.

$$S \rightarrow \quad NP \quad + \quad VP \quad + \quad NP^2$$
$$\quad\quad\quad Sj \quad\quad\quad\quad P \quad\quad\quad\quad Do$$

a. [NOUN CLAUSE AS COMPLEMENT OF AN ADJECTIVE]
> "We are **hopeful** that the NHLPA's offer will be a meaningful effort to address the league's economic problems."

> "I should be **fearful** that the court would be unwilling to pay for both."

In these examples, the adjectives have following noun clauses which are functioning as complements of adjectives. It is important to remember that noun clauses as complements of nouns or adjectives occur only after particular words.

Extra-posed noun clauses

Earlier we showed subjects and direct objects extra-posed to positions after the predicate or direct object respectively. These were noun clauses, and as noted, the expletive *it* or *there* replaced the clause in the original subject or direct object positions. When the subject or direct object is not extra-posed the phrase *the fact* can be used before the conjunction that. This shows that the clause in question is actually a noun clause (since *fact* is a noun).

a. [EXTRA-POSED NOUN CLAUSE]
> "**That he should be regarded as a suitor to herself** would have seemed to her a ridiculous irrelevance."

> "**[The fact] that he should be regarded as a suitor to herself** would have seemed to her a ridiculous irrelevance."

Extra-posed subjects

a. [EXTRA-POSED NOUN CLAUSE AS SUBJECT]
"**There** could be no doubt **that it had a very turn-up nose.**"

"**It** flashed upon me **it was enough to start a panic.**"

The *that* conjunction has been deleted in the second example. It might also read:

"**It** flashed upon me [that] **it was enough to start a panic.**"

These sentences read awkwardly if the subject noun clause is positioned before the predicate, although it is still grammatically correct.

"**That it had a very turn-up nose** could be no doubt."

"**[That] it was enough to start a panic** flashed upon me."

In the second example the *that* connector can be deleted when the clause occurs after the predicate; however, it must be reinstated when the clause is moved to the position before the predicate. One has to be very careful not to take the expletive for a subject and the extra-posed noun clause for a direct object.

At times when the predicate has no object or modifier following it, extra-position is obligatory.

a. [EXTRA-POSED NOUN CLAUSE AS SUBJECT]
"**It** appears **he was under some hazy apprehension as to his personal safety.**"

That he was under some hazy apprehension as to his personal safety appears.

In this example, the intransitive verb *appears* requires a subjective complement, predicate noun or predicate adjective. Although the noun clause is functioning as an extra-posed subject, it also covers for the missing predicate noun or predicate adjective in this case.

Extra-posed direct objects

Noun clauses occurring after the predicate as direct objects can also be extra-posed to the end of the structure. The direct object position is then filled with an expletive.

S →	**NP**	+	**VP**	+	**NP²**	+	**NP³**
	Sj		P		Do		C

a. [EXTRA-POSED NOUN CLAUSE AS DIRECT OBJECT]
"It makes **it** more likely **that these cases will actually get to trial.**"

If we reposition the direct object to that of the expletive, we have:

It makes **that these cases will actually get to trial** more likely.

Extra-posed direct objects can often be overlooked, since the expletive is so embedded into the structure that little attention is drawn to it. For extra-posed subjects the expletive is right up front, beginning the sentence and it is difficult to miss it.

RELATIVE CLAUSES

Figure 8.3 identifies the grammatical function for relative adjective clauses.

FIGURE 8.3 ✿ FUNCTIONS FOR RELATIVE ADJECTIVE CLAUSES

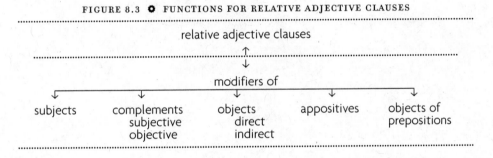

Relative pronoun conjunctions

Unlike noun clause conjunctions, relative pronouns *always* have grammatical functions within their clauses. Initially, they act as *connectors*, joining the dependent and independent clauses; secondarily they are constituents within their own clauses and carry out grammatical functions there.

Before considering the relative clause as a whole, as a sentence constituent, let us analyze the role of the connector within its own clause.

S → NP + VP + NP^2
     Sj   P

a. [RELATIVE CLAUSE]
"We are like dreamers   **who**   **walk**   **beneath a sea.**"
                    cj/sj   p   av
          cl → **cn/np** + vp + c

This is a relative adjective clause modifying the preceding noun *dreamers*. This antecedent is a subjective complement/predicate noun within the independent clause. The pronoun conjunction *who* is a *connector*, linking the dependent to the independent clause; second, this pronoun has the grammatical function of *subject* within the dependent clause. This is indicated by the dual identifiers *cj (conjunction)/sj (subject)*.

Although relative conjunctions generally introduce their clauses, they are not restricted to a particular grammatical function. They carry out all grammatical functions attributed to nouns; after all, by form they are pronouns.

1. Relative connector as subject within its own clause

a. [RELATIVE AS A SUBJECT]

	"It was I **who**		**told**		**him**	**to be off.**"
	cn/sj		p		do	av
cl →	**np**	+	vp	+	np^2	

The focus here is on the relative pronoun *who* carrying out the dual grammatical functions of clause *connector* and *subject* within its own clause.

2. Relative connector as a direct object within its own clause

a. [RELATIVE AS A DIRECT OBJECT]

"'You remember Branscon?' said Jaralson, treating his companion's wit with the inattention **that it deserved.**"

	it		**deserved**		**that**
	sj		p		cn/do
cl →	**np**	+	vp	+	np^2

3. Relative connector as an object of the preposition within its own clause

a. [RELATIVE AS AN OBJECT OF THE PREPOSITION]

"He was the first boy **with whom I had ever had any intimacy.**"

	I		had ever had		any intimacy with whom	
	sj		p		do	cn/op
cl →	**np**	+	vp	+	np^2	

In clauses such as these, the connector *whom* may or may not introduce the clause. They can occur after the preposition at the beginning of the clause, or they can begin the clause with the preposition occurring at the end of the clause, but not in both places. The above example can be rewritten to illustrate this option.

"He was the first boy *whom* **I had ever had any intimacy** *with*."

Relative connectors can sometimes be omitted, but only when they carry out the grammatical functions of objects.

a. [RELATIVE AS A DIRECT OBJECT]
"He showed a certain ethical quality that nobody else could understand."

This sentence can also be written as:

He showed a certain ethical quality **nobody else could understand**.

However, when the relative is subject we cannot delete it.

Compare the two versions of the following example.

"There are millions of people **who are illegally in the United States**."

*There are millions of people **are illegally in the United States**.

It is obvious that there is something missing from the second sentence. The first half makes sense, but the second half is lacking a sentence constituent to make sense. It is its subject.

Relative adjective clauses

Relative clauses as sentence constituents within independent sentence structures carry out the grammatical function of a modifier. They refer back to an antecedent, which is a noun or its replacement.

1. Relative adjective clause modifying the subject of a predicate

a. [RELATIVE ADJECTIVE CLAUSE MODIFYING A SUBJECT]
"***Those* whom she sentenced** were taken into custody by the soldiers."

"A new ***name* that emerged on Friday** is Detroit Lions Coach Steve Mariucci, whom an agent in college football said had been approached by Notre Dame."

"***Mr. Kuchma and Mr. Putin*, whose support for Mr. Yanukovich has provoked angry protests here and abroad**, mocked the idea of another runoff as impractical."

2. Relative adjective clause modifying a direct object

a. [RELATIVE ADJECTIVE CLAUSE MODIFYING A DIRECT OBJECT]
"His brother Roger remembers a ***boy* who was a tremendous athlete**."

"I remember once bringing back from the Cross-Roads a crumpled ***newspaper*, which my father read again and again**, and then folded up and put in his pocket."

"Kiefer offers a **comment that is consistent with his expressionistic need to 'fuse' himself with his subject**: 'I do not identify with Nero or Hitler.'"

3. Relative adjective clause modifying an indirect object

As noted earlier in our discussion of the indirect object, structures that make up its composition are very restrictive and clausal structures carrying out this grammatical function are difficult to find. I offer here a few *contrived* examples to show that structurally they can occur, even if stylistically they are not popular.

a. [RELATIVE ADJECTIVE CLAUSE MODIFYING AN INDIRECT OBJECT]
Kirk brought **young Ms Brown whom he dated** a gift.

The family sent *Mary* whom they loved a Christmas package.

They bought their *dog* that they had just trained a collar.

4. Relative adjective clause as a subjective complement/predicate adjective

Adjective modifiers can actually be subjective complements, since that is a grammatical function for adjectives—predicate adjective.

a. [RELATIVE ADJECTIVE CLAUSE AS A SUBJECTIVE COMPLEMENT/PREDICATE ADJECTIVE]
"'So THAT is **who you are**,' she added, the old look of aversion coming back to her eyes."

As well, we have examples of relative adjective clauses modifying a subjective complement.

b. [RELATIVE ADJECTIVE CLAUSE MODIFYING A SUBJECTIVE COMPLEMENT]
"It is **we who are weak** because we have deluded ourselves into thinking we are strong."

"He was **a television journalist who couldn't be bothered with ego**."

5. Relative adjective clause modifying an appositive

a. [RELATIVE ADJECTIVE CLAUSE MODIFYING AN APPOSITIVE]
"Mr. Stapleton, **a mutual friend who was much concerned at his state of health**, was of the same opinion."

"And I remember a battle with one of these urchins in the briers, **an affair which did not add to the love of their family or ours**."

6. Relative adjective clause modifying an objective complement

a. [RELATIVE ADJECTIVE CLAUSE MODIFYING AN OBJECTIVE COMPLEMENT]
"No one has ever considered *it* **an institution [which is] subject to independence and integrity**."

"Expressionism opened the window to the madness; Augustine might have called *it* **original sin that is in us all**."

7. Relative adjective clause modifying an object of the preposition

a. [RELATIVE ADJECTIVE CLAUSE MODIFYING AN OBJECT OF PREPOSITION]
"But for some ***reason* which his immature mind could not fathom**, he felt a pariah even among his coverals."

"He thought he was walking ***along a dusty road* that showed white in the gathering darkness of a summer night**."

"It was agreed that the position of the chair would be rotated, on a six monthly basis, ***between council members* 'who deplore violence and seek to pursue political progress by political means.'**"

Relative adverb conjunctions

Like relative adjective connectors, relative adverb conjunctions also have a dual role within their sentence structures. Initially, they introduce subordinate clauses, referring back to an antecedent; secondarily they carry out an adverbial function within their own clauses, expressing *time*, *place*, or *reason*.

1. Adverb of time within its own clause

```
S  →     NP     +     VP     +     C
         Sj           P            C
```

a. [RELATIVE ADVERB CLAUSE OF TIME]
"Finally the hour came   **when the sun   broke   through the clouds**."
                            m/av   sj   p
                    cl →   cn   np +   vp   + c

when the sun   broke   through the clouds
 av   sj   p
cl →   cn   np +   vp   + c

the sun broke through the clouds **when**
the sun broke through the clouds **quickly**
the sun broke through the clouds **at ten o'clock**

2. Adverb of place within its own clause

a. [RELATIVE ADVERB CLAUSE OF PLACE]
"My wish is that the Blue Flower may grow in the garden where you work."

where you work
you work **where**
you work in the garden

3. Adverb of reason within its own clause

a. [RELATIVE ADVERB CLAUSE OF REASON]
"But there was no reason why every one should not dance."

why every one should not dance
every one should not dance **because**

Relative adverb clauses

Relative adverb clauses, like adverb words and phrases, modify predicates, adjectives, other adverbs, or whole sentences. See Figure 8.4. As sentence constituents they modify or refer back to an antecedent in the independent clause.

FIGURE 8.4 ✿ FUNCTIONS FOR RELATIVE ADVERB CLAUSES

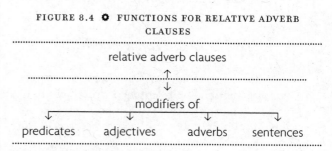

1. Relative adverb clause modifying a predicate

a. [ADVERB CLAUSE MODIFYING A PREDICATE]
"The system clearly had an impact on the composition of local authorities and few majority councils **exist where one political party holds the overall majority of seats**."

"He stopped to talk, and **asked** the old farmer **why he *sat* alone when the farm work needed to be done**."

"The problem **comes when we move too directly from the findings of a discipline to application in the real world**."

The first examples expresses *place*; the second states *reason*; and the third *time*.

2. Relative adverb clause modifying an adjective

a. [ADVERB CLAUSE MODIFYING AN ADJECTIVE]
"With *Superstar* it was very **clear where my own feelings as a composer lay**."

"I was very **aware when I was writing it**."

"'Maybe that is **just why it was glorious**,' said Bo, earnestly."

3. Relative adverb clause modifying another adverb

a. [ADVERB CLAUSE MODIFYING AN ADVERB]
"I got myself into terrible trouble back in Britain not **long ago when I said**, 'The problem with me is that I'm a maximalist.'"

"David wondered **sometimes why all the pleasant things were 'don'ts' and all the unpleasant ones 'dos.'**"

"He told us he knows **now where all the yellow dogs go to when they die**."

4. Relative adverb clause modifying a sentence

a. [ADVERB CLAUSE MODIFYING A SENTENCE]
"**When informed of reports of Meyer's deal with Florida**, White digested the information with a withdrawn look and retreated to his office."

"My last international success was *Cats,* and that may have made people forget the bleaker parts of something like *Evita,* **where I was working in a more serious way**."

"But whether Mr. Clare had spoken seriously or not, **why should she**, who could never conscientiously allow any man to marry her now."

EXPRESSED ANTECEDENTS VS. IMPLIED ANTECEDENTS

Deletions or ellipses are common in sentence structures, and this often causes a problem in identifying a relative adverb clause when it is the antecedent. The first examples here have expressed antecedents:

a. [ANTECEDENT IS PRESENT]
"On the second floor he entered a room **where Dr. Trescott was working about the bedside of Henry Johnson**."

"So he hadn't been home **when the sheriff stopped to say** he wanted Mr. Hale to come over to the Wright place."

These examples show the presence of the antecedent, which is easily identifiable, coming immediately before the relative adverb: *room* **where** and *home* **when**. When the antecedent is expressed the grammatical function of the clause is readily seen.

Now consider examples with implied antecedents:

    a. [ANTECEDENT IS MISSING]
    "You'll be **where you can't stop me**."

    "They called for reinforcements, but **when the new officers arrived**, the guerrillas entered the compound with them."

    "'Many people do not understand **why we have these bilateral agreements about confidentiality**,' she said."

In these examples the antecedent is absent; however, it is implied and we can easily reinsert it.

    a. [IMPLIED ANTECEDENT]
    "You'll be *[in the place]* **where you can't stop me**."

    "They called for reinforcements, but *[at the time]* **when the new officers arrived**, the guerrillas entered the compound with them."

    "'Many people do not understand *[the reason]* **why we have these bilateral agreements about confidentiality**,' she said."

The fact that we can insert an antecedent helps us see the grammatical function of the clause.

RELATIVE RESTRICTIVE/NON-RESTRICTIVE CLAUSES

Relative clauses are also *restrictive* or *non-restrictive*. As with appositives, the restrictive clause provides *essential* information; the non-restrictive clause gives *additional* information. The meaning of the former clause is not clear without this information; the meaning of the latter clause does not depend on this information. Non-restrictive clauses are also set off by commas.

Restrictive clauses

a. [RESTRICTIVE RELATIVE ADJECTIVE CLAUSE]
"It is interesting that an early critic **who wrote on 'Buddhist Economics' was a conservative Catholic**."

"Is atomic power the new means **by which the gods of Egypt and all other gods are to die again**?"

b. [RESTRICTIVE RELATIVE ADVERB CLAUSE]
"Gen. Abizaid, speaking to reporters at a regional security conference in Bahrain, declined to speculate on **when the Iraqi forces would be ready or say how many they now number**."

"It has been on defense **where the teams have made the most striking improvements**."

The above relative clauses restrict their antecedents by providing *essential* information to the sentence structure. Because of their significance, the clauses are not separated from the nouns they modify.

The following are features of *restrictive* clause modifiers.

1. A relative clause beginning with the *that* conjunction is always restrictive.

"It was no ordinary thing ***that* called her away**."

2. A clause with an omitted relative is restrictive.

"And she still had the Bible ***[that]* John Field had given her**."

3. If you can substitute *that* for *who*, *whom*, or *which* the clause is restrictive.

"His cheeks were pads, and the unroughened hand **which lay helpless upon the khaki-colored blanket was slightly puffy**."

"His cheeks were pads, and the unroughened hand ***[that]* lay helpless upon the khakicolored blanket was slightly puffy**."

Non-restrictive clauses

a. [NON-RESTRICTIVE RELATIVE ADJECTIVE CLAUSE]
"This inordinate growth in the population of Russia, **which has not been widely noticed in England**, has been nevertheless one of the most significant facts of recent years."

"Her mother, Berly, 47, **who migrated to the United States illegally a decade ago**, went to the immigration office on a routine visit to renew her work authorization."

b. [NON-RESTRICTIVE RELATIVE ADVERB CLAUSE]
"In consequence, **when he swung around the curve at the flower-bed**, a wheel of his cart destroyed a peony."

"This is especially true in the West, **where reflection on the faith was for centuries eagerly hosted by universities**."

The above relative clauses do not restrict their antecedents; they provide additional information to the sentence structure. Because of this they are separated from the nouns they modify by commas.

The following are features of nonrestrictive clause modifiers.

1. Non-restrictive clauses are separated from the main clause by commas.

"The shrieks gradually diminished to spasmodic sobs, **which in turn gave place to ominous silence**."

2. After personal or geographical names, John Smith or St. John's, the clause is usually non-restrictive.

"Fireworks crackled in Kiev's Independence Square, **where opposition supporters who have massed for nearly two weeks waved orange flags and chanted 'Yushchenko!'**"

3. Non-restrictive clauses can be omitted without affecting the meaning of the main clause.

"Mr. Yousef's statements signal an apparent reversal of policy for Hamas, **which has long sought to destroy Israel and replace it with an Islamic Palestinian state**."

"Mr. Yousef's statements signal an apparent reversal of policy for Hamas, ..."

ADVERB CLAUSES

Adverb clauses are formed by adding a subordinating adverb conjunction to a noun phrase (NP) verb phrase (VP) structure. These adverbs denote time (*after, before, as soon as,* etc.), manner (*as, as if, like,* etc.), contrast or opposition (*although, whereas, while,* etc.), cause and effect (*because, in that, since,* etc.), condition (in case, provided that, unless, etc.), purpose (so that, in order that, etc.), and comparison (*more than, less than,* etc.). They modify words, phrases, and clauses of a verb/adverb composition. See Figure 8.5.

Unlike relative adverb conjunctions, adverb connectors do not have grammatical functions within the clauses they introduce; in this respect they are similar to the connectors introducing noun clauses. Their only grammatical function is as a *connector* of the subordinate clause.

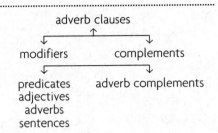

FIGURE 8.5 ✿
FUNCTIONS FOR ADVERB CLAUSES

Grammatical functions of adverb clauses

1. Adverb clause as a predicate complement

    a. [ADVERB CLAUSE OF MANNER]
    "It was not **as if Leinart and White had played poorly that day**; Leinart passed for 242 yards against U.C.L.A, and White had thrown for 254 yards against Colorado."

    b. [ADVERB CLAUSE OF CAUSE AND EFFECT]
    "He took but little interest even in the social or the athletic side of his school life, and his failures in his studies troubled him sorely, only I ***fear***, however, **because it troubled his mother and father**."

2. Adverb clause as a predicate modifier

    a. [ADVERB CLAUSE OF MANNER]
    "Supporters of present economic policies often ***speak*** **as if the alternative to global capitalism is state socialism**."

    b. [ADVERB CLAUSE OF PURPOSE]
    "He ***glared*** **so that he was terrible to look at**."

3. Adverb clause as an adjective modifier

    a. [ADVERB CLAUSE OF COMPARISON]
    "The decision came after ***dark***, **more than six hours after the judges retired to deliberate**."

    b. [ADVERB CLAUSE OF CONTRAST OR OPPOSITION]
    "The kingpin, whose hair has become ***grey and chubby*** **while in a Colombian prison over the past nine years**, faces trial in federal courts in Miami and New York."

    "Even if he threw it into the sea the action might be noticed, and thought ***noticeable***—**unless indeed he could think of some more natural way of covering the action**."

4. Adverb clause as an adverb modifier

    a. [ADVERB CLAUSE OF CONDITION]
        "I don't see what on earth keeps him *so late*, **unless, maybe, he can't sell his head**."

    b. [ADVERB CLAUSE OF MANNER]
        "He was walking up and down, **as if thinking something out**."

5. Adverb clause as a sentence modifier

    a. [ADVERB CLAUSE OF TIME]
        "**Before launching into such a critique**, I want to note that a quite similar critique could be directed to many of the academic disciplines."

    b. [ADVERB CLAUSE OF CAUSE AND EFFECT]
        "On their own, both of Shilo's conditions are incurable and hard to treat; together, they're even worse, **since they call for opposite amounts of fibre in the diet**."

Relative adverb vs. adverb clauses

Some confusion may occur between *relative adverb* clauses and *adverb* clauses. To distinguish between them structurally the following points should be remembered.

1. Relative adverb clauses begin with *when*, *where* and *why* only; adverb clauses begin with a mixture of *adverbs* and *adverb phrases*.

2. The conjunction of a relative adverb clause has two functions: one as connector of the clause to the main clause, and secondly as a grammatical function within that clause. The conjunction of an adverb clause has only one grammatical function; it is as connector of the clause to the main clause.

CLAUSE ANALYSIS

1. Noun clause

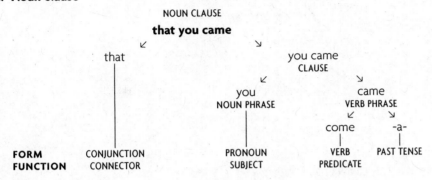

Since this noun clause has a subject and predicate, we acknowledge it for its underlying sentence-like structure. Not being an independent clause, we do not mark it with S; we would use an S^1 to mark it as the first embedded sentence and S^2 to signal a second clause when one occurs.

2. Relative adjective clause

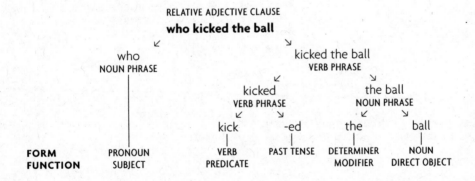

3. Relative adverb clause

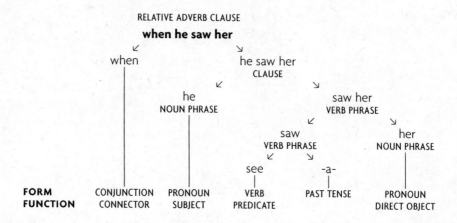

4. Adverb clause

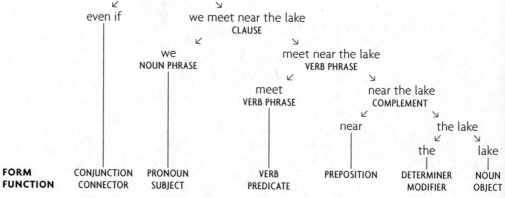

⚙ ⚙ ⚙

Having categorized words, phrases, and clauses by form and analyzed their grammatical functions, we now turn to the third category: *grammatical positions*. When analyzing sentence constituents, it is important to know their grammatical forms, functions, and positions. Each of these categories interrelates grammatically with the other.

position

9 GRAMMATICAL POSITIONS

GRAMMATICAL POSITION

restricts sentence constituents based on form and function.

Grammatical position is our third category of analysis: form, function and position, that is, *where a constituent* **GOES**. Constituents do not arbitrarily occupy any position within a sentence. We restrict them to particular positions based on form and function. Knowing the form of a sentence constituent helps us to identify its grammatical function; but together they also tell us the grammatical position of the constituent. Figure 9.1 identifies four grammatical positions.

FIGURE 9.1 ✿ GRAMMATICAL POSITIONS

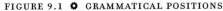
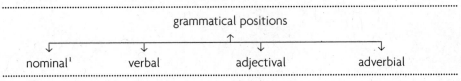

1 Note that the *-al* ending has the meaning of *like*. Hence, any word or word group that occupies a nominal positions behaves *like* a noun and can carry out the grammatical functions attributed to a noun. This is similar for the other three positions as well.

To identify grammatical positions, we change our terminology once again from that used for form and function. Noun word(s), phrase(s), and clause(s), and their replacements, occupy the *nominal* position; lexical verbs and auxiliaries occupy the *verbal* position; adjective word(s), phrase(s), and clause(s) occupy the *adjectival* position; and, adverb word(s), phrase(s), and clause(s) occupy the *adverbial* position. Beyond these, there are no other positions for identifying sentence constituents.

Again, we return to our basic sentence structure $S \rightarrow NP + VP \rightarrow NP^2/C$, where we analyzed sentence constituents in their various grammatical functions. Understanding this structure will be very helpful in identifying the grammatical positions of sentence constituents.

NOMINAL

The nominal position is reserved for the following form class categories and the grammatical functions listed in Figure 9.2.

NOMINAL POSITION

is reserved for nouns, noun phrases and clauses, and their replacements.

FIGURE 9.2 ✿ NOMINAL POSITIONS

POSITION	NOMINAL ↓	
FORMS	words ↓	phrases ↓	clauses ↓
	nouns	noun	noun
	pronoun	gerund	
	gerund	infinitive	
	infinitive		

FUNCTIONS	↓
	subject
	direct object
	indirect object
	object of preposition
	apposition
	subjective complement
	objective complement

Not all form class categories noted here carry out all identified functions. For example, the form class word *noun* can carry out all of the noted grammatical functions; by contrast, the form class phrase *infinitive* cannot carry out all of these functions. An infinitive does not occur as an indirect object, nor does it occur as an apposition, and so forth. To contrast those that *do* from those that *do not*, check the overview of *grammatical terms* by *form*, *function*, and *position* in the appendix, pages 256–57.

The following examples illustrate representative occurrences of the nominal position in sentence structures, providing examples of words, phrases and clauses. The emphasis here is on the particular grammatical position.

1. Nominal position occupied by a subject of a predicate

$$S \rightarrow NP + VP + NP^2/C$$
$$Sj \quad\quad P$$

a. [NOMINAL POSITION/NOUN AS SUBJECT]
"**Genomics** is already having a large influence on medical practice."

b. [NOMINAL POSITION/NOUN PHRASE AS SUBJECT]
"**A critique of neo-liberal economics** can emphasize either the theory or the practice."

c. [NOMINAL POSITION/GERUND AS SUBJECT]
"**This proceeding** roused the whole hive."

d. [NOMINAL POSITION/INFINITIVE PHRASE AS SUBJECT]
"**To stay** where I was would be impossible; I must either go backwards or forwards."

e. [NOMINAL POSITION/NOUN CLAUSE AS SUBJECT]
"**That he should turn around because his mood changed** seems to me unthinkable."

2. Nominal position occupied by a direct object of a predicate

$$S \rightarrow NP + VP + NP^2$$
$$Sj \quad\quad P \quad\quad Do$$

a. [NOMINAL POSITION/NOUN AS DIRECT OBJECT]
"The academic disciplines are **children** of the European Enlightenment."

b. [NOMINAL POSITION/NOUN PHRASE AS DIRECT OBJECT]
"And he hugged **the old man** and kissed him affectionately."

c. [NOMINAL POSITION/GERUND AS DIRECT OBJECT]
"Economists encourage **the ordering** of the economy to the end of increasing human satisfaction."

d. [NOMINAL POSITION/INFINITIVE AS DIRECT OBJECT]
"Van Gogh tried **to capture** what he saw of the infinite in the subjects of everyday life."

e. [NOMINAL POSITION/NOUN CLAUSE AS DIRECT OBJECT]
"You can say **what you like to me**, but remember what I've told you."

3. Nominal position occupied by an indirect object of a predicate

S	→	NP	+	VP	+	NP^2	+	NP^3
		Sj		P		Ido		Do

a. [NOMINAL POSITION/PRONOUN AS INDIRECT OBJECT]
"But when I questioned my father on these matters he would give **me** no answers."

b. [NOMINAL POSITION/NOUN AS INDIRECT OBJECT]
"And to begin my kindness, Joseph, bring **the lad** some breakfast."

c. [NOMINAL POSITION/NOUN PHRASE AS INDIRECT OBJECT]
"The House bill, which gave **the intelligence director** less authority, drew more support from the military."

4. Nominal position occupied by a subjective complement

S	→	NP	+	VP	+	C
		Sj		P		SC/P-n

a. [NOMINAL POSITION/NOUN AS SUBJECTIVE COMPLEMENT]
"This is **a copy** of the first book of mine published."

b. [NOMINAL POSITION/NOUN PHRASE AS SUBJECTIVE COMPLEMENT]
"Nancy Reagan's campaign slogan, 'Just say no,' became **the theme of the entire drug bureaucracy**."

c. [NOMINAL POSITION/NOUN CLAUSE AS SUBJECTIVE COMPLEMENT]
"It seemed **that the importance of the whole thing had taken away the boy's vocabulary**."

5. Nominal position occupied by an appositive

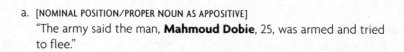

a. [NOMINAL POSITION/PROPER NOUN AS APPOSITIVE]
"The army said the man, **Mahmoud Dobie**, 25, was armed and tried to flee."

b. [NOMINAL POSITION/NOUN PHRASE AS APPOSITIVE]
"Elizabeth Weir, **the lone New Democrat in the provincial legislature**, was quick to pounce on the throne speech as lacking in substance."

c. [NOMINAL POSITION/NOUN CLAUSE AS APPOSITIVE]
"He showed a certain ethical quality **that nobody else could understand**."

6. Nominal position occupied by an objective complement

$$S \rightarrow \quad NP \quad + \quad VP \quad + \quad NP^2 \quad + \quad NP^2$$
$$\qquad\quad Sj \qquad\qquad P \qquad\qquad Do \qquad\qquad OC$$

a. [NOMINAL POSITION/NOUN AS OBJECTIVE COMPLEMENT]
"No one has ever considered it **an institution** subject to independence and integrity."

b. [NOMINAL POSITION/NOUN PHRASE AS OBJECTIVE COMPLEMENT]
"They had not, like me, made it **the subject of long contemplation**."

c. [NOMINAL POSITION/GERUND AS OBJECTIVE COMPLEMENT]
"'I call it **purring**, not **growling**,' said Alice."

d. [NOMINAL POSITION/NOUN CLAUSE AS OBJECTIVE COMPLEMENT]
"He wanted the knowledge **he lacked to drop on him**, if drop it could, by its own august weight."

7. Nominal position occupied by an object of the preposition

$$S \rightarrow \quad NP \quad + \quad VP \quad + \quad C$$
$$\qquad\quad Sj \qquad\qquad P \qquad\qquad OP$$

a. [NOMINAL POSITION/NOUN AS OBJECT OF PREPOSITION]
"The patient-doctor relationship is important **to** the **doctor** in order to obtain an accurate medical history."

b. [NOMINAL POSITION/NOUN PHRASE AS OBJECT OF PREPOSITION]
"The charm, happily, was in **other things too**."

c. [NOMINAL POSITION/GERUND AS OBJECT OF PREPOSITION]
"The interest of the government in removing this woman pales in comparison **with** her **suffering** and her family's."

d. [NOMINAL POSITION/NOUN CLAUSE AS OBJECT OF PREPOSITION]
"I'd talk to him **about** whatever he should say publicly."

All seven of these grammatical functions occupy the nominal position. This is the most varied, in grammatical functions, of the four positions. Knowing these grammatical positions helps identifies the respective grammatical functions.

VERBAL

The verbal position is reserved for the lexical verb and all auxiliary verbs used to express tense and aspect. See Figure 9.3. This can be a single verb or a verb phrase. Adverbs and prepositional phrases, because of their close association with predicates as modifiers, may appear to belong to the verb phrase and therefore to the verbal position. Although they may be found within predicate structures, as we shall see they are still adverbial by position.

The following examples illustrate a range for the verbal position.

VERBAL POSITION
is reserved for verbs and auxiliaries carrying out the function of the predicate.

S →	NP	+	VP	+	C
	Sj		P		av

1. Simple aspect

a. [VERBAL POSITION/PREDICATE IN PRESENT TENSE]
"They **call** it here 'the house' preeminently."

b. [VERBAL POSITION/PREDICATE IN PAST TENSE]
"Through the course of the twentieth century, doctors naturally **focused** increasingly on the technology."

c. [VERBAL POSITION/PREDICATE IN FUTURE TENSE]
"If we do so, we **will recognize** needs before market prices reflect them."

2. Progressive aspect

a. [VERBAL POSITION/PREDICATE IN PRESENT TENSE]
"Mr. Abbas himself **is going** to Damascus over the weekend for a rare meeting with the Syrian president, Bashar al-Assad."

FIGURE 9.3 ✿ VERBAL POSITIONS

POSITION	verbal ↓	
FORMS	words verbs	phrases auxiliaries primary modal Do
FUNCTIONS	predicate	

b. [VERBAL POSITION/PREDICATE IN PAST TENSE]
"In 1999, ICE agents received initial information that the Cali Cartel **was continuing** its drug and money laundering activities from within Colombian prisons."

c. [VERBAL POSITION/PREDICATE IN FUTURE TENSE]
"This piece will of course do well because it **will be reaching** people in various cities who would not ordinarily be able to hear this sort of thing."

3. Perfect aspect

a. [VERBAL POSITION/PREDICATE IN PRESENT TENSE]
"However, a few performers in recent years **have brought** to the industry a more substantial expression of feelings."

b. [verbal position/predicate in past tense]
"Alice **had learnt** several things of this sort in her lessons in the schoolroom."

c. [verbal position/predicate in future tense]
"They **will have forgotten** it by that time."

4. Perfect-progressive aspect

a. [VERBAL POSITION/PREDICATE IN PRESENT TENSE]
"Slowly, but with persistent courage, **we have been pushing** this question mark further and further towards that distant line."

b. [VERBAL POSITION/PREDICATE IN PAST TENSE]
"I thought there was now the possibility of being able to develop an area of my writing that I **had been** quietly **working** away on ever since I began composing."

c. [VERBAL POSITION/PREDICATE IN FUTURE TENSE]
"For they **will have been supplanting** the very process of perfection through natural selection."

The verbal position is the easiest of the grammatical positions to identify. Unlike other positions that occur in several places, verbal positions centre around the lexical verb that forms the predicate.

ADJECTIVAL

The adjectival position takes words, phrases, and clauses that carry out the grammatical function of an adjectival modifiers. See Figure 9.4. The position itself is as varied as that for the noun. In fact, its position may take on more forms as a result of its prenominal and postnominal occurrences. Wherever a noun or its replacement occurs, an adjective or its replacement can occur either before or after it, and each of these is an adjectival position. As well, we have seen that adjectives modify other adjectives; finally there is the predicate adjective as a subjective complement that follows linking verbs.

FIGURE 9.4 ✿ ADJECTIVAL POSITIONS

POSITION	adjectival ↓		
FORMS	words	phrases	clauses
	adjectives	adjectives	relative
	nouns	participle	
	determiners	prepositional	
	participles		
FUNCTIONS	modifier		

ADJECTIVAL POSITION

is reserved for adjective words, phrases, and clauses carrying out the function of a modifier as attributed to an adjective.

1. Adjectival position modifying subjects

S →   NP   +   VP   +   NP^2/C
         Sj   P

a. [ADJECTIVAL POSITION/ADJECTIVE MODIFYING SUBJECT]
"The **little** *church* on a hill had the mossy greyness of a rock seen through a ragged screen of leaves."

b. [ADJECTIVAL POSITION/ADJECTIVE PHRASE MODIFYING SUBJECT]
"In December 1993, **the British and Irish** *Governments* issued **a joint (Downing Street)** *declaration* offering Sinn Fein a place in negotiations."

c. [ADJECTIVAL POSITION/RELATIVE ADJECTIVE CLAUSE MODIFYING SUBJECT]
"American Hal Prince, **who also directed** *Evita*, is directing the show."

2. Adjectival position modifying direct objects

S →   NP   +   VP   +   NP^2
         Sj   P   Do

a. [ADJECTIVAL POSITION/ADJECTIVE MODIFYING DIRECT OBJECT]
"Leach and Stewart see the **coalition** *framework* as inappropriate for local government."

b. [ADJECTIVAL POSITION/ADJECTIVE PHRASE MODIFYING DIRECT OBJECT]
"CanWest purchased the ***National Post*** **and the Southam newspaper chain**."

c. [ADJECTIVAL POSITION/RELATIVE ADJECTIVE CLAUSE MODIFYING DIRECT OBJECT]
"All the channels and the basins were supplied with water, and men made new **channels** **which were also filled**."

3. Adjectival position modifying indirect object

S	→	NP	+	VP	+	NP^2	+	NP^3
		Sj		P		Ido		Do

a. [ADJECTIVAL POSITION/ADJECTIVE MODIFYING INDIRECT OBJECT]
"I can give **your** **question** a direct answer easily enough."

b. [ADJECTIVAL POSITION/ADJECTIVE PHRASE MODIFYING INDIRECT OBJECT]
"He gave **the old grey** **cap** a parting squeeze, in which his hand relaxed."

4. Adjectival position modifying subjective complement

S	→	NP	+	VP	+	SC
		Sj		P		pn

a. [ADJECTIVAL POSITION/ADJECTIVE MODIFYING SUBJECTIVE COMPLEMENT]
"As a result, prisoners simply **continue** **their** addiction in prison, where drugs are plentiful."

b. [ADJECTIVAL POSITION/ADJECTIVE PHRASE MODIFYING SUBJECTIVE COMPLEMENT]
"His bohemian, quasi-criminal life style—late nights in taverns and frequent brawls—**seemed** **a head-on** attack on the social status that artists had fought so hard to gain."

c. [ADJECTIVAL POSITION/RELATIVE ADJECTIVE CLAUSE MODIFYING SUBJECTIVE COMPLEMENT]
"'My son,' he answered, 'this is the *city* **which was called Ablis**, that is to say, Forsaken.'"

5. Adjectival position modifying appositive

S	→	NP	+	VP	+	NP^2
		Sj		P		Do

a. [ADJECTIVAL POSITION/ADJECTIVE MODIFYING APPOSITIVE]
"In the latter, **Sir Kenneth Bloomfield, former** head of the Northern Ireland civil service, suggested a review in the form of Macrory II."

b. [ADJECTIVAL POSITION/ADJECTIVE PHRASE MODIFYING APPOSITIVE]
"Research was undertaken in 15 councils in Northern Ireland, **the 12 power sharing** **councils** and **3 non-sharing** **councils** (Lisburn, Cookstown and Craigavon)."

c. [ADJECTIVAL POSITION/RELATIVE ADJECTIVE CLAUSE MODIFYING APPOSITIVE]
"These were the college boys who had returned home, the **ones whose individual names were known**."

6. Adjectival position modifying objective complement

S	→	NP	+	VP	+	NP²	+	NP²
		Sj		P		Do		OC

a. [ADJECTIVAL POSITION/ADJECTIVE MODIFYING OBJECTIVE COMPLEMENT]
"One of Baltovich's lawyers, James Lockyer, said he was disappointed the Appeal Court didn't declare Baltovich **an innocent *man***."

b. [ADJECTIVAL POSITION/ADJECTIVE PHRASE MODIFYING OBJECTIVE COMPLEMENT]
"Ihor Ostash called Saturday's developments in Parliament 'an attempt at revenge... **a blue-and-white *revolution*** in Parliament.'"

c. [ADJECTIVAL POSITION/RELATIVE ADJECTIVE CLAUSE MODIFYING OBJECTIVE COMPLEMENT]
"The deal makes Detroit **the first cable market in the country to broadcast Bridges TV, [which was] previously available on dish services**."

7. Adjectival position modifying object of the preposition

S	→	NP	+	VP	+	C
		Sj		P		P-ph

a. [ADJECTIVAL POSITION/ADJECTIVE MODIFYING OBJECT OF PREPOSITION]
"The local government elections of 1989 marked a turning point in **council** chambers with a degree of moderation."

b. [ADJECTIVAL POSITION/ADJECTIVE PHRASE MODIFYING OBJECT OF PREPOSITION]
"Science and technology are the evidence base for **many clinical** problems for the general population at large."

c. [ADJECTIVAL POSITION/ADJECTIVE CLAUSE MODIFYING OBJECT OF PREPOSITION]
"And I very much enjoy writing for the sound of the Latin ***language*, which obviously has something** in that it has endured as long as it has."

Prepositional phrases can also occupy adjectival positions, because they too function as modifiers.

S	→	NP	+		VP	+	NP²/C
(M)		Sj	(M)		P	(M)	Av	(M)

a. [ADJECTIVAL POSITION/PREPOSITIONAL PHRASE MODIFYING SUBJECT]
"The **science** of medicine is the body of knowledge about body systems and diseases."

b. [ADJECTIVAL POSITION/PREPOSITIONAL PHRASE MODIFYING DIRECT OBJECT]
"Britain would not block the **possible** *reunification* **of Ireland** if it was backed by a majority in the North."

c. [ADJECTIVAL POSITION/PREPOSITIONAL PHRASE MODIFYING SUBJECTIVE COMPLEMENT]
"The concert was a **disaster from the beginning**."

e. [ADJECTIVAL POSITION/PREPOSITIONAL PHRASE MODIFYING APPOSITIVE]
"In Brooklyn, similar cases cause concern for Birdette Gardiner-Parkinson, **the clinical director at the Caribbean Community Mental Health program** at Kingsbrook Jewish Medical Center."

f. [ADJECTIVAL POSITION/PREPOSITIONAL PHRASE MODIFYING OBJECTIVE COMPLEMENT]
"But could Giambi prevail on the union to compromise on the buyout issue and get **him out of an uncomfortable situation** *in New York*?"

g. [ADJECTIVAL POSITION/PREPOSITIONAL PHRASE MODIFYING OBJECT OF PREPOSITION]
"Without some long-term **progress** toward a stable political system the men of violence will, as they have in the past, reoccupy the constitutional vacuum."

ADVERBIAL

The adverbial position is reserved for words, phrases, and clauses that carry out the function of a modifier or complement that is attributed to adverbs. See Figure 9.5. While the adjective position occurs only before or after the constituent that it modifies, the adverbial position can be found just about anywhere in the sentence structure, as well as an attachment to the sentence as a whole.

FIGURE 9.5 ❂ ADVERBIAL POSITIONS

POSITION	adverbial ↓	
FORMS	words	phrases	clauses
	adverbs	absolute	relative
	nouns	participle	
	determiners	prepositional	
	participles		
FUNCTIONS		modifier	
		complement	

1. Adverbial position modifying a predicate

S →   NP   +   VP   +   NP²
         Sj   P   Do

a. [ADVERBIAL POSITION/ADVERB MODIFYING A PREDICATE]
"I **seriously** *considered* the possibility that it might soon be on the first."

b. [ADVERBIAL POSITION/ADVERB PHRASE MODIFYING A PREDICATE]
"Saturday's car bombs in Baghdad **went off** nearly simultaneously at about 9:30 a.m."

c. [ADVERBIAL POSITION/ADVERB CLAUSE MODIFYING A PREDICATE]
"I **prefer** if there would be just two trainings and then the race."

2. Adverbial position modifying an adjective

S	→	NP	+	VP	+	C
		Sj		P		P-aj

a. [ADVERBIAL POSITION/ADVERB MODIFYING AN ADJECTIVE]
"After that it was **rather** *late* in the season."

b. [ADVERBIAL POSITION/ADVERB PHRASE MODIFYING AN ADJECTIVE]
"After all, playing a determined Spaniard on his home clay can't be **too much** *tougher* than playing Roger Federer on anything."

c. [ADVERBIAL POSITION/ADVERB CLAUSE MODIFYING AN ADJECTIVE]
"The poor thing remained perfectly *quiet* **wherever I chose to put him**."

3. Adverbial position modifying another adverb

S	→	NP	+	VP	+	C
		Sj		P		Av

a. [ADVERBIAL POSITION/ADVERB MODIFYING ANOTHER ADVERB]
"Saturday's car bombs in Baghdad went off ***nearly* simultaneously** at about 9:30 a.m."

b. [ADVERBIAL POSITION/ADVERB PHRASE MODIFYING ANOTHER ADVERB]
"David, on the lowest step, was **very evidently** *not* hearing a word of what was being said."

c. [ADVERBIAL POSITION/ADVERB CLAUSE MODIFYING ANOTHER ADVERB]
"The whole front was draped in ivy, with a patch clipped bare ***here and there* where a window or a coat of arms broke through the dark veil**."

4. Adverbial position modifying a sentence structure

S	→	NP	+		VP	+	NP²/C
(M)		Sj	(M)	P	(M)	Av	(M)

As noted above, when discussing *adverb modifiers of sentences*, it is important to note that the modifier is not a syntactic part of the sentence in that it conveys essential meaning, and it is therefore separated by commas. This may occur at the beginning or end of the sentence, or is may also occur within a sentence structure. These positions are indicated by the place of (m) at various points along the sentence structure.

a. [ADVERBIAL POSITION/ADVERB INITIALLY]
"**Broadly**, it is the practical science of preventing and curing diseases."

b. [ADVERBIAL POSITION/ADVERB MEDIALLY]
"Along with the old man in *At Eternity's Gate*, van Gogh believed that he, **too**, would find an eternal home after death."

c. [ADVERBIAL POSITION/ADVERB FINALLY]
"Mystery and clarity are not necessarily mutually exclusive, **however**."

d. [ADVERBIAL POSITION/ADVERB PHRASE INITIALLY]
"**Before launching into such a critique**, I want to note that a quite similar critique could be directed to many of the academic disciplines."

e. [ADVERBIAL POSITION/ADVERB PHRASE MEDIALLY]
"Each discipline, **once established**, was free to develop the methods it found most fruitful for the study of its subject matter."

f. [ADVERBIAL POSITION/ADVERB PHRASE FINALLY]
"Each of these parts can be analyzed into its parts, **and so forth**."

g. [ADVERBIAL POSITION/ADVERB CLAUSE INITIALLY]
"**Wherever I turned my eyes**, that terrible picture was before me."

h. [ADVERBIAL POSITION/ADVERB CLAUSE MEDIALLY]
"Since then, **whenever I have had the opportunity**, I have gone to the top of the tower and enjoyed myself."

i. [ADVERBIAL POSITION/ADVERB CLAUSE FINALLY]
"It seems to me that contemporary artists and writers are more interested in truth than in beauty, **if the latter is understood in the traditional sense**."

Adjectival and adverbial positions with prepositional phrase modifiers:

S	→	NP	+			VP	+	NP²/C
(M)		Sj	(M)	P		(M)	Av	(M)

The adverbial position can also be occupied by prepositional phrases, because they can function as adverb modifiers. By position, therefore, the prepositional phrase is quite moveable within the sentence structure.

a. [ADVERBIAL POSITION/PREPOSITIONAL PHRASE MODIFYING A PREDICATE]
"The Jets **will take** the field **at Giants Stadium** with an 83 record."

b. [ADVERBIAL POSITION/PREPOSITIONAL PHRASE MODIFYING AN ADJECTIVE]
"France's Carole Montillet-Carles won both downhills last year but looked **average in training**."

c. [ADVERBIAL POSITION/PREPOSITIONAL PHRASE MODIFYING ANOTHER ADVERB]
"'You can't ever get **away from it**,' Trudy Fraser said. 'That's just the way it is.'"

d. [ADVERBIAL POSITION/PREPOSITIONAL PHRASE MODIFYING A SENTENCE]
"At present almost half of the 26 local councils share responsibility, **including some with an infamous reputation for sectarian practices**."

One adverbial position that might be overlooked because of the focus on modification is that of the complement. Adverb complements occur after intransitive and linking verbs.

a. [ADVERBIAL POSITION/PREPOSITIONAL PHRASE/ADVERB COMPLEMENT/INTRANSITIVE VERB]
"Over the past two years, a peace process **has been initiated in Northern Ireland**."

"The president's position on missile defence **has been known for quite some time**."

b. [ADVERBIAL POSITION/PREPOSITIONAL PHRASE/ADVERB COMPLEMENT/LINKING VERB]
"But he had to call the dog twice, for the dog **had remained behind quite motionless for a moment**."

"'We have established a most important fact by these questions, Watson,' he **continued in a low voice** as we went upstairs together."

In each of the first examples there is an intransitive verb predicate with a following prepositional phrase, functioning as an adverb complement, and hence in an adverbial position. Each of the second examples contain a linking verb predicate that is followed by a prepositional phrase functioning as an adverb complement, and again in an adverbial position.

POSITION VS. FORM AND FUNCTION

The key to grammatical analysis is knowing what a constituent **IS** (form), what a constituent **DOES** (function), and where a constituent **GOES** (position). Knowing one or two of these can be helpful in identifying the other(s). First identifying grammatical position is particularly useful in leading to grammatical function and then on to form. We have seen, for example, that nouns carry out seven different grammatical functions, and that gerunds and infinitives also carry out some of these functions. Because of this overlap, doubt may arise over the function of a particular constituent. Grammatical position is often the key to this doubt. Following are a number of troublesome areas where focusing on the position may be helpful.

Pronouns vs. adjectives

The demonstrative, relative, interrogative, and indefinite pronouns are pronouns by form, but they can be adjective modifiers by grammatical function, as we have seen. Here is a case where form and function overlap, and grammatical position can be very helpful in making the distinction as to when they function as pronouns and when they function as adjectives. If these pronouns stand alone, they occupy a nominal position; if they signal a forthcoming noun they are in the adjectival position. Consider the following examples to contrast *form* and *function*.

a. [NOMINAL POSITION/DEMONSTRATIVE PRONOUN]
"'My son,' he answered, '**this** is the city which was called Ablis, **that** is to say, Forsaken.'"

b. [ADJECTIVAL POSITION/DEMONSTRATIVE ADJECTIVE]
"Been and keyboardist Jim Goodwin say **this complexity** reflects their belief **that life** contains extremes that cannot be addressed with a pat approach."

In the first example, the demonstrative pronouns stand alone, carrying out the grammatical function of subject of their respective clauses. In the second example, the demonstrative pronouns function as determiners signalling forthcoming nouns, *complexity* and *life*, and carrying out the grammatical function of modifier. Knowing the position before a noun is adjectival reveals the grammatical function.

a. [NOMINAL POSITION/RELATIVE PRONOUN]
"Our whole economy is built on the basis of ever-increasing consumption, **which** in turn **adds** endlessly to the stress upon the environment."

b. [ADJECTIVAL POSITION/RELATIVE ADJECTIVE]
"If you didn't know he had surgery, you couldn't tell **which knee** it was."

The first of these examples shows a relative as subject of the clause *which ... adds*; and the second example shows a relative as an adjective modifier of the noun *knee*. The pronoun standing alone would suggest some nominal function, since pronouns can replace nouns. Again, the pronoun coming before a noun suggests a modifying function.

   a. [NOMINAL POSITION/INTERROGATIVE PRONOUN]
      "And **what** went into the decision?"

   b. [ADJECTIVAL POSITION/INTERROGATIVE ADJECTIVE]
      "Do you know **what kinds** of folks you are going to have at that
      meeting and what kinds of questions they might ask?"

These examples use interrogative pronouns; however, the grammatical functions are the same as the examples for the relatives above.

   a. [NOMINAL POSITION/INDEFINITE PRONOUN]
      "These **all** spoke of a harsh existence in a stern land."

   b. [ADJECTIVAL POSITION/INDEFINITE ADJECTIVE]
      "At **all events** Robert proposed it, and there was not a dissenting voice."

This final set off examples illustrates the same positional change for the indefinite pronouns.

Prepositions and particles

Earlier, we also covered prepositions and particles, noting that they look alike and belong by form to the same word group, prepositions; but they carry out different grammatical roles. Particles can either signal an infinitive or mark a two-word verb.

   a. [ADVERBIAL POSITION/PARTICLE]
      "His wife, his clamoring friends, sought **to** follow, but he escaped."

   b. [NOMINAL POSITION/PREPOSITION]
      "A priest referred her **to** Legal Aid, which reopened the case, stopping
      the deportation."

In the first example, *to* precedes the verbal *follow* to form an infinitive; in the second example, *to* precedes a proper noun, *Legal Aid*, to form a prepositional phrase. Identifying a particle/preposition coming before a noun or verbal leads to the grammatical function.

Signalling a two-word verb

Prepositions and particles of two word-verbs can also cause problems because they are both alike as form class words. This problem is exacerbated after transitive verbs with their direct objects. First let us consider the preposition *by* itself.

a. [PARTICLE/VERBAL]
"In a little while, however, she again heard a little pattering of footsteps in the distance, and she **looked up** eagerly."

By *form* we classified *up* as a preposition; yet, here it is carrying out a grammatical function other than signalling a noun object. In the above example, *look up* can pose a problem. Is it an intransitive two-word verb—*look up*—or is it an intransitive verb *look* plus an adverb complement *up*?

The positioning of the particle does help, because for two-word verbs the particle can generally be extra-posed to a place after words that follow. So we can have:

In a little while, however, she again heard a little pattering of footsteps in the distance, and she **looked** eagerly **up**.

Being able to reposition the particle indicates that it is a two-word verb, and not an intransitive verb plus an adverb complement. But there are *no absolutes* in language, and these are just guidelines focusing more on *position* than on *form* or *function*.

Let us consider the above example with a similar one:

a. [PARTICLE/VERBAL]
"In a little while, however, she again heard a little pattering of footsteps in the distance, and she **looked up** eagerly."

b. [PREPOSITION/NOMINAL]
"'You're crazy!' cried Helen, as Bo **looked up** the slope, searching for open ground."

Here we have the same preposition/particle *up*, following a verbal in both cases, but in one case preceding an adverbial and in the other preceding a nominal. What is the role of *up* in each of these? In the first example, the following adverbial indicates that *up* is part of the predicate and therefore a verbal; in the second example the following nominal suggests that it may be a connector and form a prepositional phrase.

We saw above that the particle *up* could be repositioned after a following word. If this were applied to our second example, we would have:

*"You're crazy!" cried Helen, as Bo **looked** the slope **up**, searching for open ground.

The sentence would be ungrammatical because the particle cannot be repositioned; therefore, it is not a participle but rather a preposition introducing a prepositional phrase—*up the slope*.

Present participles and gerunds

Present participles and gerunds are frequently confused because they both are verbals with *-ing* suffixes. Grammatical position is the key to separating these verbals.

a. [NOMINAL POSITION/GERUND]
   "Without **waiting** to observe the effect of my shot I left the house."

b. [ADJECTIVAL POSITION/PRESENT PARTICIPLE]
   "Lillian told Julia she was going over to the hospital, to sit all night in the **waiting** room."

c. [ADVERBIAL POSITION/PRESENT PARTICIPLE]
   "Mrs. Morel sat **waiting**."

In the first example, *waiting* comes after a preposition; this is a nominal position carrying out the grammatical function of object of the preposition. In the second example, *waiting* comes before a nominal, carrying out the grammatical function of modifier; this is an adjectival position. The third example shows *waiting* coming after a predicate, and functioning as an adverb complement; this is an adverbial position.

Past participles

Similarly, past participles can often be confusing. Consider the many grammatical positions of the past participle *discouraged*.

a. [ADJECTIVAL POSITION/COMPLEMENT]
   "I got **discouraged** long ago of anybody's ever making it out."

b. [ADJECTIVAL POSITION/MODIFIER]
   "David sighed in a **discouraged** way."

c. [VERBAL POSITION/PREDICATE] OR [ADJECTIVAL POSITION/COMPLEMENT]
   "Fortunately we were not **discouraged**, and we determined to try again."

d. [VERBAL POSITION/PREDICATE]
   "To say he **discouraged** me in so doing would be saying the rain is wet."

In the first example, *discouraged* follows a linking verb carrying out the grammatical function of subjective complement/predicate adjective. If we did not know the function, the position following a linking verb can only be nominal or adjectival. *Discouraged* is not a noun, so it must be an adjective. In the second example, *discouraged* precedes a nominal, and the position preceding a nominal is generally adjectival. Its function then is as an adjective modifier. In the third example, *discouraged* could again be an adjectival with a complement function, or it could be seen as part of a passive construction and thus verbal. In the fourth example, *discouraged* is clearly carrying out a predicate function and is therefore in a verbal position.

Subjects: noun, infinitive, and gerund phrases

By form we have no difficulty distinguishing among noun, infinitive, and gerund phrases. However, by function we may have some difficulty, especially with infinitives because they can carry out a few grammatical functions.

a. [NOMINAL POSITION/SUBJECT/NOUN PHRASE]
"**The only trees in flower *were*** the cherries, plums, and certain sorts of apples."

b. [NOMINAL POSITION/SUBJECT/INFINITIVE PHRASE]
"**To do** otherwise ***would not complement*** the personality of this band, or the intent of its members."

c. [NOMINAL POSITION/SUBJECT/GERUND PHRASE]
"**The Supreme Court's ruling *invalidated*** the Nov. 21 vote."

In each of these examples the form of the phrase differs and could cause problems. However, if we first consider their grammatical position, we can see that it is nominal. Coming before the predicate, the nominal position carries the grammatical function of subject.

Direct objects: noun, infinitive, and gerund phrases

Similarly for the direct object, each of these phrases can also occur in that position, as well.

a. [NOMINAL POSITION/DIRECT OBJECT/NOUN PHRASE]
"Richard and I had discovered **this tight little piece of land**."

b. [NOMINAL POSITION/DIRECT OBJECT/INFINITIVE PHRASE]
"I turned hastily round and found at my elbow a pretty little girl, who begged **to be directed to a certain street at a considerable distance**."

c. [NOMINAL POSITION/DIRECT OBJECT/GERUND PHRASE]
"Hale stopped **speaking**, and stood **staring** at the rocker."

The above words and phrases differ considerably by form, and because of this their function may be in doubt. However, if we recognize their position after a transitive verb, identifying their function as direct objects should follow.

Extra-posed subjects

a. [NOMINAL POSITION/EXTRA-POSED SUBJECT]
"**It** is interesting **that an early critic who wrote on 'Buddhist Economics' was a conservative Catholic**."

"**It** is ironic **that Bach's music, so completely biblical and evangelical, is now performed in secular environments such as concert halls**."

"**It** seems likely **that the 1992 UVa copy is the same transcription**."

In examples such as these, the expletive *it* appears to be the subject of the sentence because it occupies the nominal position, appearing just before the predicate. To deal with possible confusion, we should try to identify the verb type. This will help to determine the constituents that follow the predicate.

We have here the verb *to be* used in the first two examples and the verb *seems* in the third example; these are linking verbs, requiring a complement. Because a complement must follow, we need to identify the words following the linking verbs by *form*, which are, *interesting*, *ironic*, and *likely*, and these are all adjectives. As adjectives, we know they occupy the adjectival position. Next we focus on the *that* clauses, which follow the adjectives. These are noun clauses, because the conjunctions have no grammatical roles within the clauses other than as connector. As noun clauses they occupy nominal positions, which sheds light on our current question. Are they objects? No, they are not objects: we have here linking verbs, and we have just seen that they take complements. The link has then to be made between the expletive *it* and the noun clause, which should suggest an extra-posed subject.

Extra-posed objects

a. [NOMINAL POSITION/EXTRA-POSED OBJECT]
"I thought **it** odd **that anyone else should be in there**."

"It makes **it** more likely **that these cases will actually get to trial**."

"But Kidd made **it** clear **that he had kept up with everything said about him in his absence**."

Extra-posed objects follow a similar pattern as for extra-posed subjects. In each example above we have a predicate used transitively, *thought*, *makes*, and *made*. The direct object in each case is *it*, which is actually an expletive, occupying a nominal position. As above we need to account for the noun clauses and their constituent roles within the sentences. Again, a link has to be made between the expletive *it* and the noun clause, which should suggest an extra-posed direct object.

VERBALS

Infinitives

Grammatical position can be very helpful in identifying the function of infinitives. We have already seen that infinitives, for example, can occupy nominal, adjectival, and adverbial positions, which can cause some confusion. Let us review some examples of the infinitive in these positions.

a. [NOMINAL POSITION/SUBJECT/INFINITIVE PHRASE]
"**To be caught** at the end *is* at least no worse than to be caught at the beginning."

b. [ADJECTIVAL POSITION/MODIFIER/INFINITIVE PHRASE]
"My steel-city wife and suburbanite teen-aged children were remarkably *unanxious* **to witness this aspect of my past**."

c. [ADVERBIAL POSITION/COMPLEMENT/INFINITIVE]
"I mean calling him 'daddy' *seemed* **to kind of take the cuss off the situation**."

In the first example, the occurrence of an infinitive phrase initially in the sentence, where the subject generally is found, tips us off to its possible nominal position: hence we can note its use as subject. The second example places the infinitive phrase after an adjective, suggesting its function in modifying an adjective. The third example places an infinitive phrase immediately after a linking verb, noting a subjective complement/predicate noun and a nominal position. Where does the confusion occur? Consider the next examples.

a. [ADVERBIAL POSITION/MODIFIER/INFINITIVE PHRASE]
"**To save the country from civil war**, Pilatus finally sacrificed his prisoner, Joshua, who behaved with great dignity and who forgave all those who hated him."

Here the infinitive phrase occurs initially as the first example above; however, it is separated from the rest of the sentence by a comma. Instead of being in a nominal position, it is actually in an adverbial position as a sentence modifier.

b. [NOMINAL POSITION/DIRECT OBJECT/INFINITIVE PHRASE]
"One mother about to be deported to Nicaragua last year *was told* **to leave** her four children with her husband."

If we compare the infinitive in this second example with (c) above, *seemed to kind of take the cuss off the situation*, we might ask: is this a nominal/direct object or, as in (c), is it an adverbial complement? Again, we have to know the verb type to answer the question. In example (c) *seemed* is a linking verb taking a complement, whereas *was told* is a transitive verb requiring a direct object.

Gerunds and participles

We have already seen that participles can be confused with gerunds by form; however, they can also be confused by function because participles can modify nouns and their replacements, as well as verbs and adverbs. Hence their position can be either adjectival or adverbial.

a. [ADJECTIVAL POSITION/MODIFIER]
"I can see him now, with his **hunting** shirt and leggings and moccasins; his powder horn, engraved with wondrous scenes; his bullet pouch and tomahawk and **hunting** knife."

b. [ADVERBIAL POSITION/MODIFIER]
"'It is Mr. Jadwin,' murmured Page, **looking quickly away**."

In the first example, the participle *hunting* precedes the nouns *shirt and knife*; this is an adjectival position for modifiers. In the second sentence, the participle *looking* precedes an adverb; this is an adverbial position for modifiers.

Knowing grammatical positions does not solve all of these overlaps; but of the three—form, function, and position—it is position, along with one or the other, that most often solves the confusion.

Prepositional phrases

Prepositional phrases can also cause problems with regards to form and function. By form they have the same structure and classification; by function they can be adjective or adverb modifiers or an adverb complements. The grammatical position, however, will make the distinction.

a. [ADJECTIVAL POSITION/MODIFIER]
"A **monk**, dressed in black, **with a grey head and black eyebrows**, his arms crossed over his breast, floated by him."

b. [ADVERBIAL POSITION/MODIFIER]
"Their country-place, Styles Court, had been purchased by Mr. Cavendish **early in their married life**."

C. [ADVERBIAL POSITION/COMPLEMENT]
"His wife stood smiling and waving, the boys shouting, as he disappeared **in the old rockaway down the sandy road**."

The position of the prepositional phrase after an adjective signals its function as modifier and its position as adjectival. Similarly, a prepositional phrase occurring after an adverb signals that it is a modifier by function and adverbial by position. Lastly, a prepositional phrase coming after an intransitive verb signals that it is a complement by function and adverbial by position.

❂ ❂ ❂

We now focus on our largest syntactic structure—*the sentence*. In building up to this category of analysis, we have covered sentence constituents by form, by function, and by position. Figure 9.6 illustrates the constituents of a simple sentence and identifies their grammatical forms, functions and positions.

FIGURE 9.6 ❂ SENTENCE CONSTITUENTS

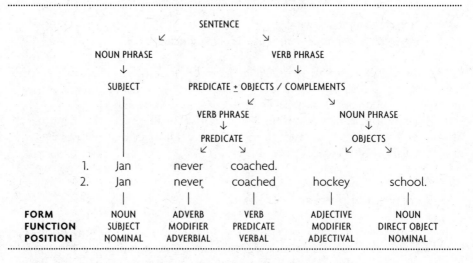

In the next chapter we turn our attention to the sentence as a complete structure, starting with the sentence as a whole and breaking it down into its possible substructures. Although we know the basic structure of the sentence is S → NP + VP + NP^2/C, we will see the many ways in which this structure can vary.

10   SENTENCES

Sentence structures are analyzed in a number of different ways, and Figure 10.1 summarizes most of these categories.

$$S \rightarrow \quad NP \quad + \quad VP \quad + \quad NP^2/C$$

FIGURE 10.1 ✿ SENTENCE STRUCTURES

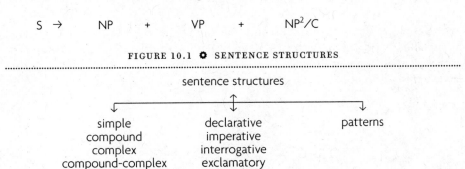

Having covered all the constituents of the sentence by *form*, *function*, and *position*, we now come to see these constituents interrelate with one another fully within the complete sentence structure. *It is the largest syntactic structure, consisting of constituents structured as a noun phrase and a verb phrase; it is not a constituent of a larger syntactic structure.* Generally, we do not write our thoughts in words or phrases, but we express them in full meaningful syntactic units—sentences. Similarly when talking, we speak our thoughts through *streams of speech*, which are more representative of sentences with completed meaning.

At this point you have already been presented with a great variety of sentence structures, varying in styles because of the many authors and their disciplines. Therefore, you already have a good basis on which to begin your analysis of the basic structures of sentences, but not the stylistic structures.

SENTENCE STRUCTURES

One common method of analyzing sentence structures is according to the *subject*, *verb*, and *object* order, which we abbreviate as *SVO*, with variations for changes in sentence patterning. Using this method of categorizing, it is generally proposed that there are six basic structures.

1. SUBJECT-VERB   →   S-V
2. SUBJECT-VERB-DIRECT OBJECT   →   S-V-DO
3. SUBJECT-VERB-INDIRECT OBJECT-DIRECT OBJECT   →   S-V-IDO-DO
4. SUBJECT-VERB-SUBJECTIVE COMPLEMENT/PREDICATE NOUN   →   S-V-SC/p-n
5. SUBJECT-VERB-SUBJECTIVE COMPLEMENT/PREDICATE ADJECTIVE   →   S-V-SC/p-a
6. SUBJECT-VERB-DIRECT OBJECT-COMPLEMENTS   →   S-V-DO-C

Another more traditional way has been to identify sentences as *simple*, *compound*, *complex*, and *complex-compound*. This is a more interesting approach to identifying these structures, because it tells us something about the structure as a whole.

Simple sentences

Simple sentences consist of only one independent clause, having a noun phrase and a verb phrase with a finite verb. Although the noun phrase/subject is not evident in imperative sentences, it is understood. Typically, sentences also have a second noun phrase or complement.

$$S \rightarrow \quad NP \quad + \quad VP \quad \pm \quad NP^2/C$$
$$ Sj P$$

a. [SIMPLE SENTENCE: TRANSITIVE VERB/DIRECT OBJECT]
   "I have described my critique as Buddhist-Christian."

b. [SIMPLE SENTENCE: INTRANSITIVE VERB]
   "The papers have been edited."

c. [SIMPLE SENTENCE: INTRANSITIVE VERB/COMPLEMENT]
   "Fireworks crackled in Kiev's Independence Square."

d. [SIMPLE SENTENCE: LINKING VERB/COMPLEMENT]
   "Canadians remain confident."

Compound sentences

Compound sentences contain two or more independent clauses linked by a coordinating conjunction. Because these independent clauses are identical to those of simple sentences, their structural variations are the same.

$$S \rightarrow \quad NP \quad + \quad VP \quad \pm \quad NP^2/C$$
$$ Sj P$$

connector

$$S \rightarrow \quad NP \quad + \quad VP \quad \pm \quad NP^2/C$$
$$ Sj P$$

a. [COMPOUND SENTENCE: TRANSITIVE VERBS/DIRECT OBJECTS]
   "I knew the accents."
   and
   I could still use the local vocabulary."

b. [COMPOUND SENTENCE: INTRANSITIVE VERBS]
   "They do not change,
   but
   our ways of perceiving and talking about them change."

c. [COMPOUND SENTENCE: LINKING VERBS/COMPLEMENTS]
   "John Flaxman's engravings from the *Iliad* are paradigms of Neoclassical clarity,
   yet
   [they] are wonderfully evocative."

Complex sentences

Complex sentences consist of an independent clause and at least one dependent clause, often more than one. It is difficult to set a pattern for the complex sentence, because the dependent clause may occur anywhere within the sentence structure. It may be a noun, relative adjective, relative adverb, or adverb clause; so, it may be found in any of the grammatical positions covering the grammatical functions for these constituents. The following sentence structures will be a representative illustration of some of these patterns.

$$S \rightarrow NP \quad + \quad VP \quad \pm \quad NP^2/C$$
$$ Sj P$$

$$cn \quad s \rightarrow np \quad + \quad vp \quad \pm \quad np^2/c$$
$$ sj p$$

a. [COMPLEX SENTENCE: NOUN CLAUSE/SUBJECT]
   "**What** we want to know
        is the nature of our proposed involvement."

b. [COMPLEX SENTENCE: NOUN CLAUSE/SUBJECTIVE COMPLEMENT]
   "The medical encounter or patient-doctor relationship is
        what medicine is about."

c. [COMPLEX SENTENCE: RELATIVE ADJECTIVE CLAUSE/MODIFIER]
"The class-action certified Friday by the Ontario court covers students
    who attended the Mohawk Institute from 1922 to 1969."

d. [COMPLEX SENTENCE: RELATIVE ADVERB CLAUSE/MODIFIER]
"I jumped the fence
    where the gate was low."

e. [COMPLEX SENTENCE: ADVERB CLAUSE/SENTENCE MODIFIER]
"**Although** the Red Cross criticized the lack of confidentiality,
    it agreed in the report that the medical care was of high quality."

Here are a few examples where more than one dependent clause is found within the complex sentence structure.

a. [COMPLEX SENTENCE: NOUN CLAUSE/ADVERB CLAUSE]
"Gen. Tolentino, the regional military commander, said
[**that**] it was not immediately clear
whether those 100 had died from the storm on Monday or from the
typhoon."

b. [COMPLEX SENTENCE: 2 RELATIVE ADJECTIVE CLAUSES]
"However, it was the crimes
that Mr. Rodriguez Orejuela allegedly committed from a Colombian
prison from 1999 to 2002
that led to the extradition."

In the first relative adjective clause the conjunction functions as the direct object of the clause; whereas in the second example the conjunction is the subject of the clause.

c. [COMPLEX SENTENCE: RELATIVE ADJECTIVE CLAUSE/NOUN CLAUSE/RELATIVE ADVERB CLAUSE]
"Canadian producers
who have lost some $5 billion Cdn during the 18-month ban
were disappointed
[**that**] Bush didn't give them a more definitive timetable
when he met in Ottawa this week with Prime Minister Paul Martin."

Compound-complex sentences

Compound-complex sentences consist of a combination of two or more independent clauses and at least one dependent clause. Again, like the complex sentence, it is difficult to give a pattern for these structures, because both the independent and dependent clauses may occur in any order within the sentence structure.

$$\text{S} \rightarrow \text{NP} + \text{VP} \pm \text{NP}^2/\text{C}$$

Sj   P

$$\textbf{cn} \quad \text{s} \rightarrow \text{np} + \text{vp} \pm \text{np}^2/\text{c}$$

sj   p

a. [COMPOUND-COMPLEX SENTENCE: 2 INDEPENDENT CLAUSES/RELATIVE ADVERB CLAUSE]
   "Henry saw it all,
   but he preserved the polite demeanor of a guest
   when a waiter spills claret down his cuff."

b. [COMPOUND-COMPLEX SENTENCE: 2 INDEPENDENT CLAUSES/NOUN CLAUSE]
   "The Chinese government said Thursday
   [that] it is testing the safety of genetically modified rice
   but denied claims by environmentalists
   that it is preparing to allow commercial sales."

c. [COMPOUND-COMPLEX SENTENCE: 3 INDEPENDENT CLAUSES/2 NOUN CLAUSES/1 ADVERB CLAUSE]
   "This 'framework of peace,'
   as it was described,
   included the assertion
   **that the ultimate decision on governing Northern Ireland would be
   made by the majority of its citizens**;
   the Republic of Ireland would, as part of an overall settlement, seek to
   revise its constitutional claim to sovereignty over Northern Ireland;
   and Britain would not block the possible reunification of Ireland
   if it was backed by a majority in the North."

SENTENCE TYPES

Apart from *sentence structures*, we also identify sentences by *type*; they are characterized by *form*. We have covered features of these sentences in our discussion of verb mood. English identifies four basic sentence types.

Declarative sentences

A simple statement, declaration or assertion is called a declarative sentence. It has a word order of *subject plus predicate plus object or complement*, which has been the same underlying structure used throughout the text. Such sentences can be either affirmative or negative.

$$\text{S} \rightarrow \text{NP} + \text{VP} \pm \text{NP}^2/\text{C}$$

Sj   P

a. [STATEMENT]

"The friends of the University in the Assembly seem to have a delicate task on their hands."

b. [DECLARATIVE]

"'I'm not going any more,' he declared."

c. [ASSERTION]

"I assure you, riding is the most healthy of exercises."

In example *a*, we have a simple statement of fact or observation; in example *b*, the statement is stronger and emphasis is indicated by the predicate *declared*. Other similar words can be used, *affirm, state, express, set down, pronounce*. Example *c* is similar to *b* in that it is the type of verb which signals the *assertion*. Here the assertion is indicated by *assure*; however, similar verbs can be used, *remark, comment, say*. An assertion appears to be a little less emphatic than a declaration.

Imperative sentences

To express a command or a request, or to forbid an action, we use an imperative sentence. They are generally used with the force of commands or directives. Such sentences can also be affirmative or negative.

a. [COMMAND]

"Open the window, then!"

"TURN round, my boy!"

b. [REQUEST]

"Oblige me!"

"Let me loose!"

c. [FORBID]

"'Don't leave me now,' he went on."

"'God forbid that he should try!' answered the black villain."

Punctuation is important in recognizing an imperative sentence; it ends in an exclamation mark (!).

Not all sentences, however, that imply commands are imperative sentences. The following, for example, are declarative sentences.

a. [DECLARATIVE]
"I want to have a talk with you."

"You should be out, whipping up the circulation like Mr. Enfield and me."

Although these are declarative sentences, there is somewhat of an implied command in their meanings.

Interrogative sentences

Interrogative sentences simply ask questions. Interrogatives can also be affirmative or negative. English distinguishes two types of interrogatives:

1. Interrogative "yes-no" questions: As indicated by its name, the question expects a simple *yes* or *no* answer. These sentences are characterized by inverted word order and the use of the auxiliary *do*.

a. [YES-NO QUESTIONS]
"Do you know why?"

"But was there a way out?"

2. *Wh*-questions: These questions are formed with interrogative pronouns. Unless the pronoun is subject of the sentence, an inverted word order is also used here.

a. [INVERTED FORMAT]
"Where had she walked that morning?"

b. [DECLARATIVE FORMAT]
"'Who has sent you so far by yourself?' said I."

English also has a *tag question* structure. This is a combination of a declarative statement followed by an inverted question that is actually tagged on. The tag structure comprises an auxiliary verb plus a pronoun. Notice that if the declarative statement is affirmative, the tag is negative, and vice versa.

a. [POSITIVE + NEGATIVE TAG]
"That is a good deal to say, don't you think?"

"You were there as a friend of young Donald, weren't you?"

b. [NEGATIVE + POSITIVE TAG]
"Your talisman didn't save you, did it?"

"But it can't be mine, can it?"

Exclamatory sentences

Exclamatory sentences denote the speaker's attitude or opinion toward the subject. Although these exclamations tend to be affirmative, negatives also occur.

a. [EXCLAMATORY]
"My God! Mr. Chace, what is the matter?"

"'But this is superb!' she cried gaily."

SENTENCE PATTERNS

A more detailed analysis of sentence structures is to identify the basic constituents according to their particular patterns. In this analysis, the verb type becomes the focus of the pattern. Consider the patterns in Figure 10.2.

Each of these divisions and substructures will now be broken down and illustrated, noting the roles and grammatical meanings for the constituents of each pattern. All structures are based on the verb type, *transitive*, *intransitive* or *linking verb*. The linking verb has three possible structures depending upon the type of complement that follows. The intransitive verb has only two possible structures both based on whether a complement follows or not. The transitive verb has three variations; however, the third pattern has eight possible variations in its fourth component. Together these structures cover the basic sentences that we use. The basic patterns may occur more than once in compound and complex sentences, but essentially it is only a duplication of a similar pattern.

FIGURE 10.2 ✿ SENTENCE PATTERNS

LINKING VERBS	1.	NP	VP / LV	SC / P-n
	2.	NP	VP / LV	SC / P-aj
	3.	NP	VP / LV	C / Av
INTRANSITIVE VERB	1.	NP	VP / InTV	
	2.	NP	VP / InTV	C / Av
TRANSITIVE VERB	1.	NP	VP / TV	NP^2
	2.	NP	VP / TV	NP^2 NP^3
	3a.	NP	VP / TV	NP^2 NP^2
	b.	NP	VP / TV	NP^2 Aj
	c.	NP	VP / TV	NP^2 Pr
	d.	NP	VP / TV	NP^2 Av (place)
	e.	NP	VP / TV	NP^2 Pp
	f.	NP	VP / TV	NP^2 Ptp
	g.	NP	VP / TV	NP^2 Prp-ph
	h.	NP	VP / TV	NP^2 I-ph + BE

Linking verbs

1. S → NP + VP + C
            Sj   LV   SC / p-n

       "The stationer   became   his banker."

FUNCTION		GRAMMATICAL MEANING
SUBJECT	The stationer	about whom an assertion is made.
PREDICATE	became	classifies.
Sj COMPLEMENT	his banker	completes the subject.

2. S → NP + VP + C
  Sj   LV   SC / p-aj

  "It   seems   hard."

FUNCTION		GRAMMATICAL MEANING
SUBJECT	It	what is described.
PREDICATE	seems	describes.
Sj COMPLEMENT	hard	completes the subject.

3. S → NP + VP + C
  Sj   LV   C / av

  "She   remained   upstairs."

FUNCTION		GRAMMATICAL MEANING
SUBJECT	She	who is identified.
PREDICATE	remained	locates.
COMPLEMENT	upstairs	completes the verb.

Intransitive verbs

1. S → NP + VP + (C)
  Sj   InTV   (C / av)

  a. "Holker   laughed...."

  b. "Holker   laughed   good-humouredly."

FUNCTION		GRAMMATICAL MEANING
SUBJECT	Holker	performer of action.
PREDICATE	laughed	independent action.
COMPLEMENT	good-humouredly	completes the verb.

Transitive verbs

1. S → NP + VP + NP^2
         Sj   TV   Do

"Alice   soon began   talking again."

FUNCTION		GRAMMATICAL MEANING
SUBJECT	Alice	performer of action.
PREDICATE	soon began	asserts an action.
COMPLEMENT	talking	affected by action.
MODIFIER	again	describes predicate.

2. S → NP + VP + NP^2 + NP^3
         Sj   TV   Ido   Do

"You   give   me   the creeps sometimes."

FUNCTION		GRAMMATICAL MEANING
SUBJECT	You	performer of action.
PREDICATE	give	asserts an action.
INDIRECT OBJECT	me	to/for whom an action is performed.
DIRECT OBJECT	the creeps	affected by action.
MODIFIER	sometimes	describes predicate.
	NP NP^2 NP^3	have different referents.

3a. S → NP + VP + NP^2 + NP^2
          Sj   TV   Do   OC

"But she   called   it   'Solitude.'"

FUNCTION		GRAMMATICAL MEANING
SUBJECT	She	performer of action.
PREDICATE	called	asserts an action.
DIRECT OBJECT	it	affected by action.
OBJ COMPLEMENT	Solitude	identifies object.

The *direct object* and the *objective complement* have the *same referent.*

All of the following variations are based on the S › NP + VP + NP² + C pattern. The only differences are found in the *complement position*.

3b.

S	→	NP	+	VP	+	NP²	+	C
		Sj		TV		Do		Aj

"Privately I   thought   it   **lucky**."

3c.

S	→	NP	+	VP	+	NP²	+	C
		Sj		TV		Do		Av(place)

"But I   found   no vacancy   **there**."

3d.

S	→	NP	+	VP	+	NP²	+	C
		Sj		TV		Do		Pp

"I just   saw   his head   **bobbing**."

3e.

S	→	NP	+	VP	+	NP²	+	C
		Sj		TV		Do		Ptp

"We   found   them   **gone**."

3f.

S	→	NP	+	VP	+	NP²	+	C
		Sj		TV		Do		Prp-ph

"He   now took   the stick   **from my hands**."

3g.

S	→	NP	+	VP	+	NP²	+	C
		Sj		TV		Do		I-ph + BE

"I   knew   him   **to be friendly**."

All of the words in the complement position suggest that an underlying infinitive phrase, *to be plus the complement*, is implied.

SENTENCE ANALYSIS

We have seen that the basic sentence S has two parts, a noun phrase NP and a verb phrase VP. Depending on the number of constituents within the sentence to be analyzed, the verb phrase VP can be further broken down into VP ± a second noun phrase NP^2 or complement C. If there are constituents occurring after the verb phrase, then one has to acknowledge them with appropriate markers. At the sentence level we must analyze all constituents.

Once the structure has been fully broken down, we identify each constituent by its form, by its grammatical function, and finally by its grammatical position. In all, after the breakdown analysis there are three identifiers: *form, function,* and *position.* Consider the following analysis:

SENTENCE
"The gorgeous night has begun again."

The gorgeous night — NOUN PHRASE

has begun again. — VERB PHRASE

	The	gorgeous	night	has	begun	again.
		gorgeous	night	has	begun	
FORM	DETERMINER	ADJECTIVE	NOUN	AUXILIARY	VERB	ADVERB
FUNCTION	MODIFIER	MODIFIER	SUBJECT	PRIMARY	PREDICATE	COMPLEMENT
POSITION	ADJECTIVAL	ADJECTIVAL	NOMINAL	VERBAL	VERBAL	ADVERBIAL

Here are some further examples. Each of the following sentences focuses on a particular phrase as part of the sentence structure.

1. Sentence with a gerund phrase

SENTENCE
"Her mother's fetching simply meant one more to fetch."

Her mother's fetching — NOUN PHRASE

simply meant one more to fetch. — VERB PHRASE / NOUN PHRASE^2

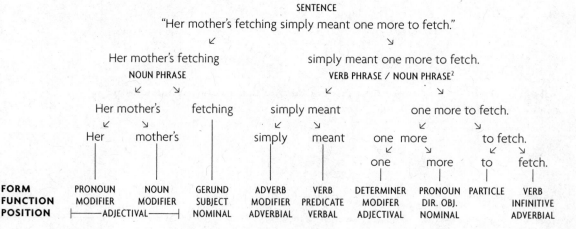

	Her	mother's	fetching	simply	meant	one	more	to	fetch.
FORM	PRONOUN	NOUN	GERUND	ADVERB	VERB	DETERMINER	PRONOUN	PARTICLE	VERB
FUNCTION	MODIFIER	MODIFIER	SUBJECT	MODIFIER	PREDICATE	MODIFER	DIR. OBJ.		INFINITIVE
POSITION	ADJECTIVAL		NOMINAL	ADVERBIAL	VERBAL	ADJECTIVAL	NOMINAL		ADVERBIAL

2. Sentence with an extended verb phrase

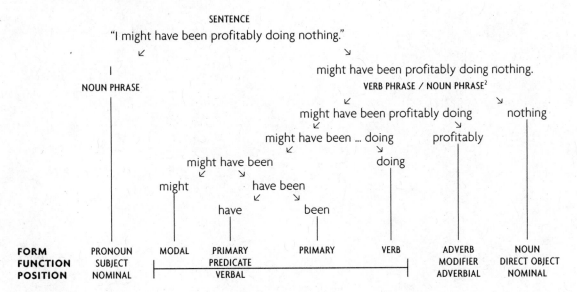

3. Sentence with a dependent clause

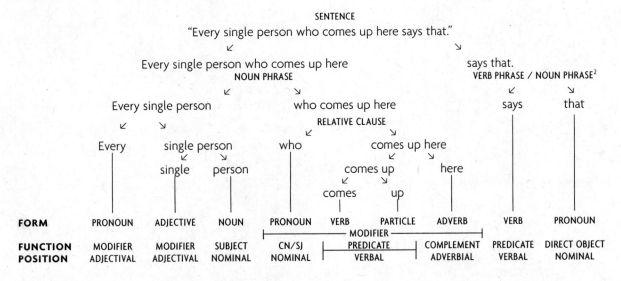

Many variations of sentences could be presented here for more complex structures. The purpose of this chapter, however, is to introduce you only to the more simple structures. The more complex structures belong to another category of language analysis.

appendices

APPENDIX A

GRAMMATICAL TERMS SUMMARY

FORMS	FUNCTIONS	POSITIONS
WORDS		
nouns	subject	nominal
verbs	predicate	verbal
adjectives	direct object	adjectival
adverbs	indirect object	adverbial
pronouns	objects of prepositions	
determiners	adjective modifiers	
auxiliaries	adverb modifiers	
prepositions	prepositional modifiers	
conjunctions	subjective complement	
	objective complement	
	adverb complement	
	connectors	
	appositives	
PHRASES		
noun		
adjective		
verb		
adverb		
participle		
gerund		
infinitive		
prepositional		
absolute		
CLAUSES		
noun		
relative adjective		
relative adverb		
adverb		

GRAMMATICAL FUNCTIONS SUMMARY

FORMS	FUNCTIONS	POSITIONS
1. nouns	subjects direct objects indirect objects objects of prepositions subjective complements objective complements appositives	nominal
2. pronouns	subjects direct objects indirect objects objects of prepositions subjective complements objective complements connectors appositives	nominal
3. noun phrases	subjects direct objects indirect objects objects of prepositions subjective complements objective complements appositives	nominal
4. noun clauses	subjects direct objects indirect objects objects of prepositions subjective complements objective complements appositives	nominal
5. gerunds	subjects direct objects indirect objects objects of prepositions subjective complements objective complements	nominal

FORMS	FUNCTIONS	POSITIONS
6. infinitives	subjects direct objects modifiers adverb complements	nominal adverbial
7. verbs auxiliaries	predicates	verbal
8. adjectives adjective phrases	modifiers subjective complements	adjectival
9. participles participle phrases prepositional phrases relative adjective clauses	modifiers subjective complements	adjectival
10. adverbs adverb phrases participles participle phrases prepositional phrases relative adverb clauses adverb clauses	modifiers adverb complements	adverbial
11. absolute phrases	modifiers	adverbial
12. determiners	modifiers	adjectival
13. conjunctions	connectors	nominal[1]

1 If the conjunction is relative and, therefore, has a grammatical function within its clause, relative conjunctions can occupy nominal positions.

APPENDIX B

IRREGULAR VERBS

The following is a list of irregular verbs still in use in Modern English.

	PRESENT	PAST	PAST PARTICIPLE
1.	arise	arose	arisen
2.	awake	awoke	awaked
3.	be	was	been
4.	bear	bore	borne
5.	beat	beat	beaten
6.	become	became	become
7.	begin	began	begun
8.	bend	bent	bent
9.	beseech	besought	besought
10.	bid	bade or bid	bidden
		bid	bid
11.	bind	bound	bound
12.	bite	bit	bitten
13.	bleed	bled	bled
14.	blow	blew	blown
15.	break	broke	broken
16.	bring	brought	brought
17.	broadcast	broadcast	broadcast
		broadcasted	broadcasted
18.	build	built	built
19.	burn	burned	burned
		burnt	burnt
20.	burst	burst	burst
21.	buy	bought	bought
22.	catch	caught	caught
23.	choose	chose	chosen
24.	cling	clung	clung
25.	come	came	come

PRESENT	PAST	PAST PARTICIPLE
26. deal	dealt	dealt
27. dig	dug	dug
28. dive	dove	dove
	dived	dived
29. do	did	done
30. draw	drew	drawn
31. drink	drank	drunk
32. drive	drove	driven
33. eat	ate	eaten
34. fall	fell	fallen
35. feed	fed	fed
36. fight	fought	fought
37. find	found	found
38. flee	fled	fled
39. fling	flung	flung
40. fly	flew	flown
41. forbid	forbad(e)	forbidden
42. forget	forgot	forgotten
43. forsake	forsook	forsaken
44. freeze	froze	frozen
45. get	got	got
		gotten
46. give	gave	given
47. go	went	gone
48. grind	ground	ground
49. grow	grew	grown
50. hang	hanged	hanged
51. hang	hung	hung
52. hold	held	held
53. kneel	knelt	knelt
	kneeled	kneeled
54. know	knew	known
55. lay	laid	laid
56. lead	led	led
57. lean	leaned	leaned
	leant	leant
58. leap	leaped	leaped
	leapt	leapt
59. learn	learned	learned
	learnt	learnt
60. leave	left	left
61. lend	lent	lent
62. let	let	let
63. lie	lay	lain

PRESENT	PAST	PAST PARTICIPLE
64. lie	lied	lied
65. light	lighted	lighted
	lit	lit
66. lose	lost	lost
67. mean	meant	meant
68. meet	met	met
69. pay	paid	paid
70. prove	proved	proved
71. read	read	read
72. ride	rode	ridden
73. ring	rang	rung
74. rise	rose	risen
75. run	ran	run
76. say	said	said
77. see	saw	seen
78. seek	sought	sought
79. sell	sold	sold
80. set	set	set
81. sew	sewed	sewed
		sewn
82. shake	shook	shaken
83. shoot	shot	shot
84. show	showed	shown
	showed	
85. shrink	shrank	shrunk
86. sing	sang	sung
87. sink	sank	sunk
88. sit	sat	sat
89. slay	slew	slain
90. sleep	slept	slept
91. slide	slid	slid
92. slink	slunk	slunk
93. smite	smote	smitten
94. sow	sowed	sowed
		sown
95. speak	spoke	spoken
96. split	split	split
97. spring	sprang	sprung
98. steal	stole	stolen
99. stick	stuck	stuck
100. sting	stung	stung
101. stink	stank	stunk
	stunk	
102. stride	strode	stridden

PRESENT	PAST	PAST PARTICIPLE
103. string	strung	strung
104. strive	strove	striven
	strived	strived
105. swear	swore	sworn
106. sweat	sweat	sweat
	sweated	sweated
107. swim	swam	swum
108. swing	swung	swung
109. take	took	taken
110. teach	taught	taught
111. tear	tore	torn
112. tell	told	told
113. throw	threw	thrown
114. tread	trod	trodden
		trod
115. wake	waked	waked
		woke
116. wear	wore	worn
117. weave	wove	woven
		wove
118. win	won	won
119. wring	wrung	wrung
120. write	wrote	written

GLOSSARY

ABLAUT WORD or *gradation* is a morphological process (internal modification) taking place in irregular verbs to extend grammatical meaning, producing different forms in the paradigm of the same word.

ABSOLUTE PHRASES are cohesive word groups not linked to the main clause syntactically or semantically by shared elements.

ABSTRACT NOUNS refer to concepts, qualities, and states.

ACTIVE VOICE describes a verbal category concerned with the relationship of subject and object; the action is expressed by the transitive verb.

ADJECTIVAL MODIFIERS occupy pre- or post-position modifying nouns, pronouns, and other adjectives.

ADJECTIVAL POSITION is reserved for words carrying out the function of a modifier as attributed to an adjective.

ADJECTIVE PHRASES are cohesive word groups that are often little more than a series of adjectives or words that go with adjectives to modify nouns or their replacements.

ADJECTIVES are form class words completing the paradigm of inflections, *-er* (or *more*) for the comparative, and *-est* (or *most*) for the superlative.

ADVERB CLAUSE is a subject and predicate (finite verb) structure carrying out the grammatical function attributed to adverbs. It is introduced by words such as *before*, *after*, *because*, or phrases, *as if*, *even if*, *as long as*.

ADVERB COMPLEMENT has the grammatical meaning of one that completes.

ADVERB MODIFIERS occupy pre- or post-modifying positions, referring to circumstances such as *how*, *why*, or *when*.

ADVERB PHRASES are cohesive word groups focusing on adverbs as their head word.

ADVERBIAL NOUNS occupy an adverbial position and carry out the grammatical function attributed to adverbs.

ADVERBIAL POSITION is reserved for words carrying out the function of a modifier as attributed to adverbs.

ADVERBS are form class words generally noted by the derivational suffixes -*ly*, -*wise*, and -*ward*.

AFFIX is a collective term for prefixes and suffixes, which means the adding of morphemes to a base or stem of a word.

AGENT is the initiator of the action in a passive sentence.

AGREEMENT is the relationship between two or more sentence constituents.

AMBIGUITY occurs when a structure has more than one possible lexical and/or structural meaning.

ANTECEDENT is the noun or nominal that a pronoun stands for.

APPOSITION has the grammatical meaning *that which renames*. An appositive is a referent to the nominal it qualifies.

ARTICLES are structure class words. The indefinite article, *a(n)*, marks only countable nouns; the definite article, *the*, marks all classes of nouns. They are also classified as *determiners*.

ASPECT expresses grammatical meanings concerned with the continuity or distribution of events in time.

AUXILIARIES are structure class words making distinctions for tense, aspect, and voice in the verb phrase.

BASE is a lexical morpheme minus all affixes.

BASE VERB or lexical verb is the uninflected form of the verb; for all verbs except *be*, it is the simple present tense.

BOUND MORPHEMES do not stand alone with meaning; they join other free or bound morphemes to create a word.

CASE is a grammatical category for inflected nouns and mostly personal pronouns showing their relationships to other sentence constituents.

CLAUSES are independent and dependent structures, consisting of a noun phrase and a finite verb phrase, that is, a subject and a predicate.

COLLECTIVE NOUNS refer to a group of persons, things or ideas.

COMMAND. See Imperative Mood.

COMMON NOUNS designate a general class of objects or concepts.

COMPARATIVE is an inflectional marker of adjectives and adverbs, noted by *-er*, this inflection can be replaced in many cases with *more*.

COMPLEMENT has the grammatical meaning of that which identifies or completes.

COMPLEMENT OF A NOUN is a noun clause, which follows a noun but behaves like a direct object of a predicate corresponding to the noun.

COMPLEMENT OF AN ADJECTIVE is a noun clause, which directly follows and completes an adjective.

COMPLEX SENTENCES consist of only one independent clause and at least one dependent clause.

COMPOUND SENTENCES contain two or more independent clauses linked by a coordinating conjunction.

COMPOUND-COMPLEX SENTENCES have two or more independent clauses and at least one dependent clause.

CONCRETE NOUNS indicate material substance.

CONJUNCTIONS are structure class words identifying *subordination, coordination,* and *conjunctiveness.*

CONJUNCTIVE ADVERBS, like coordinating conjunctions, join units of equal value but they do so with adverbial emphasis.

CONNECTORS are structure class conjunctions, used to note subordination, coordination, and conjunctiveness. The connector has the grammatical meaning of that which connects.

CONSTITUENTS are component parts of a larger syntactic structure which we analyze by grammatical form, function, and position.

COORDINATING CONJUNCTIONS join units of equal value.

CORRELATIVE CONJUNCTIONS are two-part conjunctions that connect both complete sentences and units within sentences.

COUNTABLE NOUNS are nouns where the total is determined by counting; non-countable nouns are those that cannot be similarly counted.

DECLARATIVE SENTENCES make a declaration as in a statement, contrasting with a command, a question or an exclamation.

DEFINITE ARTICLE, *the*, is a determiner that signals a forthcoming noun, specific or previously mentioned.

DEGREE is a feature of adjectives and adverbs, having forms for the positive, the comparative, and the superlative degrees.

DEMONSTRATIVE PRONOUNS, *this*, *that*, *these* and *those*, substitute for nouns and carry out the role of determiner, signaling a forthcoming noun.

DEPENDENT CLAUSES are subject and predicate (finite verb) structures needing a second clause structure for completed meaning.

DERIVATIONAL AFFIXES are bound morphemes added to bases or stems to create new words from pre-existing ones, and sometimes to change word class category.

DESCRIPTIVE means recording actual usage and observing how sentences are generated and understood.

DETERMINERS are structure class words signalling a forthcoming noun or noun phrase.

DIRECT OBJECT undergoes the action of transitive verbs. Its grammatical meaning is that which undergoes the action of the predicate, or is affected by it.

EXCLAMATORY SENTENCES note the attitude or opinion of the speaker, and are marked by the exclamation mark.

EXPLETIVES, *it* and *there*, are dummy words which have structural rather than lexical functions; we use them to replace the extra-posed subject or object.

FINITE VERBS express tense and are marked for person and number; non-finite verbs express aspect and voice.

FORM is what a constituent IS, the simplest mode of classification, the shape or appearance of a linguistic unit.

FORM CLASS WORDS readily admit new members such as nouns, verbs, adjectives, or adverbs.

FREE MORPHEMES can stand alone with meaning.

FUNCTION is what a constituent DOES, along with its syntactic relationship to other constituents within that sentence.

GENDER is a grammatical category noting masculine, feminine and neuter natural genders.

GERUND PHRASES are cohesive word groups with a non-finite -*ing* verb as head word.

GERUNDS are -*ing* verb forms that can replace nouns or nominals.

GRAMMAR. See Syntax.

GRAMMATICAL FUNCTION. See Function.

GRAMMATICAL MEANING concerns the relationships of words within sentences.

GRAMMATICAL POSITION. See Position.

HEAD WORDS (HW) are focused words around which phrases develop. HN means head noun of a noun phrase; HV means head verb of a verb phrase; HG is the head gerund of a gerund phrase, etc.

IMPERATIVE MOOD denotes the mood of a verb that expresses a command.

INDEFINITE ARTICLES, *a* or *an*, mark an unspecified countable noun.

INDEFINITE PRONOUNS form a class of words, which replace nouns without specifying which noun—often identified as specifiers and quantifiers.

INDEFINITE RELATIVE PRONOUNS end in an -*ever* suffix, for example, *whichever.* They have indefinite referents and introduce relative adjectival clauses.

INDEPENDENT CLAUSES are subject and finite verb structures that stand alone with completed meaning.

INDICATIVE MOOD states a fact or asks a question, not probability.

INDIRECT OBJECT is the second of two objects that follow transitive verbs. Its grammatical meaning is *to* or *from whom the action is performed*.

INFINITIVES are the stem forms of verbs preceded by the particle *to*, for example, *to + verb talk = to talk*; they are not limited by person, number or tense.

INFINITIVES are base forms of verbs not limited by person, number or tense, and therefore, they are also non-finite verbs. They consist of at least two words and are actually phrases by form.

INFLECTIONAL AFFIXES are bound morphemes occurring after a base or stem to extend the grammatical meaning, producing different forms in the paradigm of the same word.

INTENSIFIERS are structure-class words that qualify or intensify adjectives or adverbs.

INTENSIVE PRONOUN. See Reflexive pronouns.

INTERROGATIVE PRONOUNS, *who, whose, whom, which* and *what*, are used to ask questions.

INTRANSITIVE VERBS do not require an object, but they often take complements.

IRREGULAR ADJECTIVES have some similarities in the comparative and superlative forms, but they are generally distinctive in the positive.

IRREGULAR ADVERBS have some similarities in the comparative and superlative forms, but they are generally distinctive in the positive.

IRREGULAR NOUNS are: (1) nouns without singulars, (2) nouns with singular and plural forms alike, (3) irregular plural nouns, and (4) foreign inflections.

IRREGULAR VERBS have past tenses and past participles that do not follow the regular verb paradigm. Many take an ablaut change, and/or a past tense/participle suffix in *-d*, *-t*, or *-en*.

LEXICAL MEANING is the denotative or dictionary meaning that a speaker attaches to actual objects, events, actions, etc.

LEXICON OR VOCABULARY consists of words that make up a language.

LINKING VERBS express states rather than actions. They link the subject and complement, which have the same referent.

MAIN or **LEXICAL VERB** is the head verb.

MANNER ADVERBS (adverbs of manner) generally ending in -*ly*, focus on *how* or in *what manner* a predication is carried out.

MASS NOUNS. See Non-countable nouns.

MODAL AUXILIARIES are adjunct verbs noting such features as *probability, possibility, obligation.*

MODIFIERS give grammatical or lexical information about other words in the sentence; they have the grammatical meaning that they modify, limit or add to the meaning of a word(s). This is applicable to all words, phases and clauses that hold either adjectival or adverbial positions.

MOOD (*mode*) is the grammatical distinction in a verb form that expresses fact (*indicative*), command (*imperative*), condition contrary to fact (*subjunctive*), and probability or possibility (*conditional*).

MORPHEME ANALYSIS is the process of breaking words down into their individual morphemes and identifying them accordingly.

MORPHEME VARIANTS are contextual variations of morphemes.

MORPHEMES are the lowest standing meaningful units in our grammatical system from which words are composed and grammatical meaning extended.

MORPHOLOGICAL PROCESSES are umlauts and ablauts (internal modifications) taking place in irregular nouns and verbs respectively to extend grammatical meaning, producing different forms in the paradigm of the same word.

MORPHOLOGY is the branch of grammar concerned with the analysis of structure and the internal patterning of words, their bases and their affixes, that is, the study of morphemes.

NOMINAL POSITION is reserved for nouns, noun phrases and clauses, and their replacements.

NON-COUNTABLE NOUNS refer to mass or abstraction.

NON-FINITE VERBS express aspect and voice; they do not express person or tense.

NON-RESTRICTIVE CLAUSES do not restrict the word, phrase or clause they modify; also, they are set off by commas.

NOUN CLAUSES are subject and predicate (finite verb) structures carrying out the grammatical functions attributed to a noun.

NOUN PHRASES (NP) are cohesive word groups focusing on a head noun or its replacement.

NOUNS are form class words generally completing the paradigm of inflections: *-s* plurality, *'s* singular possessive and *'s* or *s'* plural possessive.

NUMBER is a grammatical category referring to singular and plural. Singular is used when one person is speaking or is made reference to; the plural is used when more than one person is speaking or is made reference to.

OBJECT OF THE PREPOSITION has the grammatical meaning of that which relates to a noun or its replacement.

OBJECTIVE CASE is the grammatical role of a noun or nominal functioning as direct object, indirect object, objective complement, or object of the preposition.

OBJECTIVE COMPLEMENT has the grammatical meaning of that which describes or identifies a direct object.

PARADIGM is an example or model of the variations of a base.

PARALLEL STRUCTURES have coordinated grammatical parts.

PARTICIPLE PHRASES are cohesive word groups, consisting of non-finite verb forms, present or past participles, as head words.

PARTICIPLES are non-finite forms of the verb paradigm with the present participle ending in *-ing* and the past participle ending with an *-en* or *-ed*.

PARTICLES are words similar to monosyllabic prepositions that join verbs to form a phrasal verb.

PASSIVE or **INACTIVE VOICE** is a feature of transitive sentences in which the grammatical subject of the predicate becomes the goal of the expressed action.

PAST PARTICIPLE is a non-finite form of the verb paradigm. It is noted by an *-en* or *-ed* suffix.

PAST TENSE is the *-ed* form of the verb and usually denotes a specific past action.

PERIPHRASTIC POSSESSIVE is used to attribute possessiveness to inanimate things. It is expressed in the form of a prepositional phrase.

PERSON is a grammatical category that points out the speaker (*first person*), the person or thing spoken to (*second person*), and the person or thing spoken of (*third person*).

PERSONAL PRONOUNS name specific persons or things.

PHONETICS is the system that records the actual sounds of speech.

PHONOLOGY is the study of sounds.

PHRASAL VERBS consist of a verb plus a particle having a combined meaning different from its individual parts. They are sometimes called two-word verbs.

PHRASES are cohesive word groups forming full syntactic units.

PLURAL (plurality) is a characteristic of nouns and pronouns denoting more than one. Nouns are marked by the inflectional ending *-s* (or *-es*).

POSITION (grammatical position) marks sentence constituents based on their form and function.

POSITIVE DEGREE. See Degree.

POSSESSIVE CASE is the inflected form of nouns and pronouns indicating ownership.

PREDICATE is the second of two essential grammatical functions of a sentence structure, having the grammatical meaning of that which asserts, describes, or identifies.

PREDICATE ADJECTIVES are subjective complements occurring after linking verbs.

PREDICATE NOMINATIVES or nouns are subjective complements occurring after linking verbs.

PREFIXES are bound morphemes added to the beginning of a base or stem to form new words from preexisting ones.

PREPOSITIONAL PHRASES are cohesive word groups forming syntactic units, consisting of a preposition plus a head noun or its replacement.

PREPOSITIONS are structure words introducing a phrase structure.

PRESCRIPTIVE GRAMMAR focuses on a set of rules dictating *correct usage* and how language *ought* to be used.

PRESENT PARTICIPLE is a non-finite form of the verb paradigm. It is noted by an *-ing* suffix.

PRESENT TENSE marks a present point in time, a habitual action, or the *timeless* present.

PRIMARY AUXILIARY VERBS, *be* and *have*, are adjunct verbs used to mark *tense*, *aspect*, *mood*, and *voice*.

PRONOUN–ANTECEDENT AGREEMENT. See Subject–Predicate agreement.

PRONOUNS are structure class words substituting for nouns.

PROPER NOUNS refer to specific persons, places, things, or concepts. Proper nouns are capitalized.

RECIPROCAL PRONOUNS, *each other* and *one another*, refer to previously named nouns or pronouns.

REFERENT is the person or thing a word names or refers to.

REFLEXIVE PRONOUNS refer back or intensify something.

REGULAR VERBS form the verb paradigm: *stem*, *third person singular*, *present participle*, *past tense* and *past participle*.

RELATIVE ADJECTIVE CLAUSES are subject and predicate (finite verb) structures carrying out the grammatical functions attributed to an adjectival.

RELATIVE ADVERB CLAUSES are subject and predicate (finite verb) structures carrying out the grammatical functions attributed to an adverbial.

RELATIVE ADVERBS are *where*, *when*, and *why*, and they are used to introduce adjectival clauses.

RELATIVE PRONOUNS, *who* (*whom, whose*), *which*, and *that*, relate or refer back to other words in the sentence, and they are used to introduce relative adjectival clauses.

RESTRICTIVE CLAUSES add essential information to what they modify. The restrictive modifier is *not* set off by commas.

SEMANTICS is the system and study of meaning in language.

SENTENCE is the largest syntactic structure, consisting of constituents structured as a noun phrase and a verb phrase; it is not a constituent of a larger syntactic structure.

SENTENCE MODIFIERS are words, phrases, or clauses that modify the sentence as a whole. They are separated from the rest of the sentence by commas.

SENTENCE PATTERNS are the simple skeletal structures, made up of required elements, that underlie the sentence.

SINGULAR, as opposed to plural, is characteristic of nouns and pronouns denoting one referent.

STEM is the lexical morpheme with or without affixes.

STRUCTURE CLASS WORDS are small, *closed* classes that explain grammatical relationships of the form class words.

SUBJECT is the first of two essential grammatical functions of a sentence structure, having the grammatical meanings of that which performs, describes, identifies or asserts.

SUBJECTIVE CASE is the grammatical role of a noun or noun substitute in its grammatical function as subject of the sentence.

SUBJECTIVE COMPLEMENT has the grammatical meaning of that which follows a linking verb and has the same referent as the subject.

SUBJECT-PREDICATE AGREEMENT occurs when a third-person singular subject in the present tense takes the *-s* form of the verb or when a plural subject takes the stem form. Pronoun-antecedent agreement occurs when the number of the pronoun agrees with the number of its antecedent.

SUBJUNCTIVE MOOD does not state a fact. It expresses the hypothetical, doubtful, desirable or obligation.

SUBORDINATE CLAUSES are dependent clauses introduced by a subordinating conjunction.

SUFFIXES are bound morphemes occurring after bases or stems to change word category and/or to extend grammatical meaning. (See also Derivational Affixes and Inflectional Affixes.)

SUPERLATIVE is an inflectional marker of adjectives and adverbs, noted by *-est*; this inflection can be replaced in many cases with *most.*

SYLLABLES are structures consisting of one or more phonemes of which one is generally a vowel.

SYNTAX is an infrastructure of relationships, which is the relationship between one sentence constituent and another.

TENSE is the grammatical feature of verbs relating to time.

THIRD-PERSON SINGULAR marks the personal pronouns *he*, *she* and *it*, and the *-s* form of the verb.

TRANSITIVE VERBS require a following object. Generally, they are the only ones that can be transformed into the passive voice.

UMLAUT is a morphological process (internal modification) taking place in irregular nouns to extend grammatical meaning, producing different forms in the paradigm of the same word.

UNGRAMMATICAL WORDS OR STRUCTURES are those that do not conform to the *standard* of a particular language. Dialect usage is not necessarily ungrammatical if it follows the rules of native speakers.

VERBS are form class words having distinctions for the *base, third person singular,* and the *present participle.* Verbs also have past tense and participle forms that may not be distinctive.

VERB PHRASES (VP) are cohesive word groups focusing on a lexical verb.

VERBAL POSITION is reserved for words carrying out the function of the predicate.

VOCABULARY. See Lexicon.

VOICE is a syntactic construction indicating particular relationships between the subject and object of the verb.

WH-QUESTIONS are introduced by an interrogative, such as *who, which, when, where, why,* or *how,* that asks for information or content, in contrast to a yes/no question.

WORDS are free standing forms consisting of one or more morphemes of which one is a lexical base.

YES/NO QUESTIONS are clauses or sentences not beginning with *wh-*interrogative words.

BIBLIOGRAPHY

Aiken, Conrad. *The House of Dust: A Symphony.* Boston: The Four Seas Company, 1920.

Alcott, Louisa May. "A Day." *Hospital Sketches and Camp and Fireside Stories.* Boston/Cambridge: Roberts Brothers, Applewood Books, 1986 [1863].

Andrews, Edmund L. "Social Security Reform, With One Big Catch." *The New York Times* (December 12) 2004.

Associated Press. "Bombers target police in Baghdad and Mosul." *The Globe and Mail* (December 04) 2004.

Associated Press. "Hamas are ready to accept Israel state." *The Globe and Mail* (December 03) 2004.

Associated Press. "More than 600 Dead in Storms." *The Globe and Mail* (December 02) 2004.

Associated Press. "U.S. Changes Ryder Cup Qualifying." *The New York Times* (December 02) 2004.

Barringer, Felicity. "Neighbors of Burned Homes Pained by Suburban Sprawl." *The New York Times* (December 12) 2004.

Bernstein, Nina. "A Mother Deported, and a Child Left Behind." *The New York Times* (November 24) 2004.

Bernstein, Viv. "Princeton's Steep Climb Finally Ends." *The New York Times* (December 4) 2004.

Biellik, R. "Negative Impact of Clinical Misdiagnosis of Measles on Health Workers' Confidence in Measles Vaccine." *Epidemiol Infect.* (January 2004) 1321: 7–10.

Bierce. Ambrose. *Can Such Things Be.* New York: Jonthan Cape and Harrison Smith, 1909.

Bourbeau, Jacques and Aileen McCabe. "Global National Bureau Chief Dead at 53." CanWest News Service (Canada.com) (December 02) 2004.

Braddock, R., R. Lloyd-Jones, and L. Schoer. *Research in Written Composition*. Urbana, IL: NCTE, 1963

Breck, Howard. "Magic Ends Knicks' Winning Spell." *The New York Times* (December 4) 2004.

Brontë, Emily. *Wuthering Heights*. New York: Norton, 1972 [1847].

Brooke, James and Kethi Bradsher. "Dollar's Fall Tests Nerve of Asia's Central Bankers." *The New York Times* (December 4) 2004.

Brown, Eryn. "Can For-Profit Schools Pass an Ethics Test?" *The New York Times* (December 12) 2004.

Bumiller, Elisabeth. "Bush Seeks to Begin a Thaw in a Europe Still Cool to Him." *The New York Times* (February 20) 2005.

Bumiller, Elisabeth. "Kerik's Position Was Untenable, Bush Aide Says." *The New York Times* (December 04) 2004.

Butler, Samuel. *Erewhon*. Christchurch, New Zealand: The Press, 1901.

Caldwell , Christopher. "Leinart Is Sixth Heisman Winner From U.S.C." *The New York Times* (December 12) 2004.

Canadian Press. "Bettman, Goodenow Break Bread in Big Apple, As Two Sides Start Talking." (December 03) 2004. <www.cp.org/english/hp.htm>.

Canadian Press. "Former Native Residential School Students Can Sue as a Class: Appeal Court." *The National Post* (December 03) 2004.

Canadian Press. "Francis Scores 23 Points, Hill Adds 17 as Magic Rout Raptors 129–108." (December 02) 2004. <www.cp.org/english/hp.htm>.

Canadian Press. "Quebec Farmers Make an Offer for Province's Main Slaughterhouse." (December 02) 2004. <www.cp.org/english/hp.htm>.

Carroll, Lewis. *Alice's Adventures in Wonderland*. Mount Vernon, NY: Peter Pauper Press, 1940.

Chana, Sarah. "Judging Others Favorably." Aish.com (June 04) 2000.

Checkov, Anton. "The Black Monk." *The Lady with the Dog and Other Stories*. Trans. Constance Garnett. New York: Macmillan, 1917.

Chesterton, G.K. "The Oracle of the Dog." *The Great Detective Stories*. New York: Charles Scribner's Sons, 1927.

Chopin, Kate. *The Awakening*. Chicago: Herbert S. Stone, 1899.

Christiansen, Ellen. "The Bounty of Caravaggio's Glorious Exile." *New York Times* (December 12) 2004.

Christie, Agatha. *The Mysterious Affair at Styles.* New York: National Book Co., 1920.

Churchill, Winston, Sydney Adamson, and Lilian Bayliss. *The Crossing.* London: Macmillan, 1904.

Clarey, Christopher. "Roddick Warms to the Challenge of the Davis Cup." *The New York Times* (December 02) 2004.

Cobb, John B., Jr. "Buddhist–Christian Critique of Neo-Liberal Economics." Lecture at the Eastern Buddhist conference at Otani University, Kyoto, May 18, 2002.

Conrad, Joseph. *Lord Jim.* New York: Norton, 1968.

Crane, Stephen. "The Monster." *Harper's New Monthly Magazine,* Vol 97, 1898.

Curry, Jack. "Yanks May Have to Pay to Send Giambi Away." *The New York Times* (December 04) 2004.

Daimos, Jason. "Kidd Plans to Make Debut Against Raptors." *The New York Times* (December 04) 2004.

Daimos, Jason. "N.H.L. Players Seek New Talks With League." *The New York Times* (December 03) 2004.

Dao, James. "Mystery Cloaks Couple's Firing as Risks to U.S." *The New York Times* (December 12) 2004.

Darwin, Charles. *Theory on the Origin of Species by Means of Natural Selection, or the Preservation of Favoured Races in the Struggle for Life.* Cambridge, MA: Harvard University Press, 1964.

Davis, Richard Harding. *Adventures and Letters of Richard Harding Davis.* Ed. Charle Belmont Davis. New York: Charles Scribner's Sons, 1917.

De Aenlle, Conrad. "A New Way to Hedge Your Home's Paper Profit." *The New York Times* (December 12) 2004.

De Vries, Hilary. "The Cate Who Would Be Kate." *The New York Times* (December 12) 2004.

DeBoer, J.J. "Grammar in Language Teaching." *Elementary English* 36 (1959): 413–21.

Deutsche Welle. "Ukrainian Supreme Court orders new election." Canadian Press (December 03) 2004. <www.cp.org/english/hp.htm>.

Dickens, Charles. *A Christmas Carol.* Ed. Andrew Lang. London: Chapman and Hall, 1897.

Dickens, Charles. *The Old Curiosity Shop*. Project Gutenberg. Available from the University of Virginia Library Electronic Text Center. Charlottesville, VA: University of Virginia Library, 1996.

Dillenberger, John. (Book Review) "The Visual Arts and Christianity in America: From the Colonial Period to the Present. Crossroad: New York." *Theology Today* 47.1 (1990).

Doyle, Arthur Conan. "The Adventure of the Dancing Men." *The Strand Magazine*. Vol. 26, No. 156 (December 1903).

Doyle, Arthur Conan. "The Hound of the Baskervilles." *The Strand Magazine*. Vol 2 and 23 (August 1901–April 1902).

Duenwald, Mary. "For Pain Management, Doctors Prescribe Caution." *Detroit Free Press* (February 20) 2005.

Eliot, George. *Middlemarch: A Study of Provincial Life* (1900). New York: H.M. Caldwell, 1871.

Eliot, George. *Silas Marner, the Lifted Veil, and Brother Jacob and Scenes of Clerical Life*. Chicago: Belford, Clarke and Co., 1885.

Elly, W.B., I.H. Barham, H. Lamb, and M. Wyllie. "The Role of Grammar in a Secondary English Curriculum." *Research in the Teaching of English*.10 (1976): 5–21.

Encyclopdia of Educational Research. 3rd ed. New York: Macmillan, 1960.

Erickson, Kathleen Powers. "From Preaching to Painting: Van Gogh's Religious Zeal. *Christian Century* 1990 (March 21–28): 300–302.

Erlanger, Steven. "Progress Seen on Election Break in Militant Attacks on Israel." *The New York Times* (December 04) 2004.

Eskenazi, Gerald. "After Missing 3 Games, Pennington Is Ready to Go." *The New York Times* (December 04) 2004.

Franklin, Benjamin. *The Autobiography of Benjamin Franklin*. New York: P.F. Collier and Son, 1909.

Glaspell, Susan. "A Jury of her Peers." *The Best Short Stories of 1917*. Ed. Edard J. O'Brien. Boston: Small, Maynard, 1918.

Goetz, Ronald. "Anselm Kiefer: Art as Atonement." *Christian Century* 1988 (March 23-30): 314.

Gogol, Nikolia V. *Taras Bulba and other Tales*. New York: E.P. Dutton, 1952.

Goldsmith, Oliver. *The Vicar of Wakefield*. Chicago: Fountain, 1965.

Gorham, Beth. "U.S. Appoints New Agriculture Secretary in Last Stages of Resolving Beef Ban." Canadian Press (December 02) 2004. <www.cp.org/english/hp.htm>.

Greenbaum, Sidney, and Randolph Quirk. *A Student's Grammar of the English Language.* Essex: Longman, 1990.

Grey, Zane. *The Man of the Forest.* New York: Harper and Brothers, 1920.

Hardy, Thomas. *Tess of the d'Urbervilles.* Ed. Scott Elledge. New York: Norton, 1979.

Hartman, R.R.K. and F.C. Stork. *Dictionary of Language and Linguistics.* Norfolk, England: John Wiley and Sons, 1972.

Haught, John F. "Mystery and Promise: A Theology of Revelation." The Liturgical Press, 1993.

Hawthorne, Nathaniel. *The House of the Seven Gables.* New York: World's Popular Classics, 1942.

Hayakawa, S.I. and A.R. Hayakawa. *Language in Thought and Action.* 5th ed. Orland: Harcourt Brace Jovanovich, 1990.

Hegan-Rice, Alice Caldwell. *Mrs. Wiggs of the Cabbage Patch.* The Naked Word Electronic Edition. Charlottesville, VA: University of Virginia, 1901.

Hemon, Louis. *Maria Chapdelaine: A Tale of the Lake St. John Country.* Trans. W.H. Blake. New York: Macmillan, 1921.

Hillocks, G., Jr. and M.W. Smith. "Grammar and Usage." *Handbook of Research on Teaching the English Language Arts.* Ed. J. Flood, J.M. Jensen, D. Lapp, and J.R. Squires. New York: Macmillan, 1991.

Hillocks, G., Jr. *Research on Written Composition: New Directions for Teaching.* Urbana, IL: NCTE, 1986.

Hope, Majorie and James Young. "The Homeless: On the Street, On the Road." *Christian Century* (January 18) 1984: 48.

James, Henry. *The Beast in the Jungle.* University of Virginia Library Electronic Text Center. Charlottesville, VA: University of Virginia Library, 1909.

James, Ian. "Eight Illegal Migrants Perish off Puerto Rico." *Puerto Rico Herald* (November 30) 2003.

Jefferson, Thomas. *152 Letters to and from Jefferson.* Transcribed by Frank Grizzard. University of Virginia Library, Charlottesville, VA, 1996.

Jenkins, Lee. "Another Chance for Baseball to Settle Its Score with Drugs." *The New York Times* (December 12) 2004.

Jenkins, Lee. "Newest Reports Place Bonds Back at Center of Steroid Case." *The New York Times* (December 04) 2004.

Jones, Steve. "If Jets and Steelers Are Mirror Images, It's Time for One of Them to Crack." *New York Times* (December 12) 2004.

Kaplan, Jeffery P. *English Grammar: Principles and Facts*. Englewood Cliffs, NJ: Prentice Hall, 1989.

Kenyes, John Maynard. *The Economic Consequences of the Peace*. University of Virginia Library Electronic Text Center. Charlottesville, VA: University of Virginia Library, 1919.

Kepner, Tyles. "After Talks With Torre, Pinstripes for Pavano." *The New York Times* (December 12) 2004.

Kipling, Rudyard. *The Jungle Book*. New York: Century, 1899.

Klammer, Thomas P. and Muriel Schulz. *Analyzing English Grammar*. Boston: Allan and Bacon, 1992.

Klienfield, N.R. "Bowed by Age and Battered by an Addicted Nephew." *The New York Times* (December 12) 2004.

Knox, Colin. "Emergence of Power Sharing in Northern Ireland: Lessons from Local Government." *The Journal of Conflict Studies* XVI.1 (Fall 1997).

Kolln, Martha. *Understanding English Grammar*. 4th ed. Toronto: Macmillan, 1994.

Lawless, Jill. "Stalin Must Have Had a Penchant for Reds." *Globe and Mail* (December 04) 2004.

Lawrence, D.H. *Sons and Lovers*. New York: Viking, 1913.

Leary, Warren E. "Doctor Offers Assurances That Astronauts Won't Go Hungry." *The New York Times* (December 11) 2004.

Leary, Warren E. and Dennis Overbye. "Panel Urges Shuttle Mission to Help Hubble." *The New York Times* (December 09) 2004.

Lebrun, Pierre. "NHL, NHLPA to Resume Bargaining Talks next Thursday in Toronto." Canadian Press (December 02) 2004. <www.cp.org/english/hp.htm>.

Lewis Sinclair. *Babbitt*. New York: Harcourt, Brace, 1922.

Lewis, Neil A. "Red Cross Finds Detainee Abuse in Guantánamo." *The New York Times* (November 30) 2004.

Liptak, Adam. "Colleges Can Bar Army Recruiters." *The New York Times* (November 30) 2004.

Lipton, Eric. "Audit Faults U.S. for Its Spending on Port Defense." *The New York Times* (February 20) 2005.

Lipton, Eric. "Doubts Are Raised on Push for Anthrax Vaccine." *The New York Times* (December 11) 2004.

Locke, William John. *The Fortunate Youth*. New York: John Lane, 1914.

Male, Lucas. *The History of Sir Richard Calmady: A Romance*. London: Methuen, 1901.

McCormick, Richard A. "S.J. Changing My Mind about the Changeable Church." *Christian Century*: "How My Mind Has Changed." 2000.

McDonald, Joe. "China Denies Planning Commercial Sales of Genetically Modified Rice." Canadian Press (December 02) 2004. <www.cp.org/english/hp.htm>.

McFague, Sallie. "An Earthly Theological Agenda." *Christian Century* (January 2–9) 1991.

McFarland, John Robert. "Looking for the Gospel at a Gospel Concert." *Christian Century* (June 18–25) 1986, p. 579.

McQyade, F. "Examining a Grammar Course: The Rationale and the Result." *English Journal* 69 (1980):26–30.

Melville, Herman. *Moby-Dick, or, the Whale*. Ed. Luther S. Mansfield and Howard P. Vincent. New York: Hendricks House, 1952.

Michelson, Miriam. *In the Bishop's Carriage*. New York: Grosset and Dunlap, 1910.

Moore, R. Jonathan. "Falwell and Followers." *Christian Century* (November 21–28) 2001.

Morgan, David. "Stalking the Spiritual in the Visual Arts." *Christian Century* (December 06) 1989.

Morgenson, Gretchen and Mary Williams Walsh. "How Consultants Can Retire on Your Pension." *The New York Times* (December 12) 2004.

Morris, Chris N.B. "Premier Opens Province's Purse Strings as Legislature Opens." Canadian Press (December 02) 2004. <www.cp.org/english/hp.htm>.

Morris, Jim. "Final Day of Downhill Training Cancelled, Canadians Remain Confident." Canadian Press (December 02) 2004. <www.cp.org/english/hp.htm>.

Myers, Stephen Lee. "Ukrainian Court Orders New Vote for Presidency, Citing Fraud." *The New York Times* (December 04) 2004.

Neilan Terence. "Tens of thousands of Viktor Yushchenko's Supporters Roamed Kiev for a Third Day, Chanting: 'Yushchenko! Yushchenko!'" *The New York Times* (November 24) 2004.

Norris, Frank. *The Pit: A Story of Chicago*. University of Virginia Library Electronic Text Center. Charlottesville, VA: University of Virginia Library, 1903.

O'Hanlan, Martin. "Opposition Accuse Liberals of Sponsorship Coverup." *The New York Times* (December 02) 2004.

Oppel, Richard A. Jr. and James Glanz. "U.S. Officials Say Iraq's Forces Founder Under Rebel Assaults." *The New York Times* (November 30) 2004.

Pear, Robert. "Test Finds Inaccuracies in Help Line for Medicare." *The New York Times* (December 12) 2004.

Plank, Karl A. "Broken Continuities: 'Night' and 'White Crucifixion.'" *Christian Century* (November 4) 1987.

Polkow, Dennis. "Andrew Lloyd Webber: From Superstar to Requiem." *Christian Century* (March 18–25) 1987.

Pollack, Kenneth M. "Data Mounts on Avoiding Chemotherapy. *The New York Times* (December 11) 2004.

Pollack, Kenneth M. "More Questions for Producer of Flu Vaccine." *The New York Times* (December 11) 2004.

Porter, Eleanor H. *Just David*. Project Gutenberg. University of Virginia Library Electronic Text Center. Charlottesville, VA: University of Virginia Library, 1996.

Powell, Mark Allan. "Jesus Climbs the Charts: The Business of Contemporary Christian Music." *Christian Century* (December 18–31) 2002.

Quirk, Randolph, and Sidney Greenbaum. *A University of Grammar of English*. Essex: Longman, 1973.

Rahner, Karl. *Grace in Freedom*. Herder and Herder: New York, 1969.

Reinhart, Anthony. "The Walkerton Survivors." *The Globe and Mail* (December 04) 2004.

Rich, Frank. "The Plot Against Sex in America." *The New York Times* (December 12) 2004.

Roberts, Selena. "Hockey Fans Are Silent, and Union Is Listening." *The New York Times* (December 12) 2004.

Rosenthal, Jack. "Liberal Leader From Ukraine Was Poisoned." *The New York Times* (December 12) 2004.

Rozhon, Tracie. "Even if Just a Bauble, Luxury Counts for Holidays." *The New York Times* (December 12) 2004.

Salmaso S., Bruzzone B.M., Bella A., Crovari P., and the Serological Study Group. "Epidemiology of Measles, Mumps and Rubella in Italy." *Epidemiol Infect.* (December 2002): 543–50.

Sanders, Gregory P. "Weather Hinders Search for Ship's Crew as Oil Spill Widens." *The New York Times* (December 11) 2004.

Schmitt, Eric. "Abuse Inquiry Finds Flaws." *The New York Times* (December 04) 2004.

Shakespeare, William. *Othello*. New York: Signet Classics, 1986.

Shanker, Thom and Richard Steveson. "White House Seeks Deal to Save Intelligence Bill." *The New York Times* (November 04) 2004.

Short, Brent. "The Calls Cry in the Wilderness." *Christian Century* (September 19–26) 1990.

Stackhouse, Max L. "Fundamentalism around the World." *Christian Century* (August 28–September 4) 1985.

Stageberg, Norman. *An Introductory English Grammar*. Orlando, FL: Holt, Rinehart and Winston, 1981.

Stevenson, Robert Louis. *The Strange Case of Dr. Jekyll and Mr. Hyde*. London: Penguin, 1979.

Szklarski, Cassandra. "Ontario Court Orders New Trial for Baltovich 12 Years after Murder Conviction." Canadian Press (December 02) 2004. <www.cp.org/english/hp.htm>.

Thamel, Pete. "Meyer Spurns Irish for Gators." *The New York Times* (December 04) 2004.

Thorne, Stephen. "Martin says Bush Assured Him no Plans for Space-Based Weapons." Canadian Press. (December 02) 2004. <www.cp.org/english/hp.htm>.

Trotter, F. Thomas. "On Being Alive to the Arts and Religion: Music." In *Loving God With One's Mind*, F. Thomas Trotter 1987.

Tutu, Bishop Desmond. "South Africa's Blacks: Aliens in Their Own Land." *Christianity and Crisis* (November 26) 1984.

Twain, Mark. *Adventures of Huckleberry Finn*. New York: Harper and Brothers, 1912.

Twiddy, David. "National Beef Packing Officials 'Optimistic' on Beef Sales Next Year." Canadian Press (December 02) 2004. <www.cp.org/english/hp.htm>

Van Dyke. Henry. *The Blue Flower*. New York: Charles Scriber's Sons, 1911.

Van Loon, Hendrik. *The Story of Mankind*. New York: Boni and Liveright, 1921.

Wales, Katie. *A Dictionary of Stylistics*. Singapore: Longman, 1989.

Walkin, Daniel J. "The Juilliard Effect: Ten Years Later." *The New York Times* (December 12) 2004.

Wells, H.G. *God the Invisible King.* Electronic Text Center. Charlottesville, VA: University of Virginia Library, 1967.

Wikipedia Medicine. http://en.wikipedia.org/wiki/Main_Page.

Wink, Walter. "Drug policy: The Fix We're In." *Christian Century* (February 24) l999.

Worth, Robert F. and Richard A. Oppel, Jr. "27 Civilians Die in New Attacks by Iraq Rebels." *The New York Times* (December 04) 2004.

Yoffe, Emily "Tennis Star, Singer Are Happily Married. *U.S. News and World Report* (December 15) 2004.

Ziegenhals, Gretchen E. "Robert Shaw's Ministry of Music." *Christian Century* (March 22–29) 1989.

INDEX